# 1000 American History Facts and 101 True Tales

A Journey Through America's Defining Moments and Figures

# Table of Contents

# Part 1: American History

## 1000 Interesting Facts About the United States

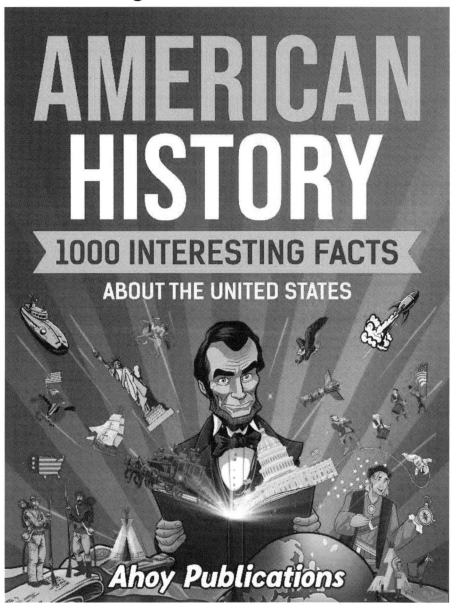

# Introduction

**Are you interested in uncovering the secrets of American history?** Do you want to explore the depths of America's past and learn about events, people, and technological advancements that shaped this great nation?

If so, *1000 Interesting Facts of American History* is your perfect guide. Our facts cover America's earliest history to recent events. Uncover fascinating facts related to major political events, sports achievements, military conflicts, technology, social movements, immigration, music, art, and literature. Discover some of the major Supreme Court cases, African American culture and heritage, and presidential elections.

With *1000 Interesting Facts of American History* at your fingertips, it's never been easier to learn all about America's rich past! Read on to start your journey!

## Section 1: Exploring the Core Facts of American History

# Native Americans and Life Before European Exploration

This chapter will explore the fascinating history of **Native Americans and life before European colonization**. Let's take a look at thirty interesting facts about Native American cultures, beliefs, languages, tools, and art. We'll also discover how the indigenous people utilized nature to survive in harsh conditions and develop complex trade networks between different tribes across **North America**.

1. **Native Americans** have lived in **North America** for around twenty thousand years.

2. The term **"Native Americans" is broad**. There were likely over one thousand different tribes and cultures before European colonization. Each one had different beliefs and systems.

3. Many tribes had a concept called **"Sacred Hoop,"** where all living things were linked together and needed to be respected by each other. It represents the seasons, the universe, and **the life cycle. It has no beginning or end.**

4. Tribes used **sophisticated tools** made from stone, bone, shell, wood, and antlers, allowing them to hunt animals or fish more efficiently. They could also **build homes** faster.

5. Native Americans created **pottery out of clay.** The pottery was used for food storage or cooking purposes. They could last up to generations within some families.

6. The indigenous people **relied heavily on nature.** They grew plants such as corn and squash. They also hunted buffalo, deer, elk, and ducks.

7. **Native American cultures developed complex trade systems** between different groups across North America. They exchanged goods like copper jewelry or animal skins for things they needed from other tribes.

8. Native American tribes developed **their own languages**. The indigenous people in North America did not have writing systems, so they passed their histories down orally and through other means, such as wampum belts.

9. **Tribes believed** in many different spiritual beliefs, which were often based on nature or animals. These beliefs guided most of their daily life decisions.

10. Some tribes practiced **farming techniques** like terracing, which allowed them to grow food more efficiently with limited resources. This same technique is still used by farmers today!

11. Music was an integral part of native cultures. People would **sing, dance, drum, and play flutes** and other instruments. Music connected individuals in spiritual ceremonies and celebrations.

12. Some Native American religious practices included vision quests. A person would go off alone into nature to have visions or dreams **inspired by spirit guides**. These guides would provide guidance and direction on essential matters within one's life.

13. Native American cultures practiced various forms of art, including pottery, basket weaving, and painting on hides. **Art was usually meant to be spiritual**, although some things, like baskets, were used for practical purposes. Art could also be used to record stories and histories within the tribe.

14. **Tribes had their form of organized societies with leaders** who would oversee critical decision-making processes like how to distribute food. Each tribe was different, so not all tribes had the same kind of societal structure.

15. Most tribes believed that **land did not belong to an individual** but to all the people living on it. This concept was known as **communal property** and allowed different groups to share common resources.

16. Ancient native peoples **developed intricate systems of medicine** that included herbs, massage therapies, and sweat lodges. Many of these treatments are still used today by modern doctors worldwide due to their effectiveness in **healing certain conditions**.

17. Native American **women were usually responsible for gathering food**, making clothing, and tending to the home. They also held various spiritual roles. They could be medicine women, healers, or leaders of ceremonies.

18. **Natives utilized astronomy** to predict seasonal changes and to understand the migration patterns of animals when certain plants would become ripe for harvesting. **This knowledge was essential for their survival**. They would plan activities around what nature provided them each year.

19. **Many tribes used deep-seated philosophies** that revolved around the balance between humans and nature, which they believed created harmony and happiness within one's life. This belief system has been passed down through generations of native peoples and is used even today!

20. **Native Americans** were known for their intricate beadwork designs, which could be found on moccasins, blankets, and other items. They **also made beautiful jewelry out of shells or stones** that had symbolic meanings attached to them. These pieces served a functional purpose and acted as powerful symbols. They represented something important about someone's identity within their tribe.

21. **Medicine men and women were significant within tribal societies**. These healers understood herbs and ritual and spiritual practices that could be used to treat illnesses or injuries. They passed this knowledge down to the next generation.

22. **Ancient tribes utilized the buffalo for more than just food**. They used the buffalo's hide for clothing, shelter, and tools like bows and arrows! Today, some native communities still practice traditional **buffalo hunting ceremonies** as part of their cultural identity.

23. **Native Americans followed migratory patterns** of animals throughout different seasons, allowing them access to fresh game on an ongoing basis. This was essential for their **survival during leaner months** when other resources might have been scarce due to a lack of rainfall or cold weather.

24. **Tribes relied heavily on the cycles of nature** when it came time to plant crops or harvest certain plants. They understood how their actions impacted the environment around them, so they took great care not to waste anything.

25. Three of the **most important crops in early North America were squash, maize (corn), and beans**. These three crops were called the Three Sisters. They were usually planted together. The cornstalk would act like a trellis for the beans. The squash's leaves would shade the ground, keeping the moisture in the soil so the **beans and maize could grow** without any problems.

26. **Fishing was an essential part of many native diets**. The indigenous people used unique methods like fish weirs (a trap made out of sticks), spears, and nets.

27. Ancient tribes developed ingenious ways of transportation. **They used canoes, which allowed them to travel across rivers easily**. They also used snowshoes which helped them traverse snowy paths and mountains.

28. **Some tribes built towns with palisades** (walls made out of wood) to protect themselves against potential threats. Palisades also provided protection during harsh winter months **when food might have been scarce** due to the lack of sunlight and cold temperatures.

29. **Native Americans believed in communicating respect between different cultures.** Traders exchanged not only goods but also stories, songs, and ideas, which allowed them to learn more about each other's customs and beliefs!

30. **Ritual dances** were often performed within native cultures as part of significant ceremonies or festivities. **These dances varied from tribe to tribe** but had some shared similarities, such as their reverence for nature and ancestors.

# European Exploration and Colonization of the United States

This chapter will explore the **history of European exploration and colonization** in the United States. We'll look at thirty interesting facts about how various countries claimed parts of North America, what they brought to the region, and why some colonies decided to declare independence. We'll also learn about other acquisitions, **such as Alaska, Hawaii, and Puerto Rico**, all of which eventually became part of the United States!

31. **The first European to explore North America was Leif Erikson**. He was a Viking. He traveled to what is now Newfoundland in 1000 CE.

32. By the time of **Christopher Columbus**, people had forgotten about Leif's voyage. Most early explorations were centered on Central and South America. The first European explorer to reach the present-day US was **Ponce de León.**

33. **Amerigo Vespucci**, who explored South America, is where we get the name "America."

34. **In 1607, England** established its first permanent settlement in North America at Jamestown.

35. **France settled colonies in Canada** and Louisiana in the 1600s.

36. **Spain** claimed much of the Southwest, from **California to Texas**.

37. **Dutch** colonists settled in New Netherland (present-day **New York**) in 1624.

38. **Pilgrims** came to Plymouth, **Massachusetts**, in 1620 on the *Mayflower*.

39. **Quakers** began settling in **Pennsylvania** in 1681.

40. **European settlers brought horses, cattle, pigs, and other animals to the Americas.** Settlers also introduced new plants like wheat, barley, oats, and rye for farming.

41. By the mid-1700s, **Britain's Thirteen Colonies** had been established along the Atlantic coast from Maine to Georgia.

42. **African slaves were brought to the United States** by European traders to work the plantations.

43. **The French and Indian War (1754–1763)** was fought between France and Britain with their respective Native American allies.

44. **Britain won the war** and gained control of much of eastern North America.

45. After the war, the **British attempted to increase taxes** on the colonists to pay off the war. The colonists were upset because they were not given representation in Parliament.

46. **The American Revolution** broke out in 1775 because of tensions between the Thirteen Colonies and Britain.

47. **The Thirteen Colonies declared independence** from Britain in July 1776.

48. **The Revolutionary War officially ended in 1783** with the Treaty of Paris. The treaty formally recognized the United States as an independent nation.

49. **Great Britain ceded most of its land** east of the Mississippi River to the United States.

50. **The Northwest Ordinance was passed in 1787.** It organized the area northwest of the Ohio River into the Northwest Territory, which would later become several states.

51. **The Louisiana Purchase of 1803** doubled the size of the United States.

52. **The Lewis and Clark Expedition**, which lasted from 1804 to 1806, was led by Meriwether Lewis and William Clark. With the help of a young Shoshone woman named Sacagawea, the party traversed the country from the Missouri River to the Pacific Ocean. They encountered Native American tribes and brought back valuable information, which expanded the knowledge of the American West.

53. **Florida became part of the United States** after the Adams-Onís Treaty with Spain in 1819.

54. After **the Mexican-American War**, Mexico ceded present-day California to the United States through the Treaty of Guadalupe Hidalgo in 1848.

55. **The Gadsden Purchase added land in southern Arizona** and southwestern New Mexico in 1853.

56. **Alaska was purchased from Russia** in 1867.

57. The United States acquired Hawaii and Guam in 1898. **Hawaii became a state in 1959.** Guam is a US territory today.

58. **Puerto Rico became a US territory** in 1898 following the Spanish-American War.

59. The **Panama Canal Zone** was leased to the US in 1903.

60. The **US acquired the Virgin Islands from Denmark** in 1917.

# The Great Awakening

**You might be wondering how we got through America's history so quickly**. Don't worry! We will take a closer look at the big events of US history. This chapter will explore the **Great Awakening, a religious movement that swept across America** in the early to the mid-18th century. We'll take a look at how this spiritual revival challenged traditional Puritan beliefs and brought new **denominations of Christianity into the colonies**, such as Methodism. Additionally, we'll learn about why **George Whitefield** was so important to this period and discover why the Second Great Awakening sparked social movements, including abolitionism, temperance, and women's rights. These movements helped shape much of what **defines the people's sense of morality in the US today.**

61. **The Great Awakening was a religious movement** in the early to the mid-18th century.

62. It began with an emotional sermon by preacher **Jonathan Edwards in 1734**. The ideas from his sermon quickly spread, leading to a large turnout at revival meetings throughout America.

63. His sermon talked about how people were natural-**born sinners and how they needed to be forgiven** to attain salvation. He urged people to accept God into their lives.

64. **This spiritual awakening challenged traditional Puritan beliefs**. Puritans believed that only priests could interpret the Bible.

65. In the past, **free-thinking Puritans, like Anne Hutchinson**, had been banished from Puritan society for going against the norm.

66. **George Whitefield** was one of the leading preachers of the Great Awakening. He traveled up and down the East Coast, preaching his message of religious revival to thousands at a time.

67. **Whitefield's stirring sermons** promoted self-determination for individuals instead of depending on group consensus. His ideas inspired people to become more independent thinkers, not just believers or followers.

68. For example, he encouraged colonists to take control of their own lives by making decisions about **what kind of values they wanted.**

69. **The Great Awakening significantly impacted American intellectual life**, inspiring people to create their own interpretations of the Bible and helping them move away from traditional Puritan beliefs.

70. It also helped spark a **sense of national unity**, as colonists from different backgrounds united in their belief in God's power.

71. **The Great Awakening was an essential factor in the American Revolution.** It helped spread ideas about self-determination and liberty throughout the colonies before hostilities began with Britain.

72. **It encouraged people to think for themselves**, question authority, and stand up against oppressive forces, ultimately leading them toward independence from a monarchical system.

73. **New Protestant denominations** arrived in America because of the Great Awakening, such as Methodism.

74. **John Wesley founded Methodism** in the 1730s. In 1784, Methodism took root in America, with immigrants from Ireland bringing the religion with them.

75. **Baptists were also affected by the Great Awakening.** Baptists had been around since the 17th century, but the religious revival brought about a new kind of Baptist, one that broke away from Puritan (or Congregationalist) views.

76. There had been few Baptists in America before the Great Awakening. By 1804, there were over **three hundred Baptist churches in New England** alone.

77. Many prominent figures, including **Thomas Paine**, wrote extensively about religious liberty, **the separation between church and state**, and other topics related to individual rights and freedom of expression.

78. **The Great Awakening was a reaction to the Enlightenment**, which began in Europe. The Enlightenment was based on reason, while the Great Awakening was based more on emotion and beliefs.

79. **The Enlightenment affected religion.** Since the ideas of the movement were based on reason, there was increasing skepticism toward traditional Christian beliefs. Some **intellectuals rejected biblical theology** altogether, influencing what is now known as secular humanism today. Most Enlightenment thinkers called for religious tolerance.

80. **Deism emerged during the Enlightenment**. It rationalized the existence of God. Deists believed in God but did not believe he interfered in daily life. Some famous Deists were **Thomas Jefferson and Thomas Paine.**

81. Although the religious revival movement did not focus on rationalism, it still left a lasting impact on education in America. **Several famous universities opened because of the Great Awakening**, such as Princeton, Dartmouth, and Brown.

82. These universities were originally intended to be places **where men could learn about the Bible** and train to become ministers.

83. This movement was significant for **African Americans**. They were encouraged by preachers like Whitefield to **reject slavery and pursue freedom through faith** in Christ's teachings about love and justice for all people, regardless of race or class status.

84. **The Second Great Awakening** happened during the early 19th century. It is generally believed to have lasted from 1790 to 1840. It was another major Protestant revival.

85. The Second Great Awakening spurred several social reform movements, including **abolitionism, temperance, and women's rights.**

86. The Second Great Awakening preached that **all men were equal under the eyes of God**, leading to increased calls for abolitionism.

87. It also revived **the belief that one should live a life free of sin**. Temperance movements took this idea and applied it to the vice of drinking in excess.

88. The increased religious enthusiasm of the period empowered **women to take on a more active role in religious life, including teaching and preaching**. While women were still largely excluded from formal positions in religious institutions, the Second Great Awakening allowed them to gain greater autonomy and influence in religious matters.

89. The Second Great Awakening also contributed to a **growing sense of religious equality between men and women**, paving the way for the early women's rights movement.

90. **The Third Great Awakening took place from the late 1850s to the early 20th century.** This revival also focused on social issues like abolitionism. It also focused on the end times and the Second Coming of Christ.

# The French and Indian War

This chapter will explore the **French and Indian War**, which was a theater of the Seven Years' War. We'll take a look at **thirty interesting facts** about how this conflict began, who was involved in it, and what the outcome was. Learn about famous figures like **George Washington and Benjamin Franklin**, who played important roles during this war.

91. **The French and Indian War** was fought between 1754 and 1763 in North America.

92. This war was a theater of **the Seven Years' War,** which broke out over territorial disputes.

93. **The French and Indian War pitted the British** against the French. Both sides had Native American allies.

94. The war started because of disputes over land ownership of **the Ohio River Valley.**

95. **France helped its Native American** allies by providing weapons to prevent British colonists from expanding into new lands.

96. **The first battle** during this war took place at **Jumonville Glen** near present-day Pittsburgh, Pennsylvania, **in May 1754**. It only lasted about fifteen minutes.

97. **George Washington** commanded the colonists in the Battle of Jumonville Glen.

98. **Jumonville was the leader of the French forces** in the battle. He was sent to warn Washington to leave the area, not to engage in combat. **Jumonville died in the battle.**

99. **The first political cartoon in US history** was printed in 1754. The cartoon was designed **by Benjamin Franklin**. It showed the colonies as parts of a chopped-up snake.

100. **The Battle of Fort Necessity** was the first major battle of the war. It took place in July 1754. **George Washington** was forced to surrender the fort.

101. **British General Edward Braddock** was killed while leading a force against Fort Duquesne (now located within modern-day Pittsburgh) on July 9th, 1755, making him one of many casualties during this long and bloody conflict.

102. Initially, the **French** did better in the war. But the tides began to turn when the **British scored a victory** at Fort Niagara in July 1759. Their win allowed them to begin plans to invade Canada from the west.

103. **The Battle of Quebec** took place in September 1759. **The British had laid siege** to the city for three months before they were finally able to declare victory. Generals from both sides were killed from injuries they received while fighting.

104. **The French tried to retake Quebec**, but they failed.

105. Due to a lack of resources, both sides resorted to using **guerilla warfare tactics.**

106. **Over forty thousand colonists and British soldiers took part in the war**. The French had around ten thousand regulars. However, the French had more Native American allies than the British.

107. In September 1760, **the British successfully took Montreal**. The seizure of Montreal meant that all of New France was in British hands.

108. **In 1763, a peace treaty was signed in Paris between France, Britain, and the other countries that fought in the Seven Years' War**. The treaty ended that war and the French and Indian War. It gave all lands east of the Mississippi River to Britain. France withdrew from North America, although it kept some territories in Canada.

109. **Louisiana was split in half**, with Britain getting the eastern side. France got the western side.

110. **France would not hold Louisiana for long**. Before the 1763 Treaty of Paris, France signed a secret agreement with Spain. **France agreed to give Louisiana to Spain**. Shortly after the war, Spain received its half of the territory. It did not contest the terms of the Treaty of Paris.

111. The British were worried about its new residents in Canada, namely Catholics in Acadia. **In 1755, the British began expelling the Acadians**. Hundreds of them settled in Louisiana. The name "Acadian" turned into "Cajun." Cajuns still live in Louisiana to this day.

112. **The Treaty of Paris also gave all of Spanish Florida to Britain**. Spain had fought with France in the Seven Years' War and was forced to give up territories in the treaty.

113. Although this conflict was fought **primarily between Great Britain and France**, Native American tribes were significant participants. Most tribes supported France. Some even tried to remain neutral during the war.

114. **The Iroquois Confederacy was initially neutral in the war**. The Iroquois later allied with the British. However, members joined forces with the French. It really depended upon who offered better terms at any given moment.

115. **The French and Indian War** opened up opportunities for colonists from Europe to begin settling newly acquired territories. To do so, they had to push the indigenous people out.

116. **Native Americans** were not included in the peace treaty between France and Britain. They continued facing displacement from their lands until treaties were made directly with tribes or governments set up specifically for them.

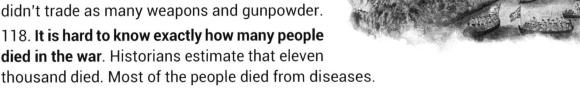

117. **When France left, the Native Americans** lost an important trading partner. Although the colonists still traded with the natives, they didn't trade as many weapons and gunpowder.

118. **It is hard to know exactly how many people died in the war**. Historians estimate that eleven thousand died. Most of the people died from diseases.

119. British officers like **George Washington** gained experience and respect in the French and Indian War. His accomplishments in this war later led him to be commander of the Continental Army.

120. Other prominent figures in US history, such as **Benjamin Franklin**, played significant roles in the war as well. **Franklin became a commander in the war.**

# The Boston Tea Party

This chapter will cover the events and causes of **the Boston Tea Party**, which was a **pivotal moment in United States history**. The American Revolution would break out less than two years later. We'll look at **thirty interesting facts** about this historical event, from who organized it to what happened afterward. Learn why **Americans boycotted tea from England**.

121. **The Boston Tea Party was a political protest** that happened on December 16th, 1773, in the city of Boston, Massachusetts.

122. **Three ships carrying tea from England were sent to the harbor in Boston.** Colonists were upset about the fact they had representation in the British Parliament. To show their displeasure, they threw all 342 chests of tea into the water!

123. **The tea that was dumped** would have been worth almost two million dollars today!

124. The tea would have weighed over ninety thousand pounds.

125. In May 1773, **Britain passed the Tea Act**. This was one of many acts that upset the American colonists.

126. **Colonists already paid taxes on tea** because of the Townshend Acts, which were passed in the late 1760s. Colonists also paid taxes on glassware, stamps, and paper, to name a few.

127. During that period, **tea was very popular in America**. The colonists drank over one million pounds of tea a year in the late 18th century!

128. **The Tea Act gave the East India Company a monopoly on tea**. Smuggling was a big problem in the colonies. Almost 90 percent of the tea the colonists drank had been smuggled. It became clear to the colonists that the tax on tea would stand.

129. **Thomas Hutchinson was governor of Massachusetts** at the time of the Boston Tea Party. He wanted the taxes paid on the tea. He refused to let the ships leave the harbor with the tea.

130. **The colonists made it clear they would not pass the tax**. The captains didn't want to risk any potential damage to their ships, so they stayed in the harbor.

131. Over **one hundred people participated** in the historic **Boston Tea Party**. Only about sixty of them boarded the ships.

132. Most participants wore disguises, such as masks. Some even **dressed up as Mohawks!**

133. Participants used hatchets and ropes to dump the chests into the water. **It took them almost three hours in the dark to unload all the tea!**

134. The main organizer of this event was **Samuel Adams**. He is considered one of the Founding Fathers. He was also an active member of a political **group called the Sons of Liberty.**

135. **The Sons of Liberty** fought for the colonists' rights. This group could sometimes be violent. For instance, **they tarred and feathered officials**. A person would be stripped naked. Tar would be poured on them. And then feathers would be thrown at them.

136. Some of the famous Sons of Liberty include **Samuel Adams, Benjamin Church, John Hancock, Paul Revere, and Benedict Arnold.**

137. The Boston Tea Party was called the **"Destruction of the Tea"** at the time. Other cities had their own "tea parties," but the one in Boston was the most destructive.

138. Even though no fatalities or injuries were reported during this event, **the British were still furious**. They demanded compensation for the loss of the tea.

139. Britain passed several acts known as the Intolerable Acts. These acts restricted colonial rights even more, leading to more protests.

140. The Boston Port Act was passed first. The colonists had to repay the cost of the destroyed tea. Until they did, the port of Boston would be closed.

141. The Massachusetts Government Act put Massachusetts under the control of the British government. Prior to this act, Massachusetts had a charter. People in Massachusetts could also only have one town meeting a year.

142. The Administration of Justice Act allowed **British officials to be tried in Britain**, not in Massachusetts.

143. People were upset about this act because British soldiers had been given a fair hearing after **the Boston Massacre.**

144. In the Boston Massacre, **British soldiers fired into a large crowd of colonists**. The colonists had been pelting the soldiers with rocks and other objects. The captain never gave orders to shoot. Most of the soldiers were acquitted.

145. **The Quartering Act** required that housing be provided to British troops. This act applied to all Thirteen Colonies.

146. This historic act of rebellion **caused a lot of tension between Britain and America**. The Intolerable Acts did not ease the tensions. A revolution would eventually break out in April 1775.

147. **The Intolerable Acts** were meant to break the colonists' spirit. Instead, it **drew the colonists closer together**. In September 1774, twelve colonies sent representatives to the First Continental Congress.

148. **After the Boston Tea Party**, many Americans began drinking coffee instead of tea. Coffee was already popular in America, but coffee drinkers eventually outpaced tea drinkers!

149. Today, you can visit **several museums** dedicated to teaching visitors about the history behind what happened at **the Boston Tea Party**. You can even take boat tours where they dumped those 342 chests into the harbor waters!

150. To commemorate the anniversary of the Boston Tea Party, **a reenactment is held in Boston**. Participants wear traditional colonial clothing and even throw tea into harbor waters just like they did back then!

# The American Revolution

This chapter will examine the **American Revolution and its lasting effects on the United States**. We'll explore how it began, who was involved, and what events led up to it.

Learn some **facts about the key battles** fought during this war, like Bunker Hill and Yorktown. Discover France's involvement, the treaty signed in Paris after the **colonists won their freedom from Great Britain**, and the contributions made **by African Americans and women.**

151. **The American Revolution began in 1775** and officially **ended in 1783.**

152. It was primarily fought between **the British and the colonists** of what would become America. Both sides had help from allies. The US had help from France, Spain, the Netherlands, and the Native Americans. The British had help from the Native Americans. They also received help from the Hessians.

153. **The leading cause of the conflict was taxation without representation.** Many acts had been passed that placed taxes on everyday goods. However, the colonists had no voice in Parliament. As the years passed, it became clear to them that their opinion had little weight in Britain.

154. One major event that propelled the colonists to fight a revolution was **the Boston Massacre.** On March 5th, 1770, **British troops fired upon a crowd of angry colonists.** Five colonists were killed, creating more anti-British sentiment.

155. Another major event happened on December 16th, 1773. A group of colonists disguised as Mohawks threw hundreds of crates of tea into Boston Harbor to protest the Tea Act. This event is known as **the Boston Tea Party.**

156. **The First Continental Congress** was formed on September 5th, 1774. The representatives talked about effective ways to deal with the British government. **They sent a petition to the king**, asking him to remove the Intolerable Acts. The men agreed to meet again if things did not change. The First Continental Congress disbanded almost two months after it had started.

157. **John Adams wrote the Novanglus** essays, which were first published in 1774. These essays defend the constitutionality of the Stamp Act but argue the colonies had a right to **self-government**. His writing showcased his intellectual prowess, earning him the respect of his peers. John Adams was a noted figure in colonial America and would later become president.

158. On March 23rd, 1775, **Patrick Henry** gave his famous **"Give me liberty or give me death"** speech at St John's Church in Richmond, Virginia, while urging Virginia to raise troops for the American Revolution. He wanted people to realize that war was inevitable.

159. In 1775, **Thomas Paine** began writing his famous pamphlet called **Common Sense.** This work argued for American independence from Britain. It was not published until January 1776. Common Sense became one of the most widely read documents. By the end of the war, it is estimated that 500,000 copies had been sold!

160. **Paul Revere made his famous ride from Boston to Lexington** to warn Americans about British troops on April 18th, 1775.

161. **The British were planning** to take weapons and other supplies because they feared the colonists were on the verge of rebelling violently. Their actions **started the American Revolution.**

162. **The "shot heard 'round the world"** happened at the Battles of Lexington and Concord. The battle at Lexington was minor. At Concord, the two sides were at a standoff until someone fired a shot. To this day, no one knows which side fired first.

163. Shortly after the Battles of Lexington and Concord, **the Second Continental Congress was convened.** It essentially acted as the government while the colonies fought for their independence.

164. **George Washington was appointed commander** in chief of the Continental Army on June 15th, 1755.

165. **The Battle of Bunker Hill** was fought on June 17th, 1775, and is one of the most famous battles of the American Revolution. Although the British won, they suffered heavy casualties. The British soon realized this **rebellion would not be put down easily.**

166. **The Declaration of Independence** was adopted on July 4th, 1776, with Thomas Jefferson being its principal author. John Adams, Benjamin Franklin, Robert Livingston, and Roger Sherman edited or wrote portions of it.

167. **Thomas Jefferson** also wrote the Virginia Statute for Religious Freedom in 1776. The statute proclaimed that no one should be persecuted based on religion, despite their beliefs or lack thereof. This document was a precursor to the **First Amendment of the United States Constitution.**

168. The Battle of Trenton was fought on December 26th, 1776, when **George Washington's** forces crossed the Delaware River. **The colonists surprised the Hessian soldiers** stationed in the city. It was one of the most significant victories for the Americans during its war of independence. Winning the battle boosted morale greatly, which was suffering after defeats in New York.

169. On July 31st, 1777, **a French aristocrat named Lafayette became a major general** in the Continental Army. Lafayette played a major role in securing help from France.

170. Although the **French didn't really get involved in the war until 1778**, France played an essential role in helping the Americans win their freedom. For instance, French fleets helped blockade seaports so that British soldiers could not sail to America. In 1780, **French general Rochambeau's army arrived** to help the colonists. His assistance in the Battle of Yorktown was invaluable.

171. **Native Americans** were caught in the middle of the war, with many tribes fighting for both sides. For instance, **the Cherokee and Choctaw sided with Britain**. The Iroquois Confederacy was divided, although most tribes supported the British.

172. **Women also played an active role in the American Revolution** by serving their country. They nursed wounded soldiers, acted as spies, and even took up arms against the enemy!

173. **Betsy Ross is credited with creating the first United States flag** with stars and stripes representing the Thirteen Colonies. However, there is no firm evidence that she was the first to make the design. **This flag was adopted on June 14th, 1777.**

174. During the American Revolution, **African Americans played a crucial role in the war** effort. About 100,000 enslaved African Americans escaped. **Many joined the British forces**, hoping to find freedom. Other African Americans served as spies, messengers, and scouts. African Americans also served as soldiers in the **Continental Army.**

175. In 1777, **the Articles of Confederation** were created by the Continental Congress. The articles established the **first form of government for the United States**. A little over ten years later, the Articles of Confederation were replaced with the US Constitution after realizing too much power rested with individual states. The Constitution created the foundation of the **federal system of the US today!**

176 **The Battles of Saratoga** were fought between British and American forces in September and October of 1777. These conflicts turned the tide of the war in favor of the Americans and led them **to gain support from France.**

177. **The siege of Yorktown** lasted from September 28th to October 19th, 1781. American and French troops laid siege to the town for three weeks. **British General Cornwallis** was eventually forced to surrender. The end of the siege ended the major military operations of the American Revolution.

178. **The Treaty of Paris** was signed on September 3rd, 1783. It officially recognized **the United States as an independent nation**. The new nation gained everything north of Florida, south of Canada, and east of the Mississippi River.

179. **Benjamin Franklin, John Adams**, and **John Jay** helped negotiate **the Treaty of Paris.** France, Spain, and the Netherlands signed separate treaties with Britain.

180. **After winning freedom from Great Britain**, America began establishing its government and drafting laws and regulations, leading to what we know today as the present-day US.

# The Constitutional Convention and the Constitution of the United States

This chapter will explore the history and key elements of **the Constitutional Convention and the Constitution of the United States**. With these **thirty facts**, you'll gain insight into how **the Founding Fathers** created a document to ensure citizens had rights, freedom from oppression, and unfair treatment by others and the government. We will also examine the **Bill of Rights**, which outlines important freedoms. Finally, we'll learn why understanding this **revolutionary document** is so critical to keeping America strong.

181. **The Constitutional Convention** was a meeting of delegates from the former Thirteen Colonies in 1787 to discuss and form a plan for how the new nation would be governed.

182. **Rhode Island did not attend** the Constitutional Convention. It was worried that the new document would take away the state's power. Rhode Island was the last state to ratify the Constitution.

183. Many of the men who met at the Constitutional Convention became known as the **Founding Fathers**. These men helped establish the new nation. Some scholars believe all the men at the Constitutional Convention were Founding Fathers because they helped work on the US Constitution.

184. Some important **Founding Fathers** did not sign the Constitution. **Thomas Jefferson and John Adams** were away in Europe during the Constitutional Convention, so they did not get to sign the document.

185. The men who met at the convention wanted to ensure **citizens had rights**, including freedom from oppression and unfair treatment by others or governments. It was important to them that the new nation did **not become like Britain.**

186. At first, there were arguments about **how much power each state should have** and what kind of laws should apply across America.

187. But eventually, they agreed on a system. **Congress would have specific powers**, while individual states would have some control over their affairs. This is known as **federalism.**

188. It took the men at **the Constitutional Convention** four months (from May to September) to write their ideas down into one document. This document became **the Constitution of the United States**.

189. **Jacob Shallus**, a clerk from Pennsylvania, transcribed the document. He was paid $30, which would be around $730 today.

190. It took **ten months for enough states** to ratify the Constitution so it could become law. Some people were worried that the Constitution gave too much power to the central government.

191. Although seventy delegates were appointed to **the Constitutional Convention**, only fifty-five showed up. And of those fifty-five, only thirty-nine signed. Some became sick, and others left. But some outright refused to sign the document because of the lack of a **Bill of Rights.**

192. **The Constitution** set up three branches of government: **executive** (the president and his staff), **legislative** (Congress), and **judicial** (the Supreme Court).

193. This system ensures that no branch can become too powerful over the other. It's called the **separation of powers** or the system of checks and balances.

194. **The Constitution** also allowed for amendments, which are changes to the Constitution to suit the nation as time goes on.

195. The original **Constitution** did not mention **women** or **enslaved** African Americans.

196. **The Bill of Rights** was written four years later to ensure that everyone had access to basic rights. These rights include the **freedom** of **speech, religion, protest**, and more. However, some groups of people, like women, African Americans, and Native Americans, didn't get to enjoy these rights until later on. **The Bill of Rights is the first ten amendments to the Constitution.**

197. **The Constitution** replaced **the Articles of Confederation**. The Articles of Confederation gave more power to the states, and the US needed a stronger central government after the war.

198. The Constitution also set up **the Electoral College**. Today, people in the US cast their votes for president. Each state gets a certain number of electoral votes, depending on its presence in Congress. The new president is determined by how many electoral votes they receive. So, it is possible for a president to lose the popular vote (the vote of the people) while still winning the electoral vote.

199. **The Constitution** also outlines the process for electing senators and representatives to Congress. These people act as a state's voice in government.

200. However, **the original Constitution did not state that everyone had the right to vote**. The decision on who could vote belonged to the states.

201. This document helps to **protect us from the abuse of power by federal, state, and local governments** so that no one person could ever rule over the people without their consent.

202. **The Constitution states** that both houses of Congress must approve laws before they can become official laws.

203. **It forbids states** from making certain agreements with each other or foreign countries without permission from Congress first.

204. **The Constitution** can only be changed if more than three-fourths of the states agree to it. This was done so that small **groups couldn't just make changes** whenever they wanted.

205. **Since 1787, there have been twenty-seven amendments** added to the original document. Many of them give Americans more rights or expand on the original ones.

206. **The Constitution is the cornerstone of the United States**. It's what makes the nation a democracy. It also ensures that everyone has equal rights in the country.

207. **Although the US is not credited with inventing democracy**, it invented the kind of democracy we are familiar with today. The US is also the oldest continuous democracy in the world.

208. **The Constitution was revolutionary** when it was written and continues to be so today. Almost every nation in the world was not free when the Constitution was signed.

209. **Constitution Day is** celebrated on **September 17th**, the day it was signed.

210. In 1789, **George Washington** stated that **November 26th** would be a day of **thanksgiving for the Constitution**. It was the first time a president acknowledged the holiday of Thanksgiving.

# The First President of the United States

This chapter will explore the life and legacy of George Washington, the first president of the United States. We'll look at thirty interesting facts about his early life, military career, political career, and retirement at Mount Vernon. Additionally, we'll learn some fun facts about the man himself!

211. **George Washington** was the first president of the United States. He served from **1789 to 1797.**

212. He is known as the **"Father of His Country."**

213. Washington's face appears on the **US one-dollar bill** and the quarter.

214. **George Washington was born in Virginia** on February 22nd, 1732, into a wealthy slave-holding family. He lived on a plantation called Mount Vernon.

215. He had no middle name. But he did have **three younger brothers**, two of which, John Augustine and Samuel, became officers in the American Revolutionary War. He also had other siblings and half-siblings.

216. At the age of eleven, Washington's formal schooling ended because his father died. Instead of going to England for an education, **he worked as a surveyor in the US** before joining the military just before the French and Indian War broke out.

217. **Washington was largely self-educated.** In 1744, he transcribed a manual about etiquette. Washington's exercise became known as **Rules of Civility & Decent Behavior in Company and Conversation.** It details advice on how one should act with others. It is believed these guidelines played a crucial role in how Washington conducted himself.

218. **Washington married Martha Dandridge Custis** when he was twenty-six years old. She brought two children from her previous marriage whom they raised together. **Washington had no biological children.**

219. **George Washington was one of America's Founding Fathers**. Other popular Founding Fathers include Thomas Jefferson, Benjamin Franklin, and John Adams.

220. **Washington was a crucial leader in the American Revolution.**

221. He is known **for crossing the Delaware River** with troops to take Trenton during the Revolutionary War due to a famous painting. The battle helped turn morale around.

222. He was **appointed commander in chief of the Continental Army** in 1775. He officially resigned from his position in December 1783.

223. In June 1787, **George Washington attended the Constitutional Convention**. He was nominated as its president. He presided over debates among delegates about how best to organize a new government for the United States of America.

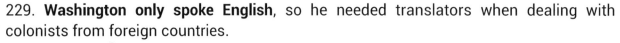

224. In 1789, George Washington became **the first US president.**

225. During his presidency, **he set precedents that are still followed today**. For example, he appointed Cabinet members to advise him on policy decisions and formed an executive department. He gave the first State of the Union Address and **created diplomatic relations between the US and other countries**. Under his presidency, a national bank was created.

226. Almost six hundred slaves worked at Mount Vernon during his lifetime. **He eventually spoke out against slavery**, calling it "a reproach upon human nature." However, he never denounced the practice in public. He advocated for gradual emancipation rather than a sudden, drastic change that could lead to social unrest or revolt among freed slaves who had no means of support. George Washington freed all of his slaves in his will.

227. **He was a Freemason** and served as the Worshipful Master of his Lodge in Alexandria, Virginia. The Freemasons were a secret order that only men could join. They are still around today!

228. **Washington owned a large collection of books** on topics like philosophy, math, politics, and more.

229. **Washington only spoke English**, so he needed translators when dealing with colonists from foreign countries.

230. **George Washington was a founding member of the Society for Promoting Agriculture.** This organization encouraged people living in rural areas to become better farmers by sharing ideas about crop rotation methods and other farming techniques.

231. **He was a keen horseman** and owned many horses over his lifetime, even having some specially bred for racing.

232. **George Washington had false teeth made from ivory**, which were held together by springs. People tend to say he had wooden teeth, but that is a myth. His false teeth often caused him great pain while eating or speaking, so it wasn't unusual to see him without them.

233. **He loved fishing** and would go out regularly at Mount Vernon. Fish was his favorite food.

234. **Washington enjoyed drinking** and had several favorite alcoholic beverages. However, he drank in moderation, as he knew the effects of drinking too much alcohol in one sitting.

235. **Washington was unanimously elected for a second term**. He retired from office at the age of sixty-five after serving two terms as president. He set a precedent. The only person to serve more than two terms was Franklin Delano Roosevelt. After Roosevelt died, an amendment created a two-term limit on the presidency.

236. **When Washington first became president**, there were only thirteen states. By the end of his life, there were sixteen states in the Union.

237. **Washington's** Farewell Address in 1796 warned Americans to stay away from foreign entanglements and to avoid the formation of political parties. He also advised against the accumulation of debt by individuals and governments.

238. **After his presidency, he moved back to Mount Vernon**, where he spent the rest of his life overseeing business operations at the plantation. He also cultivated wheat for export. He died on December 14th, 1799, from an illness related to a throat infection.

239. **George Washington is consistently listed as one of the best US presidents.** He was known for his integrity, honesty, and strong leadership skills. His qualities earned him great respect from both sides of the political divide during America's early days as a young nation.

240. **In 1885, Congress created an annual holiday named after Washington to recognize all that he had achieved as president**. Initially, the holiday was celebrated on Washington's birthday. The date was later changed to the third Monday of February and morphed into Presidents' Day.

# The War of 1812

This chapter will explore the history and key elements of the War of 1812. This war was fought between **the United States and Great Britain**. With these thirty facts, you'll discover how this conflict helped solidify US independence from British rule. We'll also learn **about American heroes,** such as **Andrew Jackson and Oliver Hazard Perry,** who led battles during this war. Discover the important outcomes resulting from the War of 1812, including a boundary line still in place today.

241. The War of 1812 was fought between **the United States and Great Britain.**

242. It lasted for two years and eight months, **from June 1812 to February 1814.**

243. Both sides were trying to gain more control over territories in **North America and at sea.**

244. The impressment of sailors was a big problem. The British would forcefully **recruit US sailors to serve on British ships.**

245. **The US was also upset over the British blockade of France.** America was a new nation and needed trading partners to sustain itself. **The Napoleonic Wars were in full swing in Europe.** It became clear that America could not remain neutral, especially when France blockaded Britain.

246. On June 18th, 1812, **President James Madison** signed the declaration of war.

247. **Britain was busy fighting France in Europe** at the start of the war. It sent around five thousand people at the beginning of the war. By the end of the war, almost fifty thousand men were fighting.

248. **The US had around seven thousand soldiers at the start of the war.** By the end, nearly thirty-six thousand men were engaged in conflicts.

249. **The War of 1812 largely took place in Canada,** although several key battles happened in the Great Lakes region of the US.

250. The first battle in the war was **the siege of Fort Mackinac in July 1812**. "Battle" might be too strong a word. The soldiers on Mackinac Island, Michigan, didn't even know the war had broken out. They surrendered to the British without a fight.

251. **Many Native Americans fought alongside the British during the war**. After the war ended, they realized Britain would no longer help shield them from the influx of settlers heading west.

252. **Tecumseh was a Shawnee chief who led a confederacy of tribes**. He aided the British during the war and was instrumental in taking Fort Detroit from the US.

253. **Tecumseh died during the Battle of the Thames in October 1813**. His death caused the confederacy to fragment.

254. **General Andrew Jackson led some of the American forces in the war**. He won crucial victories, such as the Battle of New Orleans in January 1815. This battle was actually fought after the peace treaty had been signed overseas.

255. **Jackson would later become the president**. And he was not the only future president that fought in the War of 1812. John Quincy Adams, James Monroe, and William Henry Harrison also fought in this war.

256. **At the beginning of the war, the US Navy only had sixteen ships!** It had hundreds of smaller vessels, though. The British navy was much larger, but it also had the Napoleonic Wars to deal with in Europe.

257. **The US Navy experienced great success in the War of 1812**. The British Royal Navy was considered the best in the world, but the US Navy defeated the British in several key battles, such as the Battle of Lake Erie in September 1813.

258. **Commodore Oliver Hazard Perry led the US Navy to victory at the Battle of Lake Erie.** The US held control over the lake for the rest of the war. This win allowed them to win the Battle of the Thames and end Tecumseh's confederacy. The US was also able to take back Fort Detroit.

259. **In August 1814, the British set fire to the White House, the Capitol**, and other buildings. First Lady Dolley Madison is believed to have saved the portrait of George Washington, which still hangs in the White House to this day.

260. **Four days later, a huge storm and a tornado** swept through the area, extinguishing the flames. Although the weather put the fires out, it also caused more destruction.

261. During the war, **Francis Scott** Key wrote a poem called **"Defence of Fort M'Henry."** The poem turned into the lyrics for "The Star-Spangled Banner," which later became the US national anthem.

262. He wrote the poem after witnessing the **Battle of Baltimore**, which was fought in September 1814. The poem has four stanzas. The first stanza is the one that is commonly sung today.

263. Although neither side achieved an overall victory, it became known as **the Second War of Independence** because it solidified US independence from British rule.

264. **The Treaty of Ghent** was signed in December 1814, officially ending the war. Since neither side had technically won, the treaty restored the "status quo ante bellum" (meaning both sides agreed to return any land or goods captured during the war).

265. **The Treaty of Ghent** established a boundary line between Canada and the US. This line still exists today.

266. **After the war, American trade with Britain increased**. More settlers came to America looking for new land and a new life.

267. **The period after the war saw rapid growth in America's industry and economy** due to improved trade relations with Britain and other European countries.

268. **The War of 1812 also helped to shape the country's military and naval forces.** For instance, Winfield Scott introduced a training system that improved the US Army's performance.

269. Many monuments dedicated to those who served or died during this conflict still stand today **to remind us of what they achieved** for future generations.

270. **The War of 1812** helped forge a more robust national identity and increased pride in being an American.

# The Indian Removal Act and the Trail of Tears

**This chapter will explore the Indian Removal Act** and its devastating impact on Native American tribes in the United States. We'll look at how this act led to forced relocations and the **Trail of Tears**, a long journey that saw thousands suffer hardships.

271. **The Indian Removal Act** was passed by US Congress **on May 28th, 1830,** during the presidency of Andrew Jackson.

272. **The act forcibly removed Native Americans from their lands** east of the Mississippi River. They were to be relocated to lands west of the river that had been acquired through treaties with other tribes.

273. **President Andrew Jackson** is widely regarded as one of the main figures responsible for passing the Indian Removal Act and authorizing its implementation. The act did have opposition from Congress members like **Henry Clay, Daniel Webster, and Davy Crockett.**

274. **Jackson believed removal was the best way to grow the American economy**. He said getting rid of the Native Americans would allow states like Alabama and Mississippi "to advance rapidly in population, wealth, and power."

275. After the passage of the Indian Removal Act, many **Native American leaders tried to resist removal** by appealing directly to the US Supreme Court. They also petitioned President Jackson himself, although their pleas fell on deaf ears.

276. **In 1832, the Supreme Court declared that the "Indian Nations" were separate nations** and that the US needed to treat the Native Americans as it would any other nation. Although the ruling was never enforced, it did lay the foundations for tribal sovereignty.

277. **More than forty-six thousand Native Americans were forced to leave their ancestral homes due to this act**. The five main tribes the Indian Removal Act affected were the **Cherokee, Muscogee (Creek), Choctaw, Seminole, and Chickasaw.**

278. These people embarked on a journey known as the **Trail of Tears**. They traveled over five thousand miles, although the amount the Native Americans traveled depended on where they lived.

279. The trail went across rugged terrain. **The Native Americans endured harsh conditions with little food** or supplies provided by the federal government agents who were assigned to oversee their relocation process.

280. **The number of deaths on the Trail of Tears is not known.** It is estimated that at least ten thousand Native Americans died during this long trek due to exhaustion, malnutrition, disease, and exposure.

281. **The Cherokees alone suffered at least four thousand deaths.** The death toll goes as high as six thousand.

282. **John Ross was the chief of the Cherokee**. He was one-eighth Cherokee, but he grew up with the Cherokees. The Cherokees are matrilineal, and his mother was Cherokee. He fought hard for the Cherokee to remain in their homeland. His wife died on the trail.

283. **Most Native Americans traveled on foot**, although some traveled by boat, in wagons, or on horseback.

284. **The Trail of Tears took place for several years.** People were removed from the Southeast from 1830 to 1850.

285. **The Indian Removal Act led to a war.** The Second Seminole War was fought because the US had voided a previous treaty with the passing of the act. The Seminoles were defeated in this war.

286. After removal, **the property** previously held **by Native Americans** was confiscated and **given to white settlers** or taken by the government.

287. This period in history remains controversial to this day. **It led to great suffering for Native Americans** and their families, many of whom were forced from their homes at gunpoint.

288. **Despite this hardship, some Native Americans resisted removal through legal means.** Others used guerrilla tactics, such as sabotage or escape attempts, when confronted with US troops.

289. **The Indian Removal Act did not remove all of the Native Americans from the Southeast.** For instance, some eluded the US Army and melted into the backwoods of the Southeast. Some Cherokee were allowed to stay in North Carolina after assisting the US Army.

290. Those who were removed **lived on established reservations, which were mostly located in Oklahoma**. The land was different from what they had been used to, and they also had to deal with other tribes already living there.

291. **Today, there are around five million Native Americans in the US**. About 30 percent of them live on reservations.

292. **The Indian Removal Act** had far-reaching consequences. Native American communities on either side of the Mississippi River have experienced economic disparities and land disputes for generations.

293. It is not known for sure where the name **"Trail of Tears"** came from. The name was first printed in 1908.

294. **The Indian Removal Act was repealed in 1980.**

295. **The Trail of Tears National Historic Trail** was established in 1987. It stretches over nine states, from Georgia to Oklahoma and north to Illinois.

296. **The trail is a memorial for those who lost their lives**. It also serves as a reminder that the US government's policy toward Native Americans has not always been fair.

297. **The trail** preserves critical cultural sites along the route, such as burial grounds, villages, and sacred places.

298. **Every year, many people visit parts of the original path** that Native Americans were forced to take when they were forcibly removed from their homes.

299. **Many Native American activists have condemned the Indian Removal Act** over the years. Historians have also looked down on the act due to its devastating impact on indigenous populations.

300. **The Indian Removal Act was also seen as a violation** of several treaties signed between the US government and tribes. The treaties were supposed to protect their rights but led to their displacement without compensation or adequate protection.

# The Civil War

This chapter will explore **the history of the Civil War**, a conflict that lasted from 1861 to 1865. Over three million soldiers fought for their beliefs. We'll take a look at thirty interesting facts about how the **North (the Union) and the South (the Confederacy)** fought one another, what strategies were employed by both sides, and why the South decided to secede from the Union in the first place. Additionally, we'll examine the impact this had on African Americans who gained freedom during this period.

301. **The Civil War was fought between 1861 and 1865** in the United States of America.

302. It was a war **between the North** (the Union) **and the South** (the Confederacy).

303. The leading cause of the **war was slavery**, as many disagreed on whether it should be allowed.

304. **Abraham Lincoln became president** in 1860 and was inaugurated (entered office) in 1861.

305. Although **Lincoln** never expressed a desire to abolish slavery outright, the South was worried the new Republican government might do that. Before Lincoln was inaugurated, seven **Southern states had already left the Union.**

306. On February 8th, 1861, the **Confederate States of America was officially founded**. In total, eleven states seceded from the Union.

307. The first battle **of the Civil War** occurred at **Fort Sumter** in South Carolina in April 1861 when Confederates fired upon US troops stationed there. No one died from the fighting, and the US evacuated the fort.

308. **The First Battle of Bull Run took place in Virginia** on July 21st, 1861. The Union expected an easy victory; the Confederates won the day. Thomas J. Jackson earned his famous nickname, "Stonewall," in this battle for holding the line.

309. **The Battle of Shiloh**, which took place in northern Tennessee in 1862, saw approximately twenty-three thousand casualties in just two days, making it one of the bloodiest battles of **the Civil War.**

310. **The Battle of Antietam** occurred in September 1862 in Maryland. Prior to this battle, **the Confederacy had just scored an important victory** at the Second Battle of Bull Run and expected another win. The Union was able to repel the Confederacy's invasion of the North.

311. **The Battle of Antietam** paved the way for President Lincoln to issue his famous Emancipation Proclamation in January 1863. It freed all slaves in the "rebellious states." The border states (slave states that did not secede) were not affected by the Emancipation Proclamation.

312. In July 1863, one of the most important battles of the Civil War took place: **the Battle of Gettysburg**. This battle is seen as the turning point in the war. **The Union stopped any Confederate** plans of invasion and put the Confederates on the defensive.

313. The famous Pickett's Charge was ordered by Confederate **General Robert E. Lee**. He wanted to break through the Union lines at Gettysburg, but it failed and cost thousands of casualties. Gettysburg was the bloodiest battle in the war.

314. **Abraham Lincoln** gave his memorable Gettysburg Address about four months after the Union victory at that battle site, cementing its place in history.

315. In 1862, **Congress passed an act that freed enslaved people whose masters fought for the South.** African American volunteers joined the Union Army in droves. Almost 180,000 African Americans served in the army, while 19,000 served in the navy.

316. **Women played an essential role on both sides**. Nurses like Clara Barton helped wounded soldiers at battlefield hospitals and held fundraisers for relief efforts.

317. **Both sides used new naval technology,** such as ironclad ships and submarines. Ironclad ships were used for war for the first time in the US Civil War. And a Confederate submarine was the first submarine to sink an enemy ship.

318. **The Civil War** also saw the introduction of new weapons, such as new versions of repeating rifles like the Spencer rifle and Gatling guns. These weapons would change the face of warfare forever.

319. **Generals William Sherman and Philip Sheridan** are famous for their scorched-earth policy, which saw them burn down villages in the South to deprive Confederate troops of shelter and supplies.

320. On April 9th, 1865, **General Robert E. Lee** surrendered at Appomattox Court House, marking an end to hostilities between the North and South.

321. **Approximately 620,000 soldiers died** during the four years of fighting. The Civil War is considered to be the bloodiest war in US history.

322. Following the defeat, **some Confederates fled across the border into Mexico and Brazil**, where they formed communities known as Confederados.

323. **President Lincoln** was assassinated on April 14th, 1865, shortly after winning reelection for a second term and shortly after the Civil War ended.

324. After Lincoln's death, **Andrew Johnson** became president and oversaw the Reconstruction efforts. He also granted pardons to many former Confederates who had fought against Union forces.

325. **The Reconstruction era** began shortly after the war's conclusion and lasted until 1877, when US government troops withdrew from former Confederate states.

326. **After four years of war,** many cities and towns were destroyed throughout the South. It would take decades for some to rebuild.

327. **The Thirteenth Amendment was passed in** 1865, officially outlawing slavery throughout the United States of America.

328. **In 1866, Congress passed the Fourteenth Amendment,** which gave former slaves the same rights as listed in the Bill of Rights. The amendment did not apply to women of any race.

329. **In 1869, the Fifteenth Amendment was passed.** This amendment protected voting rights for black males.

330. **Today, it is debated how much the Reconstruction helped the country**. The country was put back together after the war, but African Americans still faced discrimination and segregation. Things would not start to get better for them until the 1960s.

# The Old West

This chapter will explore **the history of life in the Old West between 1865** and 1895. We'll take a look at thirty interesting facts about what happened during this iconic time period, such as **the gold rushes, famous outlaws** who earned their notoriety through daring **heists and robberies**, details on how **cowboys lived** while herding cattle on long journeys, and more! Discover famous chiefs like **Sitting Bull**, who fought bravely against US forces and other important aspects of life out west that helped shape the US into what it is today!

331. **The Old West** was a period in the United States between 1865 and 1895.

332. **Cowboys were men** who herded cattle on long journeys called cattle drives. They also did other things, such as care for horses and repair fences.

333. **Cattle drives took cowboys** months to complete. They often faced danger along the way from rustlers trying to steal their cattle!

334. Other dangers like mountain lions, rattlesnakes, wolves, and bears lurked around every corner, so **cowboys needed to be careful** while out on the range.

335. **Cowboys slept under the stars**. They also carried a canvas tent with them in case the weather didn't cooperate.

336. **Cowboys wore big hats** that kept the sun off their faces while herding cattle during long days in hot or rainy weather.

337. **Cowboys ate a lot of beans and beef** while herding cattle. They also ate hard biscuits and dried fruit. Coffee was their preferred beverage.

338. **Buffalo Bill Cody** held the first big rodeo in 1882. In rodeos, people could show off their skills by roping calves or riding wild horses. These events attracted large crowds of spectators looking for entertainment of a different kind.

339. **Gunslingers were expert marksmen who could shoot accurately**, sometimes even from horseback. Sharpshooting became very popular during this time. Buffalo Bill even made a traveling show involving fancy gun tricks and plays. His shows starred **Annie Oakley, Sitting Bull, and Wild Bill Hickok.**

340. **People who moved west faced a lot of challenges.** Getting to their new home was difficult, as everything had to be moved by wagon. And once the new family got there, they had to build a cabin and barn and then plant crops. And that was on top of other chores, like cooking, cleaning, and repairing items.

341. **Life was hard on the frontier.** There were few stores or doctors, so one had to be prepared for anything that could happen.

342. **Wells Fargo** was an important mail delivery service established in California in 1852. It used stagecoaches instead of horseback riders for long distances.

343. **The Pony Express** was a way to send letters and news across the country. It was established in 1860. Riders would **travel on horseback while carrying mail** for long distances. Pony Express stations would provide a place to rest, eat, and get a fresh horse for the next leg of the trip.

344. **The Transcontinental Railroad** was built between 1863 and 1869. It connected the eastern states of America with California, which made it much easier for people to travel westward.

345. **Settlers also ran into problems with Native Americans**, who had lived off the land long before settlers arrived. The tribes hunted, farmed, fished, and gathered food in the West.

346. The influx of settlers led to clashes with the Native Americans. US forces were called in to fight Native Americans. **The tribes were upset the settlers were taking away their land** and hunting buffalo to near extinction.

347. **Millions of buffalo once roamed freely in large herds in the West**, but as settlers moved westward, they killed them for food and sport. The buffalo also suffered from disease and drought.

348. In 1889, there were less than **six hundred buffalo left in the Great Plains.**

349. **Native Americans formed powerful alliances** as settlers continued moving westward. Chiefs like **Sitting Bull fought against US forces** to protect their people.

350. **Sitting Bull was a Hunkpapa Lakota leader**. He led the native forces against Lieutenant Colonel George Custer in the Battle of the Little Bighorn. Everyone in Custer's battalion died.

351. **Crazy Horse also fought in the Battle of the Little Bighorn,** which took place in 1876. Crazy Horse is most remembered for his tragic death. He was killed by a US soldier after resisting arrest. To this day, it is not known for sure if he ever resisted.

352. **Buffalo Soldiers were African American cavalry** units of the US Army who fought in many battles against Native Americans and protected settlers during westward expansion. The American Indian Wars started long before the time of the Old West and would not end until the 1920s.

353. **The discovery of gold** in states like California, Montana, and Colorado led many people to travel westward to become wealthy, displacing Native Americans in the process.

354. People from all over the world came to take part in these **gold rushes**. Around sixty-seven thousand **Chinese immigrated to California** during the gold rush years.

355. **Towns grew quickly** as more people moved westward to look for land, adventure, and wealth. More than 300,000 people moved to California during the gold rush!

356. **Sheriffs kept law and order in towns** by arresting criminals or outlaws, sometimes with help from deputies or even posses that tracked down wanted men!

357. **Vigilante justice was common in the Wild West**. Law enforcement couldn't keep up with criminals, so posses would hunt down wanted men, sometimes without legal authority from a judge or jury of peers.

358. **Jesse James was a famous outlaw in the Old West**. He led men in the first daytime bank robbery during a time of peace.

359. Other famous outlaws include **Billy the Kid and Butch Cassidy and the Sundance Kid.**

360. **The Wild West** was full of **adventure, danger, and excitement**. It has been immortalized by books, movies, and television shows for generations to come.

# The Industrial Revolution

This chapter will explore **the history and impact of the Industrial Revolution.** We'll look at thirty facts about how this period changed life in America and around the world, from new inventions that made production faster to advances in communication and transportation. **We'll also discuss how it sparked a population boom in cities** across America while creating new jobs and opportunities for people.

361. **The Industrial Revolution** began in the United States around 1790 and ended around 1870.

362. **During this period, many changes took place** to make production easier and faster. **New machines were invented,** which allowed people to produce more items in shorter amounts of time than ever before.

363. **Many new inventions during the Industrial Revolution made life easier for Americans.** Sewing machines could make clothes quicker, and cotton gins could separate fibers quickly so they could be made into textiles like clothing or blankets.

364. One crucial invention was **the steam engine, which allowed machines to be powered by steam.** The steam engine helped power factories in cities across America at unprecedented speeds.

365. With the help of these **new technologies**, industries started booming. Businesses flourished like never before!

366. **The Industrial Revolution** saw the rise of large-scale factories and production centers, allowing for the mass production of items. This was particularly important in developing textiles. Machines could produce more cloth faster than ever!

367. **Coal and iron ore mining also boomed during this period**. Coal fueled steam engines, and iron ore was needed to make steel.

368. **New industries emerged, such as steel** (which provided materials needed for buildings) and oil production (which powered new machines and vehicles).

369. **A big part of the Industrial Revolution was transportation.** New roads were built so goods could be transported quickly from one place to another. Steamships revolutionized sea travel. They were much faster than ships powered only by sails!

370. **New railroad tracks** made it possible for people to travel longer distances at greater speeds.

371. **The construction of the Erie Canal** finished in 1852. The canal connected the Atlantic Ocean to the Great Lakes, which cut the costs of transporting goods to the US interior.

372. **The telegraph also became widely available** during this time. Telegraphs allowed people to communicate over vast distances without waiting days or weeks for letters like they did before.

373. **Newspapers and magazines were also mass produced** and distributed during the Industrial Revolution. People could more easily be informed about worldwide events.

374. **Advances in medicine** helped reduce deaths from diseases. For instance, in 1800, Dr. Benjamin Waterhouse gave his children the first smallpox vaccine in the US. The vaccine had been developed four years earlier by an English doctor named Edward Jenner.

375. **Financial services grew rapidly** during this time due to increased demand from businesses looking for investments or loans. In 1790, the Philadelphia Stock Exchange became the first stock exchange in the US.

376. **The Industrial Revolution changed how Americans worked**. It made everyday life easier for some while creating new jobs and opportunities.

377. However, **working conditions were not great** for those in the factories or coal mines. People worked in cramped spaces and dealt with heavy machinery.

378. Although the wealthy enjoyed the increase in goods, **poorer people worked twelve-to sixteen-hour days**, six days a week, just to scrape by.

379. **Children worked in factories** and coal mines as well. Their small fingers were perfect for working on delicate yet dangerous machinery.

380. Coal mining was a very dangerous job. **Mines could collapse unexpectedly**, and coal dust caused serious breathing problems.

381. **The newsies were young boys who sold newspapers** on the corners of busy streets. They were typically orphaned and were paid pennies for selling newspapers.

382. **Child labor laws** were eventually signed into law. For instance, the Cotton Factories Regulation Act of 1819 set the minimum working age to nine. Children in the textile industry could work up to twelve hours a day.

383. **Adult workers fought for their rights** in the workplace. They began forming unions, allowing them to fight for better working conditions, including higher pay or shorter hours.

384. **The American Federation of Labor** was formed by Samuel Gompers in 1886. Although it made some strides, working conditions for most Americans would not get better until the early 20th century.

385. **Women's roles also started changing**. They gained increased access to education, jobs outside the home, and even voting rights in some places.

386. **The US economy grew significantly** during the Industrial Revolution, creating new wealth through trade and industry.

387. It also led to a **population boom in cities** across America, with people flocking from rural areas in search of work opportunities.

388. **Immigration also increased** during this period. Many Europeans were attracted by the possibilities the growing American economy offered!

389. Some people were angry about the influx of immigrants. **Immigrants were willing to take a job with lower pay** and deal with poor working conditions. This led to much resentment.

390. The US had more than one Industrial Revolution. **The Second Industrial Revolution took off soon after the First Industrial Revolution ended**. The Third Industrial Revolution happened during the mid- to late 20th century. Some historians believe we are in the Fourth Industrial Revolution right now.

# The Spanish-American War

This chapter will explore **the Spanish-American War**, a conflict between the United States and Spain that lasted from April to August 1898. We'll look at thirty interesting facts about **how this war began** and why it's an important milestone in American history. Discover some fascinating facts about **Theodore Roosevelt's** volunteer cavalry unit and a journalist named **Richard Harding Davis**.

391. **The Spanish-American War** was a conflict between the United States and Spain that lasted from April to August 1898.

392. It began when an **American warship**, the USS Maine, blew up in Havana Harbor, Cuba, while on a diplomatic mission.

393. **Yellow journalism** (similar to modern-day tabloids) pointed the finger at Spain. Recent examinations have determined that the Maine exploded because something went wrong on the ship.

394. Over a month later, **President William McKinley asked Congress to declare war on Spain**. He wanted to support the Cuban rebels fighting for independence from Spanish control. The country was also still upset over the sinking of the Maine, with most people believing Spain was behind it.

395. The **US wanted to help Cuba gain its freedom**. There were also many US citizens living on the island. The US invested money in businesses in Cuba and relied on trade with it.

396. **The Spanish-American War was an important milestone in US history,** as it marked the first time that a large part of its military forces was used overseas.

397. **The Battle of Manila Bay** took place on May 1st, 1898. The Americans headed to the Philippines to ensure the Spanish naval forces there would not go to Cuba to aid in the war effort. The Spanish were crushed, ending their colonial rule over the islands.

398. **The Battle of San Juan Hill** occurred on July 1st, 1898. The Americans trounced the Spanish and practically ensured they would be the victors in Cuba.

399. Future **American president Theodore Roosevelt** led his volunteer cavalry unit known as the Rough Riders into battle at San Juan Hill near Santiago de Cuba. This helped solidify him as a national hero!

400. Although they were called the **Rough Riders**, only the officers rode horses into battle!

401. **The Buffalo Soldiers,** which were units comprised of African Americans, also served with distinction on the battlefield. Although they faced racial tensions at home, white commanders in the US Army praised the Buffalo Soldiers' bravery.

402. **The Battle of El Caney** happened on the same day as **the Battle of San Juan Hill**. The Americans technically won this battle, but El Caney did not prove useful to them, especially in light of the causalities they suffered.

403. On July 3rd, 1898, the Battle of Santiago de Cuba took place. **All of the Spanish ships were destroyed**, while the US Navy remained intact. This battle ended the Cuban theater of the war.

404. **The Spanish-American War had a large impact on journalism**. Richard Harding Davis became the first US war correspondent. He went to the front lines of the war in Cuba to give readers back home a better understanding of the events happening so far away.

405. **Davis was not the only journalist to travel to the front lines**. Others traveled to Cuba as well to get the latest scoop.

406. Newspaper owners like **William Randolph Hearst** and **Joseph Pulitzer** competed to see who could sell the most papers.

407. Around **three thousand Americans died in the war**, although most of those deaths were from yellow fever. It is not known for certain how many Spanish died, but the best estimate is between fifty-five thousand and sixty thousand.

408. **The war ended with the signing of the Treaty of Paris**, which was signed in December 1898.

409. **The treaty gave America control over Cuba.** Spain ceded Guam, Puerto Rico, and the Philippines to the US.

410. **The US occupied Cuba** until the Republic of Cuba was formed in 1902.

411. **Although the US left Cuba in 1902**, it ensured it would still have a say in Cuban politics. In 1903, the Platt Amendment was passed, allowing the US to interfere with international and domestic Cuban affairs if it impacted the island's independence.

412. **The Treaty of Paris of 1898** stated that the US would pay twenty million dollars for the acquisition of the Philippines.

413. **The Philippine-American War** would break out in February 1902 because the Filipinos sought their independence, not another ruling colonial power.

414. The war would last for over **fourteen years** and end in an American victory.

415. The **Philippines** would be granted its independence after World War II.

416. **Guam and Puerto Rico are still US possessions today.**

417. **The Spanish-American War** is seen as the beginning of an American empire, although the US has never announced its designs on creating an empire.

418. As a result of the war, **Spain no longer had possessions in the Western Hemisphere**. The Spanish Empire was officially on the decline.

419. About ten years after the war, **the Great White Fleet**, an impressive collection of sixteen battleships painted all white, sailed around the world to demonstrate America's growing naval power.

420. **New technologies were being developed** around the time of the Spanish-American War, such as machine guns, improved naval ships, and larger-scale military maneuvers. This allowed enemies to be defeated much more quickly, leading to a new era of warfare seen during the world wars.

# World War One

This chapter will explore **the history of World War One**. We'll take a look at thirty interesting facts about how America became involved in the conflict and what it brought to the European war effort.

**We'll also learn about advances in technology** and the development of new tactics like trench warfare and submarine attacks.

421. **World War I began in Europe on July 28th, 1914,** and ended with an armistice signed on November 11th, 1918.

422. The war began for several reasons, but the main trigger was the assassination of **Franz Ferdinand on June 28th, 1914**, by a Bosnian Serb radical.

423. **The United States joined the war** after Germany attacked several American ships carrying goods to England in 1917.

424. **The Zimmermann Note** was another reason the US decided to declare war.

425. This was a **secret piece of German intelligence** sent to Mexico in early 1917. The note said that if the US entered the war, **Germany would enter into an alliance with Mexico** and help it retrieve territories it had lost to the US. The telegram was intercepted and led to outrage in the US.

426. **President Woodrow Wilson declared war against Germany on April 6th, 1917**, for their attack on American ships at sea and violations of US neutrality rights.

427. In May 1917, **Wilson signed a bill introducing military conscription**, otherwise known as "the draft."

428. Over **four million Americans served in the military** during World War I.

429. **The first American soldiers** to fight on European soil during WWI arrived in France on June 26th, 1917.

430. **African American soldiers** made up 13 percent of the US forces during WWI. They fought for their country but had limited rights back home.

431. **Women served as nurses** in the armed forces during WWI but not as officers or enlisted personnel until WWII.

432. **The Allies in Europe were exhausted from the fighting.** The conflicts were harsh and bloody. The arrival of the US soldiers greatly boosted morale.

433. Perhaps the most well-known **aspect of WWI was trench warfare**. Instead of fighting in the open, the soldiers in Europe dug trenches and fought from there.

434. **The trenches provided some safety**, but disease ran rampant. The main killer of the men in the trenches was artillery fire from the enemy. Debris from the blast could hit men who were close by, causing fatal wounds.

435. **Chemical warfare was used in WWI,** with the most popular being mustard gas. The US did not produce any chemical weapons during the war.

436. **During World War One, aviation played an important role** in military operations. By the end of the war, almost thirty-three thousand men had been enlisted to fly in aviation missions.

437. **The US Air Force was not around during World War One**. It was created after World War II.

438. **Submarines were used much more significantly** than in the past. A lot of "firsts" for submarines happened during World War One, such as the first submarine to sink a ship with a self-propelled torpedo and the first true submarine (submarines that were fully submerged in the water).

439. **The US government issued war bonds** to help fund their involvement in WWI. Money from these bonds went toward purchasing weapons and other necessary supplies for troops overseas, among other things.

440. **The United States Food Administration**, which was led by Herbert Hoover, made sure enough food was available at home and abroad throughout the war effort.

441. **America's involvement caused rapid growth in industry**. War production increased employment opportunities, especially for women at home.

442. **WWI had a significant impact on industrial production in the United States**. Manufacturers and producers moved away from producing consumer goods and focused more on war production, such as munitions, weapons, and other military equipment.

443. This resulted in an **increased demand for raw materials**, which led to the rapid expansion of the nation's industrial sector and a surge in industrial employment.

444. **The United States** participated in several battles, such as Château-Thierry, Belleau Wood, Saint-Mihiel, and the Meuse-Argonne Forest offensive.

445. **In November 1918, President Wilson set forth his Fourteen Points**, which proposed a new international system of peace and security for all nations after World War I.

446. **On November 11th, 1918, Germany signed an armistice with the Allied forces, ending WWI in Europe.**

447. **The Treaty of Versailles** was signed on June 28th, 1919, by representatives from 32 countries. This treaty marked the official end of World War One.

448. **An estimated twenty million soldiers died in WWI**, making it one of the deadliest wars in history. The US was only in the war for a little over a year. The other countries fought for over four years.

449. **More than 116,000 Americans died during WWI.**

450. **After the war, the Spanish flu broke out**. Around 675,000 people died of the flu. Contrary to the name, the Spanish flu didn't originate in Spain. Researchers believe it started in the state of Kansas.

# The Women's Suffrage Movement

This chapter will explore the **history of the women's suffrage movement** and how it impacted life in the United States.

We'll take a look at **thirty facts** about this important movement, including its origins, leaders, key events, and victories.

451. **The fight for women's voting rights** in the United States began in 1848 at a convention held in Seneca Falls, New York.

452. **The Seneca Falls Convention** was the first organized gathering of people dedicated to fighting for women's rights and is often considered the start of the women's suffrage movement.

453. More than three hundred men and women gathered to hear people speak about **the suffrage movement**. One hundred of them signed the Declaration of Sentiments, which declared **"all men and women are created equal."**

454. There were earlier **fighters for women's rights**, such as **Mary Wollstonecraft**, who wrote books about how women were not inferior to men in the 18th century. She believed if women could have proper education, they could achieve great things.

455. **Elizabeth Cady Stanton and Lucretia Mott** were two crucial leaders during the Seneca Falls Convention. They spoke out against gender inequality and worked to establish voting rights for all citizens.

456. **The American Equal Rights Association** was founded in 1866. It fought for the right to vote, no matter one's gender or race.

457. **Many suffragists** were abolitionists and fought for the end of slavery.

458. When **the Fifteenth Amendment was proposed**, some suffragists were upset because there was no mention of women.

459. **Susan B. Anthony** and **Elizabeth Cady** Stanton protested the amendment and formed an organization called the National Woman Suffrage Association in 1869. This move caused a rift in the women's rights movement.

460. **The American Woman Suffrage Association (AWSA)** was founded in 1869 by Lucy Stone and focused on winning voting rights at the state level. It promoted black and women's suffrage.

461. By 1890, the suffrage movement had worked out their differences and combined to form **the National American Woman Suffrage Association.**

462. **The women's suffrage movement** brought together people from all walks of life. Wealthy white women were able to dedicate the most time, but poor women also joined the cause.

463. **African American suffragists like Ida B. Wells and Sojourner Truth** fought for their rights and those of other oppressed groups.

464. **Many men fiercely opposed the movement**. Women also joined anti-suffragist movements. Before 1916, more women joined anti-suffragist movements than suffragist organizations.

465. **Many brave women risked arrest** when they participated in protests demanding equal rights. For instance, **Susan B. Anthony** was arrested in 1872 for voting in an election.

466. **Suffragists created leaflets and newspapers** to spread their message and organized marches in cities all over the United States.

467. **In addition to voting rights**, suffragists fought for other women's rights, such as access to higher education, better working conditions, and labor laws that would protect them from discrimination based on gender. Some groups also advocated for discrimination against race.

468. In 1913, **Alice Paul and Lucy Burns led the first women's rights parade in DC**. Thousands of people marched through the capital, demanding voting rights for women.

469. **During World War I**, many suffragists campaigned hard for the right to vote. Woodrow Wilson publicly announced his support for women's suffrage in 1918, becoming the first president to do so.

470. **Women played an essential role in WWI**. Many historians believe their aid in the war effort led the vast majority of women to realize they deserved the right to vote.

471. **Jeannette Rankin from Montana** was the first woman elected into Congress in 1916, four years before the Nineteenth Amendment took effect in 1920.

472. **The Nineteenth Amendment** was passed in 1919 and ratified in 1920. It stated, "The right of citizens of the United States to vote shall not be denied or abridged by the United States or any State on account of sex."

473. **The Nineteenth Amendment** is sometimes referred to as **the Susan B. Anthony Amendment** due to her tireless work and dedication toward women's rights.

474. **Several states already allowed women to vote before 1920**, such as Arkansas, New York, Michigan, and Oklahoma, just to name a few.

475. **The League of Women Voters was formed in 1920**. It succeeded the National American Woman Suffrage Association. Instead of fighting for the right to vote, the League of Women Voters seeks to educate people about upcoming elections. It registers voters and promotes voting rights, as well as other issues.

476. **The Equal Rights Amendment** was proposed in 1923, but it wasn't approved by Congress until 1972. The ERA prohibits discrimination based on gender and would invalidate outdated laws regarding women.

477. **The ERA** did not receive enough votes for ratification, even after the deadline was extended to 1982. In 2020, Virginia ratified the ERA. If Congress decides to adopt the amendment, it will become the Twenty-eighth Amendment to the Constitution.

478. In 2020, **Kamala Harris** became the first female vice president of the United States. This historic moment would not have been possible without the suffrage movement, which allowed women full citizenship and voting rights.

479. As of today, **women in countries all over the world can vote, except in Vatican** City, which only allows the College of Cardinals to vote for the leader (the pope).

480. Although women can vote around the world, **women still face discrimination** and voting restrictions in many countries.

# The Roaring Twenties

This chapter will explore **the Roaring Twenties**, a decade of **economic growth** and excitement **in the United States.**

Discover thirty interesting facts about popular music, new inventions, and Prohibition. Meet other iconic figures who made their mark during this time period, like **Babe Ruth** and **Al Capone!**

481. **The Roaring Twenties lasted from 1920 to 1929.** It was a period of economic growth and prosperity.

482. **Automobiles became more affordable** for middle-class Americans. At the beginning of 1920, there were eight million drivers. That number nearly tripled by the end of the decade!

483. Many famous brands that we know and love today first appeared in the 1920s, such as Wonder Bread, Kool-Aid, Rubbermaid, and Reese's peanut butter cups.

484. **Television was invented** in the 1920s but wouldn't become popular until after WWII.

485. **The first commercial radio news program** in the US aired in 1920. Radios grew in popularity during the Roaring Twenties. People could sit at home and listen to music, variety shows, and the news.

486. **Scientists discovered insulin** in 1921. It was first used in the US in 1922. Before this discovery, people with severe diabetes typically only lived for a few months at most.

487. **The first transatlantic telephone call** was made between the president of AT&T, Walter Gifford, and the head of the British post office, Evelyn Murray, in 1927.

488. **The first crossword puzzle book** was published in 1924 by Simon & Schuster, increasing the popularity of this activity.

489. **The Scopes Trial occurred in 1925** when John T. Scopes was accused of violating Tennessee state law. Scopes taught evolution in his classroom. He was ultimately found guilty, although the verdict was overturned.

490. **Women gained the right to vote** with the ratification of the Nineteenth Amendment in 1920.

491. **Women began working outside the home** in larger numbers than ever before. They attended college and enjoyed more freedom.

492. **Flappers were stylish young women** who wore their hair short. They enjoyed dancing, drinking alcohol, smoking cigarettes, and wearing makeup and short skirts. They went against the idea of how a proper woman should dress and act.

493. **Women's fashion changed significantly** during this time. Hemlines rose to above the knee, and new fabrics became available.

494. **The Art Deco style of architecture** and design defined the look of this era with its bold geometric shapes and bright colors.

495. **People enjoyed new dances** like the Charleston and the Lindy Hop at parties and nightclubs across the country.

496. Fads like **flagpole** sitting and **marathon dancing** became popular among young adults looking for excitement.

497. **The Harlem Renaissance** was a period of great cultural and artistic expression for African Americans.

498. Some well-known **African American** authors include Zora Neale Hurston, Langston Hughes, and Claude McKay.

499. **Jazz music** became popular in the United States, with musicians like Louis Armstrong and Duke Ellington leading the way.

500. **The Ku Klux Klan**, a violent hate group, grew in size throughout this decade due to anti-immigration sentiment. The KKK in the 1920s believed that native Protestant whites should be the ones to live in the US. Although the KKK was initially founded in the South, it became very popular in the Midwest during this time.

501. **Working conditions began to improve** during the 1920s. In 1926, Ford introduced the five-day workweek.

502. **Charles Lindbergh** became the first man to fly a solo, non-stop across the Atlantic Ocean in 1927. He flew his plane called the Spirit of St. Louis.

503. Charles Lindbergh is also well known for the **kidnapping of his son** in 1932, sparking a nationwide search for him. The baby was killed, although theories abound on who really killed him.

504. **Babe Ruth** broke baseball records, including hitting sixty home runs in one season. He became one of America's most beloved athletes!

505. **In 1926, American Gertrude Ederle** swam across the English Channel, becoming the first woman ever to do so. She was an Olympic champion and held multiple world records. She was one of many female sports heroes in the 1920s.

506. **Prohibition began when Congress ratified the Eighteenth Amendment** in 1919, banning alcohol production and distribution within US borders.

507. **Speakeasies sold liquor illegally.** They became popular during the Roaring '20s. In the late 1920s, there were around thirty-two thousand speakeasies in New York alone!

508. **Al Capone became one of America's most notorious gangsters** during this time. He was part of the bootlegging business, which means he illegally distributed alcohol to speakeasies. Capone led an organized crime syndicate out of Chicago.

509. On October 24th, 1929, **the American stock market crashed**. This day, which is known as Black Thursday, marked the highest number of sold shares in US history. On Black Tuesday (October 29th, 1929), the stock market crashed again, with investors trading millions of shares in just one day.

510. **The stock market crash marks the end of the** Roaring Twenties and the start of the Great Depression.

# The Great Depression

This chapter will explore **the history of the Great Depression in the United States**. We'll look at thirty interesting facts about how this period of economic hardship began, what it meant for people living through it, and how various government initiatives attempted to alleviate suffering during this difficult time.

Learn about **new forms of entertainment** that developed during this era and other issues, such as **migration patterns** and **labor rights.**

511. **The Great Depression** was a time of **economic hardship** in the United States that lasted from 1929 to 1939.

512. It began after the **stock market crashed** on October 29th, 1929, which was known as Black Tuesday.

513. During this time, **millions lost their jobs and homes** due to business failures and bank closures.

514. It is believed that a third to **a half of all banks closed** during the Great Depression.

515. Nearly **25 percent of American workers were unemployed** in 1933.

516. Many homeless men, known as **hobos**, rode freight trains from city to city, **looking for work.**

517. **The Dust Bowl** further intensified the effects of the Depression on farmers in America's **Midwest and Great Plains**. Drought and severe dust storms damaged crops and people's health.

518. Many people **fled the regions affected by the Dust Bowl**. An estimated 2.5 million people moved out of the Great Plains by 1940.

519. To offset the effects of prolonged drought caused by the Dust Bowl, **the Soil Conservation Service** was established in 1935.

520. **Herbert Hoover** was the president from 1929 to 1933. He initially believed that economic recovery should be left to the private sector, but he eventually implemented programs and policies. Although some of his policies were sound, they took too much time to become useful.

521 One of the most iconic symbols of the Great Depression is **Hoovervilles**. Unemployed people built shantytowns that they named after the president.

522. **Crime increased** after the Great Depression, but it fell once successful programs were put in place.

523. In 1933, **the Twenty-first Amendment was ratified**. It repealed the Eighteenth Amendment, which made Prohibition the law of the land.

524. Organized crime continued to be a problem even after the Twenty-first Amendment was passed. Instead of bootlegging, **crime syndicates turned to gambling and racketeering.**

525. **President Franklin D. Roosevelt** was elected in 1932 on a platform of relief and reform.

526. **With the New Deal and the Second New Deal**, FDR created employment opportunities for millions of Americans. These workers built infrastructure projects, such as roads and dams.

527. **The Tennessee Valley Authority** was formed in 1933. It provided hydroelectric power production and flood control to seven states.

528. **The Social Security Act** was passed in 1935, which provided financial security to older people.

529. **The Works Progress Administration** (WPA) put unemployed people back to work by providing jobs in construction.

530. **The WPA also employed** people who were involved in **art and theater**, ensuring that American culture could still grow during this trying time.

531. **Artists created works that reflected American hardships**. Some of the most famous artists of this period include photographers **Dorothea Lange** and **Walker Evans** and the painter **Jackson Pollack.**

532. Some people were inspired by self-help books like Think and Grow Rich, which stressed personal responsibility over government intervention during hard times.

533. Despite economic hardship, **baseball was a popular pastime**. The New York Yankees won a World Series Championship in 1932.

534. **Women had a more significant presence in the workforce during this era** due to necessity. Some women worked in factories. Many worked in the domestic sphere or took government or clerical jobs.

535. **Women also often took on the role of caregiver, providing care** for the elderly and children while their husbands worked. Women took on the responsibility of managing the household budget and finding ways to make ends meet.

536. **The Great Depression saw a drop in the birth rate** due to economic hardship and a lack of available resources.

537. **In 1935, President Roosevelt signed the National Labor Relations Act into law**, which gave laborers more rights, including freedom of collective bargaining with employers.

538. **The Fair Labor Standards Act was passed in 1938**. It set a national minimum wage and placed restrictions on child labor. **Many children worked** dangerous factory jobs.

539. Despite attempts at recovery from various government initiatives during the 1930s, **the US economy only fully recovered during WWII.**

540. **World War II significantly impacted the Great Depression in the US.** It provided a resurgence of economic activity, employment opportunities, and wages. Additionally, the war provided a large influx of capital, which allowed the government to fund public works and social welfare programs that helped create today's prosperous economy.

# World War Two

This chapter will explore **the history of World War II**, one of the most devastating wars in human history. We'll take a look at thirty **interesting facts about why it started** and what its lasting impacts were.

**Learn about battles** that changed the course of history, the technology developed during this time, and the human cost of the war.

541. **World War II** was fought from **1939 to 1945** and involved over fifty countries, including **the United States of America, Britain, Japan, and Germany.**

542. **President Franklin Delano Roosevelt (FDR)** wanted to join the war, but he knew the public would not support the idea. Many believed they should not join a war that did not involve the US.

543. **In 1941, FDR signed the Lend-Lease Act**. The act allowed the United States to supply materials to Allies fighting the Axis (Germany, Italy, and Japan).

544. **The aid was given to the Allies for free**. The US spent a little over $50 billion (around $720 billion today) to help the Allies win the war.

545. **The United States supplied more tanks and aircraft** to the Allies than any other country in World War II.

546. **Japan's attack on Pearl Harbor, Hawaii,** on December 7th, 1941, led the United States to join WWII against the Axis powers.

547. **After the Japanese attacked** Pearl Harbor, **FDR issued Executive Order No. 9066**, allowing the military to place people of Japanese ancestry living on the West Coast to internment camps.

548. **Over sixteen million Americans served in the US Armed Forces** during WWII. Over 400,000 of them were killed in battle or died due to other causes, such as illness or injury.

549. **In 1940, Congress approved the Selective Training and Service Act.** It was the first peacetime draft in the US. When WWII broke out, the draft's terms were amended. Over ten million men had been drafted into military service by 1945.

550. More than one million African Americans served during WWII. The war also saw the first African American officers.

551. Beginning in 1942, **women began contributing in full force to the war** effort. They joined the Army Nurse Corps, Women's Auxiliary Corps (WAC), Marine reserves, and the Navy WAVES unit during WWII.

552. **During WWII, women began to take on traditionally more masculine roles**. Women worked in factories, shipyards, and mines. During the war, women ensured the US economy continued to flourish and created military equipment for the war effort.

553. During the war, the US public felt a sense of patriotism and the desire to aid in the war effort. **Food and gas were rationed**. People planted **"victory gardens"** to grow their own food. Propaganda films increased the people's need to support their country during the war.

554. In December 1943, **the Cairo Conference was held in Egypt** by three major Allied powers (the US, the UK, and China). The three powers agreed that Nazi Germany needed to be destroyed for the war to end. The Allies also needed Japan's unconditional surrender.

555. On June 6th, 1944 (D-Day), 133,000 Allied troops **landed on beaches at Normandy,** France, beginning Europe's liberation from Nazi Germany.

556. **General Dwight Eisenhower** was the supreme commander of the Allied forces in Europe. He was in charge of the successful **D-Day operation**, which turned the tide against the Germans. He would go on to become the president of the United States.

557. **The G.I. Bill** was passed in 1944. It provided returning veterans with funds to pursue college degrees or start businesses after the war ended.

558. **The Holocaust occurred during World War** II. Six million European Jews were murdered under the Nazi regime. Another five million other minorities and Soviet prisoners of war were killed by the Germans during the war.

559. **American soldiers liberated several concentration camps**, which was where Jews and other minorities were sent to work and die. One of the most infamous concentration camps they liberated was Dachau. Liberating these camps made the soldiers realize the true horror of the war.

560. **On April 12th, 1945, FDR** passed away from a cerebral hemorrhage at Warm Springs, Georgia, leaving **Vice President Harry S. Truman** to assume office as the thirty-third president of the United States.

561. **Eisenhower** accepted Germany's unconditional surrender ending WWII in Europe on May 7th, 1945.

562. **Although the war in Europe was over**, the war in the Pacific was still ongoing. **The US Navy played a huge role in the Pacific** theater, winning important battles like **the Battle of Midway** and **the Battle of Leyte Gulf**.

563. One of the more famous Pacific battles was **the Battle of Iwo Jima**. It was a brutal fight between US and Japanese forces on the Pacific island of Iwo Jima. The battle lasted from February 19th to March 26th, 1945. The US won this battle.

564. **The Manhattan Project** was a top-secret program by the US government to build the first atomic bomb. It was carried out by tens of thousands of scientists and engineers from 1939 to 1945. It didn't officially start until 1942, though.

565. On July 16th, 1945, the US performed the first successful **atomic bomb test** in New Mexico.

566. A little over a month later, on August 6th, 1945, an **atomic bomb** was dropped by US military forces on **Hiroshima, Japan.**

567. **When Japan didn't surrender**, US forces dropped another **atomic bomb on Nagasaki** three days later. It is difficult to know how many died because of the aftereffects of the bombs. Hundreds of thousands died because of radiation effects and from the blast itself.

568. On August 14th, 1945, **Japan announced its surrender**. On September 2nd, 1945, Japan signed the Instrument of Surrender, officially ending the war.

569. Almost **five hundred Medals of Honor** were awarded to American soldiers who fought during WWII. The Medal of Honor is the highest award a soldier can receive.

570. After **World War II ended in 1945**, the United Nations was founded to help maintain peace among countries.

# The Cold War and the Space Race

This chapter will explore **the history of the Cold War and the Space Race**. We'll examine thirty interesting facts about how this period impacted global relations, space exploration, scientific breakthroughs, and more! Learn about important figures like **Neil Armstrong** and **Yuri** Gagarin, who played a major role in outer space exploration. We'll also discuss key moments like **the Cuban Missile Crisis** and the building of the **Berlin Wall.**

571. **After WWII ended in 1945**, people from all over Europe came to live in major American cities like New York, Chicago, and Los Angeles. These immigrants brought their cultures, which shaped future generations.

572. **The Cold War** was a period in history when tensions escalated between the democratic **United States** and the communist **Soviet Union.**

573. **The Cold War lasted from 1945 to 1991**, which is around forty-six years.

574. During this time, many new technologies were invented or improved. **Computers became more powerful**, allowing officials to access information more quickly. **Televisions became more popular** and allowed people to see news events happening far away as if they were right there themselves!

575. Throughout **the Cold war**, American scientists made many breakthroughs, such as launching communication **satellites like Telstar 1 in July 1962.**

576. **During the Cold War, the US and the Soviet Union competed** to show who was more powerful by developing new technologies like missiles and rockets faster than the other.

577. **This competition led to space exploration**, with both countries launching rockets into space.

578. **In 1957, the Soviet Union launched Sputnik 1**, the first artificial satellite ever put into orbit around Earth. It made beeping noises on its way up that people in the US could hear on the radio.

579. **This shocked the Americans** because they had fallen behind the communists. So, in 1958, President Dwight D. Eisenhower **created NASA** (the National Aeronautics and Space Administration).

580. **On April 12th, 1961, Russia sent Yuri Gagarin into space**. He was the first human to reach space, doing so aboard Vostok 1.

581. **A few weeks later, on May 5th, 1961, America sent Alan Shepard** as the first American into space aboard Freedom 7.

582. **Although many accomplishments happened during the Space Race,** it is important to be reminded that what these people were doing was very dangerous. In 1967, American astronauts Gus Grissom, Roger Chaffee, and Ed White died during a pre-launch test when a fire broke out.

583. In 1969, American **Neil Armstrong** became the first person to walk on the moon when he stepped out of Apollo 11. This was a massive milestone for US space exploration and officially ended the Space Race.

584. Although **the Space Race ended in 1969**, there are a few other important achievements to talk about in regard to US space exploration. In 1975, the US sent a probe called **Voyager 1** into space to study the outer solar system and discover the outer limits of the sun's magnetic field.

585. In 1983, **Sally Ride became the first American female astronaut** in space when she went up on the Challenger. This feat shows how far women had come since WWII ended!

586. Also, in 1984, **President Ronald Reagan** proposed his Strategic Defense Initiative (SDI), also known as "Star Wars," which called for building an impenetrable force field around Earth using lasers, satellites, and other weapons! The plan was a bit too complicated for technology at the time and was scrapped in 1993.

587. **After WWII, Germany was split between the democratic West and communist Russia.** The Berlin Wall was built in 1961 by East Germany to separate its people from West Germany. In 1987, President Reagan gave his famous speech, uttering, "Mr. Gorbachev, tear down this wall!" The Berlin Wall would be dismantled about two years later.

**588. The Cold War led to an arms race** (a competition between countries to build bigger and better weapons) between the US and the Soviet Union. Each wanted to protect its people from an attack by the enemy.

589. Although there was an arms race, **the US and the Soviet Union** would not directly war against each other.

590. Instead, they fought in **proxy wars (a war where major powers use another country to fight the war for them).** One proxy war was the Korean War. It is seen as the first proxy war between democratic and communist powers. **The Korean War** was fought from 1950 to 1953. The war resulted in the division of Korea.

591. **Another proxy war was the Vietnam War,** which took place between 1955 and 1975. The fighting was brutal, and many died. The Vietnamese were ultimately able to reunite the country under a communist regime.

592. **The Cuban Missile Crisis** is one of the most famous events from the Cold War. It was a thirteen-day standoff where Cuba allowed USSR missiles on its soil. The US threatened military action if the missiles stayed there. The crisis brought the Cold War to America's doorstep. Luckily, war was averted.

593. **For years during the Cold War**, the US government created hideouts in case of a nuclear attack, stockpiling food and supplies that could last for months!

594. **The Soviet Union** had a similar plan. Its government built secret cities, some underground, that were designed to hold millions if something ever happened between US and Russia.

595. **During the Cold War, both sides used propaganda** (information meant to influence people's opinion) to spread fear and mistrust among citizens living within their borders.

596. Beginning in the late 1940s, **Senator Joseph McCarthy** went on a witch hunt to find communists and socialists in the United States. Many false accusations were flung, and notable people were targeted. Some famous people who were victims of McCarthyism include **Helen Keller, Charlie Chaplin, Leonard Bernstein, Orson Welles, and Lucille Ball.**

597. There was also an intense **rivalry in the Olympic Games** between American athletes and Russians during this time. In **1980, the Olympics was held in Moscow**. America and sixty-four other nations refused to participate.

598. In 1969 and 1979, **the US and Russia signed treaties called SALT I and II** (Strategic Arms Limitation Talks). The treaty limited the number of nuclear weapons each country could have.

599. Although relations could be tense one moment and better the next, the Cold War thawed under the leadership of **Mikhail Gorbachev**. The Cold War ended in 1991 when **the Soviet Union collapsed**. This shift in the international order enabled increased cooperation between the two countries, leading to the International Space Station in 1998. The end of the Cold War also opened the door for the sharing of resources and new technologies.

600. **After the Cold War ended in 1991, America became the only superpower in the world**. It had achieved great success in space exploration and experienced many technological advancements, proving itself to be a powerful nation compared to the rest of the world's countries.

# The Civil Rights Movement

This chapter will explore **the history of the civil rights movement in America**. We'll take a look at thirty interesting facts about how African Americans and other minority groups fought for their right to equal treatment under the law.

Discover inspiring heroes like **Rosa Parks** and **Martin Luther King** Jr. We'll also learn more about organizations like the NAACP and SNCC that helped advance civil rights through peaceful protests and legal action!

601. **The civil rights movement** was a struggle for social justice that began in the 1950s and lasted until the late 1960s.

602. It notably sought to **end racial discrimination** against African Americans. Other minority groups, such as Native Americans and Hispanics, also fought for equal rights.

603. The **NAACP** (National Association for the Advancement of Colored People) was formed in 1909. It is still an active organization today and advocates for civil rights and racial justice through legal action, education, and outreach programs.

604. The **Greensboro Four** staged sit-ins at segregated lunch counters throughout North Carolina.

605. Sit-ins were an integral part of **the civil rights movement**, as they helped desegregate public spaces like restaurants and movie theaters with peaceful protests. Tens of thousands of people participated in sit-ins during this era.

606. In April 1960, **the Student Nonviolent Coordinating Committee** (SNCC) was formed. It began organizing sit-ins at segregated lunch counters throughout the South in the 1960s.

607. **The Freedom Riders** were groups of people who rode buses across the South in 1961. They challenged the Jim Crow laws. These riders even faced death threats and violence as they protested for equal rights!

608. **The Jim Crow laws** began in the late 19th century and were predominant in the South. These laws discriminated against African Americans. For instance, African American children had to attend a separate school from white children. African Americans had separate drinking fountains and lived in different neighborhoods than whites.

609. In 1896, in **Plessy v. Ferguson**, the US Supreme Court ruled that the Jim Crow laws did not go against the Constitution as long as things were "separate but equal."

610. This law was mostly overruled by the decision of **Brown v. Board of Education**. In 1954, the Supreme Court ruled that racial segregation in public schools went against the Constitution.

611. In 1957, nine African American students, known as the Little Rock Nine, attempted to integrate **Little Rock Central High School in Arkansas.** They received death threats and physical abuse. The National Guard refused to let the students enter until President Eisenhower got involved.

612. **Six-year-old Ruby Bridges** became a symbol of courage when she became African American student at William Frantz Elementary School in New Orleans, Louisiana, in 1960. Despite facing extreme racism, she stayed strong throughout her journey to fight for equality education system United States.

613. **The Black Panther Party** was founded by Huey Newton and Bobby Seale in Oakland, California, in 1966. Members of this group sought to protect African Americans from police brutality through grassroots organization and self-defense tactics, such as armed patrols of neighborhoods.

614. Almost every Black Panther believed that **the Black Power movement** could make a difference in how African Americans were treated. Instead of depending on the government to make changes, the Black Power movement believed blacks should be self-sufficient, which included taking justice into their own hands.

615. **Malcolm X** was a huge proponent of the Black Power movement. He championed social justice through his radical ideology and unapologetic speeches that aimed to empower African Americans and other people of color.

616. **Martin Luther King Jr**. was an activist who sought a more peaceful resolution. While he wasn't part of the Black Power movement, he understood their pain and frustration. King notably gave his iconic **"I Have a Dream"** speech at the March on Washington in 1963, which called for equality among all races and people worldwide.

617. **Rosa Parks is known for refusing to give up her seat on a bus to a white person**, sparking the Montgomery bus boycott, which lasted for more than one year.

618. In 1962, Cesar Chavez formed the **United Farm Workers of America**, a labor union, to fight against unfair wages and working conditions faced by farm workers, specifically those of Hispanic descent living in California. Chavez was part of the Chicano movement, which was similar to the Black Power movement in regard to ideas of nationalism and community empowerment.

619. **The Birmingham church bombing** in 1963 was a turning point for the civil rights movement. Four African American girls died, sparking nationwide outrage and finally pushing President Lyndon B. Johnson to sign the Civil Rights Act of 1964 into law.

620. **The 1964 Civil Rights Act** outlawed segregation nationwide by prohibiting discrimination based on race or color in public places like schools, parks, and businesses.

621. **The Freedom Summer of 1964** saw thousands of activists from all walks of life travel to Mississippi to register African American voters. In 1962, a little over 5 percent of blacks were registered to vote. The Freedom of Summer project was ultimately unsuccessful in its goal, but it did raise attention to the issue blacks faced at the polls.

622. **In February 1965, Malcolm X was assassinated**. He had renounced the Nation of Islam, a US group that is different from traditional Islam, and formed a new group for Muslims. The Nation of Islam was not happy about this, and three members of the group shot him during an assembly. People still wonder if the government was somehow involved in his death.

623. **The 1965 Selma to Montgomery march** was a historical event demonstrating the power of peaceful protest. It ultimately led to Congress passing the Voting Rights Act, which prohibited discrimination when people voted.

624. In August 1965, Congress passed the Voting Rights Act. **African Americans could finally vote** without facing unfair obstacles like literacy tests or poll taxes. The Voting Rights Act was a landmark piece of legislation that outlawed discrimination based on race or color when voting.

625. **On April 4th, 1968, Martin Luther King Jr. was assassinated**. His death spurred nationwide mourning and outrage. His message inspired many to keep fighting for civil rights until justice had been achieved.

626. **In 1968, Congress passed the Fair Housing Act**, which outlawed discrimination based on race or ethnicity when renting, selling, or financing housing across America.

627. In 1969, the Stonewall riots marked the beginning of **the LGBTQ movement**. The riots were sparked when police raided a popular gay bar in New York City. LGBTQ activists united to protest against discrimination and fight for equal rights for all, regardless of sexual orientation.

628. **In 1969, hundreds of Native American activists and supporters occupied Alcatraz Island** for nineteen months. They wanted the island to be returned to them since it had once belonged to the Lakota. Alcatraz had been home to a notorious prison, but it closed in 1964. The protest was not successful, but it did set a precedent for Native American activism.

629. **The 1971 Supreme Court case Swann v Charlotte-Mecklenburg Board of Education** ruled against racial segregation on buses. The Supreme Court ruled that busing students of different races together across district lines promoted integration.

630. **The election of Barack Obama** as the forty-fourth president of the United States showed how far the US had come since the civil rights movement. As the first African American president, Obama's election was a major step forward in terms of racial equality in the nation.

# The Gulf War and the War on Terror

This chapter will explore **the history of the Gulf War and the War on Terror**, two significant conflicts that are still impacting the world today. We'll look at some key events, such as Iraq's invasion of **Kuwait** in 1990 and **Operation Desert Storm**. Additionally, we'll cover other related topics like **drone strikes** and **human rights** violations caused during military interventions.

631. **The Gulf War** was a conflict between Iraq and an international coalition led by the United States that lasted from 1990 to 1991.

632. It began when **Iraq invaded Kuwait** on August 2nd, 1990, and ended with the liberation of Kuwait on February 28th, 1991.

633. **Saddam Hussein** ordered Iraq's invasion of Kuwait. He wanted control over its oilfields and ports for trade purposes and to expand Iraq's power.

634. **Iraq had a powerful military**. Its soldiers took over Kuwait in just two days!

635. **Operation Desert Storm** was the US-led military intervention to liberate Kuwait from Iraqi occupation during the Gulf War in early 1991.

636. Almost a **million soldiers** from the coalition fought in the Gulf War. Most of them were from America. Iraq sent over 650,000 soldiers.

637. After forty-two days of relentless bombing campaigns, **President George H. W. Bush** ordered a ceasefire to be drawn up since most of the Iraqis had surrendered or were killed by that point.

638. **The UN Security Council** declared that Iraq must pay for the damages caused during the war and give up all weapons of mass destruction (WMDs). Iraq eventually agreed. Its military power was greatly reduced.

639. **The war resulted in high casualties among civilians** and the destruction of infrastructure in Iraq and Kuwait. Estimated deaths for civilians range as high as 100,000. Millions of people had to move because of the fighting. A little **over two hundred American soldiers** died in the war.

640. Americans saw **live broadcast news** from the front lines for the first time during the Gulf War.

641. **The War on Terror** is a term used to refer to the global military campaign against terrorist organizations and individuals, especially **Osama bin Laden** and his al-Qaeda network.

642. The War on Terror began shortly after the **September 11th attacks in 2001**. The attacks took nearly three thousand lives.

643. Four planes were hijacked. **Two were flown into the World Trade Center in New York City. One hit the Pentagon.** And another was taken over by the passengers and crashed down in Pennsylvania. It was likely headed to the Capitol.

644. In October 2001, **NATO** invoked its collective defense clause for the first time due to 9/11. This clause states that a NATO country being attacked should be treated as if all the NATO countries are being attacked.

645. The War on Terror has resulted in numerous military interventions **in Afghanistan, Iraq, Pakistan, and Somalia**. For the most part, these interventions have been led by the US.

646. **US forces have conducted air strikes** targeting militant groups in these and other regions in the Middle East.

647. **Several successful missions** have been carried out by international coalition forces. The forces aid local governments in countering terrorist activities.

648. **In 2003, US forces entered Iraq** in search of WMDs and to bring democracy to the people of Iraq. To this day, no major stores of WMDs have ever been found in Iraq.

649. **Saddam Hussein** was overthrown and killed in 2006, ending his reign of terror.

650. In 2011, **Osama bin Laden** was killed after being found hiding in Abbottabad, Pakistan, by US Navy Seals during a raid operation. Osama bin Laden orchestrated 9/11 and was the leader of the terrorist organization called al-Qaeda.

651. Every day, thousands of soldiers face dangers posed by **improvised explosive devices** (IEDs) and **suicide bombers.**

652. The use of **unmanned drones to target terrorists** has been highly debated due to civilian casualties resulting from this practice. It is estimated that in Pakistan alone, drone strikes killed over two thousand civilians between 2004 and 2014.

653. The wars associated with this conflict have received **widespread criticism over human rights** violations and civilian casualties. Both sides are guilty of committing war crimes.

654. In 2014, **NATO declared the war in Afghanistan to be over**. Many US troops stayed in the country. In 2021, the American soldiers left. The Taliban took over the Afghan government.

655. **The War on Terror** has resulted in almost **one million deaths** and tens of millions of displaced people. So far, the US has spent an estimated eight trillion dollars to fight terrorism.

656. It is believed that countries with strong **US military presence** have significantly decreased terrorism-related activities since 2001.

657. This conflict significantly **impacted international relations** between different nations, especially those directly involved or affected by it.

658. Since 2001, **the War on Terror** has caused governments to put stricter surveillance laws in place, which has led to restrictions on civil liberties in many countries.

659. **US Special Forces** continue operations in Iraq, providing training and support to local security personnel tasked with countering terrorist threats.

660. After a two-decade-long conflict between coalition forces and terrorist factions, such as al-**Qaeda and ISIS**, there are still active conflicts occurring in many regions worldwide. There is currently **no precise end date set for this war**. Many believe it is unlikely terrorism will ever end.

# The United States of America in the 21st Century

This chapter will explore the many important events that have taken place **in the United States in the 21st century.** With these thirty facts, you'll gain insight into how this nation has developed over a major world power. We'll discover their advances in technology, global relationships, health care reform, and more. Discover why understanding this country's **recent history is so critical to understanding its future!**

661. **In 2003, the United States invaded Iraq** and overthrew Saddam Hussein in a little over a month.

662. **The United States has been involved in multiple international conflicts** in the 21st century in places like Syria and Libya as part of its efforts toward global stability and peace.

663. **After Hurricane Katrina** struck New Orleans in 2005, President George W. Bush signed off on $10.5 billion worth of relief aid for victims affected by this disaster.

664. In 2005, Americans were hit by three major hurricanes within weeks: **Katrina** (August), **Rita** (September), and **Wilma** (October).

665. **The US elected** its first African American president, **Barack Obama**, in 2008.

666. In 2009, the **US government passed an economic stimulus package** to help revive the economy from a financial crisis that had caused massive unemployment rates across America and serious stock market declines.

667. In 2009, **President Obama won his Nobel Peace Prize** for promoting nuclear disarmament while leading negotiations with foreign leaders on international issues of major importance.

668. **The Obama administration passed a vital health care reform** bill commonly known as "Obamacare" in 2010, which increased access to medical coverage across America.

669. In 2010, US scientists created the world's first synthetic organism from DNA strands in a laboratory.

670. The "**Occupy Wall Street**" movement was a protest against corporate greed and economic inequality. It spread quickly throughout cities across America, including New York City, where it began.

671. **The NASA rover Curiosity landed on Mars** for exploration in 2012. The project cost an estimated 2.5 billion dollars, making it one of the most expensive space missions ever undertaken.

672. In 2013, **Edward Snowden** leaked government documents revealing information on US surveillance programs against citizens and foreign countries.

673. **Marriage equality was finally approved nationwide** after legal battles that lasted nearly ten years. The Supreme Court ruled on the Obergefell v. Hodges case, declaring that same-sex marriage was a constitutional right in June 2015.

674. **After several years** of negotiations between various parties, Iran reached a nuclear agreement with world powers, including America, in 2015. **Iran agreed to reduce its stockpile of uranium**.

675. On August 21st, 2017, **a total solar eclipse crossed fourteen states**, providing millions with a unique view of this natural phenomenon.

676. **The US has seen significant advances in technology** during this century, from smartphones to self-driving cars. Artificial intelligence (AI) applications are being developed all over the country.

677. **Apple Inc. was founded by Steve Jobs** and others in 1976. In 2010, it was worth over $65 billion. Two years later, it was worth $156 billion.

678. **Social media networks**, such as **Twitter** and **Facebook**, have become ubiquitous worldwide since they were launched at the start of the 21st century. These platforms allow billions to connect instantly across continents without barriers.

679. **In 2014, Google purchased Nest Labs,** making it one of the first large companies to invest heavily in home automation techs like smart thermostats, security systems, and other devices.

680. As of 2022, **the US is home to the world's largest economy**, accounting for over 15 percent of the global GDP (gross domestic product).

681. In 2019, almost **165.5 million people visited the United States**, making it one of the most popular tourist destinations in the world.

682 **America's per capita GDP is one of the highest in the world**. It is estimated at around $65,000 in 2020, making it an attractive destination for those seeking economic opportunities abroad.

683. **The US has seen a surge in mass shootings** across the nation since 2007, leading to numerous debates and discussions on gun law legislation.

684. **The US is a major contributor to greenhouse gas emissions**. As part of the Paris Climate Agreement, the US committed to reducing its emissions by 26 to 28 percent from 2005 levels by 2025. Although the US planned to leave the Hillary Paris Agreement, Biden recommitted to the agreement when he became president.

685. **In 2016, America elected its first female candidate for president, Clinton**, although she ultimately lost to Donald Trump.

686. In 2020, **NASA launched the Perseverance rover**, which landed on Mars in 2021. As of this writing, it is successfully collecting data from the red planet to help study its environment.

687. In 2020, **the United States experienced** an unusually high number of cases and deaths due to **a virus outbreak**. In response to this pandemic, the United States took action in 2021 to provide relief for citizens in terms of health and economic stability.

688. As of 2022, **the US had distributed 613 million doses.** The country also enacted the American Rescue Plan in 2021, a $1.9 trillion economic stimulus package. The government also passed additional initiatives aimed at providing relief during these difficult times.

689. On January 6th, 2021, **pro-Trump supporters stormed Capitol Hill to protest** and stop the certification of Joe Biden's win against Trump. As of this writing, investigations are being made into whether President Trump encouraged them.

690. In 2022, **the US continued addressing major challenges** such as climate change while working toward restoring international relations through investments in renewable energy sources and cyber security projects, among others.

# Section 2: Uncovering More Fascinating Facts of American History
# Major Political Events That Shaped Modern-day Politics

This chapter will delve into **the major political events of the world and the US**. These thirty facts will explore key moments in history, such as **the American Revolution, the Civil War**, and more recent occurrences like the **MeToo movement**. We'll also look at how these events impacted US foreign policy, civil rights movements, and economic power. By understanding these pivotal moments in time, we gain a greater appreciation for their role in shaping the current political landscape.

691. **The Magna Carta** of 1215 was an important document in English history that limited the power of the king and established fundamental rights for all people, including nobles. **The Magna Carta** greatly influenced the US Constitution.

692. **In 1776, America declared independence from Britain** and became a new nation with its own laws and government system

693. **The US Constitution was written in 1787** and is the supreme law of the United States. It is the oldest written constitution still in use today and outlines the structure of the federal government.

694. **The French Revolution began in 1789,** with people seeking to overthrow the monarchy and establish a democratic republic instead. Other revolutions followed, many of which were inspired by the American and French Revolutions.

695. **The Louisiana Purchase** was a significant land transaction in 1803. The United States paid France $15 million for 828,000 square miles west of the Mississippi River. This purchase more than doubled the size of the United States and opened up the country's westward expansion.

696. **The War of 1812** was fought to gain control of the Great Lakes and the Canadian border. The conflict resulted in a stalemate. However, it established the US as a powerful nation, as the country was able to show its strength to the rest of the world.

697. **The Mexican-American War** lasted from 1846 to 1848. The war resulted in the US gaining more than 500,000 square miles of land, including parts of modern-day California, Arizona, New Mexico, and Nevada, among others.

698. **The Communist Manifesto** was written by Karl Marx and Friedrich Engels in 1848. The text argued for a classless society based on common ownership of production forces, eventually leading to uprisings across Europe in the 19th century.

699. **During the Industrial Revolution** (1760–1850), machines replaced manual labor around the world, leading to increased economic growth and poverty among certain groups of workers.

700. **Slavery was abolished in many countries** in the 19th century, as people began to increasingly view it as morally wrong.

701. **The Civil War** was fought **between the Northern and Southern states** of the United States from 1861 to 1865. The war was fought over the issue of slavery, and it resulted in the abolishment of slavery and the reunification of the United States.

702. **The Berlin Conference** of 1884/85 saw European nations carve up Africa for their interests, leading to a long period of colonization and exploitation by foreign powers on the continent. Although the US did not colonize Africa, it did play a role on the continent with the formation of Liberia.

703. **The Spanish-American War** was fought over Cuban independence in 1898. It resulted in the US gaining control of several Spanish territories, including Puerto Rico and the Philippines.

704. **World War I** (1914–1918) was fought between the Central powers (Germany, Austria-Hungary, Turkey, and Bulgaria) and the Allied forces (Britain, France, Russia, and the US). It resulted in millions of deaths and changed many borders, creating the map we are familiar with today.

705. **The Great Depression** was a severe economic recession that began in 1929 and lasted until the early 1940s. The Great Depression had a devastating effect on the world's economy and resulted in widespread unemployment and poverty.

706. In 1963, **President John F. Kennedy was assassinated**. The news shocked the US. Three other notable people would be assassinated in the 1960s: Malcolm X, Martin Luther King Jr., and Bobby Kennedy (JFK's brother), who was running for president.

707. **The Vietnam War** was a conflict between North and South Vietnam. It lasted from 1955 to 1975. The US became involved in the war in 1965, and its involvement was highly controversial. The war had a lasting impact on the US economy, politics, and foreign policy.

708. **The Watergate scandal** was a political scandal in the 1970s. A group of men broke into the Democratic National Committee headquarters at the Watergate Hotel and Office building in Washington, DC. The scandal resulted in Republican **President Richard Nixon's resignation** and impacted US politics for decades to come.

709. **The Iranian hostage crisis** was a diplomatic crisis that lasted from 1979 to 1981. Iranian militants took over the US Embassy in Tehran, holding fifty-two diplomats and civilians hostage for 444 days. When Iraq invaded Iran in 1980, Iran reached out to the US for help. The hostages would all be released by 1981, although the militants began releasing groups of hostages in 1979.

710. **Reaganomics is the term used to refer to President Ronald Reagan's** economic policies. He implemented several conservative policies, including tax cuts, deregulation, and a firm anti-communist foreign policy. Reaganomics had a lasting impact on US politics and economics.

711. **The Iraq War** was a conflict between the United States and Iraq that lasted from 2003 to 2011. The war was fought over Iraq's weapons of mass destruction and Saddam Hussein's brutal regime. The war resulted in the overthrow of Saddam Hussein and the establishment of a democratic government in Iraq.

712. **The Arab Spring** was a series of protests and uprisings in the Middle East and North Africa that occurred between 2010 and 2012. The protests resulted in the overthrow of several dictatorships and had a profound impact on US foreign policy in the region.

713. The 2012 **presidential election was between incumbent President Barack Obama and Republican challenger Mitt Romney**. The election was highly contested, but President Obama was reelected, making him the first African American president to serve two terms in office.

714. **In 2015, the US Supreme Court's decision on same-sex marriage was a landmark victory for LGBTQ** rights and served as a stepping stone for further progress in the area of civil rights.

715. **The 2016 presidential election was between Democratic nominee Hillary Clinton and Republican nominee Donald Trump**. The latter was elected president, making him the first president in US history to be elected without prior political or military experience.

716. **The 2016 presidential election was notable for the role of social media**. Both campaigns used social media platforms, such as **Twitter and Facebook**, extensively, and the election has been described as the "first social media election" in US history.

717. **The MeToo movement is an international movement that seeks to end sexual violence and harassment**. The movement began in 2006 but picked up momentum in 2017. MeToo has brought awareness to the everyday issues girls and women face.

718. **The 2017 Tax Cuts and Jobs Act was a sweeping tax reform package** passed by Congress and signed into law by President Trump in December 2017. The package was highly controversial, but it significantly impacted the US economy and led to a large reduction in taxes for many Americans.

719. **In 2018, the US became the world's largest producer of crude oil** and kept its position until 2021, revolutionizing the global energy market and increasing America's financial and political clout on the world stage.

720. **The 2020 presidential election was between incumbent President Donald Trump and Democratic challenger Joe Biden.** The election was highly contested, but Joe Biden was elected president, making him the oldest person to be elected president in US history.

# Sports Achievements during US History

This chapter will explore some of **the incredible sports achievements made by US athletes throughout history**. We'll take a look at thirty facts to gain insight into how **Americans have dominated Olympic and World Cup competitions** and broken records in baseball, basketball, and boxing.
Learn **why US teams continue to be so successful today** due to their commitment to excellence through dedication and hard work!

721. **The United States** has been one of the most successful countries in the modern Olympic Games. As of this writing, it has won over one thousand gold medals!

722. **Women's sports** have made a major impact on US history. Babe Didrikson Zaharias became one of the greatest American female athletes, winning two gold medals in track and field. Wilma Rudolph also found success in the same category in the 1960 Rome Olympics, winning three gold medals.

723. **Bob Beamon broke his long jump world record** and current Olympic mark with a leap of 8.90 meters (29 feet, 2.5 inches) at the Mexico City Olympics in 1968, setting a record that wouldn't be broken until 1991!

724. **Dan Gable** is considered one of **wrestling's best athletes** after **winning the 1972 Summer Olympics** without giving up a single point. He pinned every one of his opponents and scored a gold medal, the first American wrestler to do so in twelve years.

725. In 1980, a hockey game called the **"Miracle on Ice"** took place. It was one of the biggest upsets in sporting history. **The US men's hockey team, composed mostly of amateurs, beat the Soviets**, who were heavy favorites for that year's Olympics Games! The "Miracle on Ice" became an iconic underdog story.

726. **The 1984 Los Angeles Olympics was sensational for the US.** American athletes won 174 medals, including 83 gold, 61 silver, and 30 bronze medals, making it one of America's most successful Olympic performances.

727. **Tonya Harding** made history by becoming the first American female figure skater to land a triple axel jump in the 1991 US Figure Skating championships competition. Her accomplishments on the ice tend to be overshadowed by her controversies off the ice.

728. In 1992, the **US Dream Team was created**. This team consisted of active NBA (National Basketball Associate) players. Some of the members included **Larry Bird, Michael Jordan, Magic Johnson, Charles Barkley, Patrick Ewing, and Scottie Pippen**. It has been called the greatest sports team ever assembled.

729. In 1996, **Michael Johnson** became an iconic athlete for his performance in the Atlanta Olympics when he won the 200m and 400m races. He is the only male athlete so far who has been able to do so in the same Olympics.

730. **The Boston Marathon** is an annual marathon that started on April 19th, 1897. It is traditionally held on Patriot's Day, which commemorates Paul Revere's ride.

731. **Jack Johnson** became America's very first African American world heavyweight boxing champion in 1908.

732. **Joe Louis** became a world heavyweight **boxing champion for twelve years**, from 1937 to 1949, becoming an iconic figure for African Americans. He defended his title twenty-five times!

733. **The first professional football game** was played in 1892. The Allegheny Athletic Association was pitted against the Pittsburgh Athletic Club.

734. **The American Professional Football Association** was formed in 1920. Two years later, it changed its name to the National Football League (NFL). Football is considered to be the most-watched sport in the US.

735. **The Super Bowl** is the final playoff game between the best of the best in football. It is one of the most-watched TV programs in American history and is second only to Thanksgiving for food consumption.

736. **The New York Yankees baseball team** is one of the most successful sports teams in the US. The team has won twenty-seven World Series championships. Some of the most iconic players in the history of baseball played for the Yankees, including **Babe Ruth, Joe DiMaggio, Mickey Mantle, and Lou Gehring.**

737. **Willie Mays** is considered one of the greatest baseball players, with 660 career home runs, a 1954 Most Valuable Player Award, and 23 All-Star selections throughout his 22-year-long career!

738. **Baseball legend Hank Aaron** hit 755 home runs over 21 seasons, which set the record then. He is known as the "Home Run King" of Major League Baseball (MLB).

739. In 2004, **the Boston Red Sox** ended an eighty-six-year-long drought when they finally won their first World Series title since 1918 by sweeping the St. Louis Cardinals in four games, giving fans reason to celebrate after so many years of misery.

740. **Basketball was invented** by James Naismith in Springfield, Massachusetts, in 1891 and is now a popular sport around the world.

741. In 1996, **the Chicago Bulls** won seventy-two of eighty-two games during the regular season, setting the NBA record for most wins in a single year! The Golden State Warriors upset that record in their 2015/16 season, winning seventy-three games in a single season.

742. **Michael Jordan played for the Chicago Bulls** and is one of the most celebrated US athletes today. He has many accomplishments, two of which are winning the NBA championship six times and being the NBA MVP five times.

743. **The US Women's National Basketball Association** has been incredibly successful since its formation in 1996. As of this writing, the US Women's National Team has one of the best records in the Olympics, suffering no losses since 1992. It is also first in the FIBA rankings.

744. **Women's team sports** have grown significantly in US history, especially after Title IX legislation passed in 1972 that allowed female athletes access to equal educational opportunities and funding in sports.

745. **The US Women's National Soccer Team** (USWNT) has been incredibly successful since its formation in 1985, winning four Olympic gold medals from 1996 to 2012. It has also won four Women's World Cups in 1991, 1999, 2015, and 2019.

746. **Billie Jean King** became one of the most iconic female tennis players after she won a legendary match against Bobby Riggs at the Houston Astrodome in 1973, known as the "Battle of the Sexes."

747. **Venus and Serena Williams** both made history by becoming the two highest-ranked female tennis players in 2002. The sisters have achieved amazing things on the court. Venus Williams has won four Olympic gold medals, seven Grand Slams, and five Wimbledon championships. Serena Williams also holds four Olympic gold medals and thirty-nine Grand Slams. The sisters set an example for young women all over the world.

748. Although **hockey (the NHL)** is not as popular as football or basketball, it is still one of the major sports franchises in the US. In the 1995/96 season, **the Detroit Red Wings had** the most wins in a single season. The Tampa Bay Lightning tied the Wings' sixty-two wins in the 2018/19 season.

749. **Tiger Woods** set several records during his historic win at the 1997 Masters Tournament by becoming not only the youngest winner but also the first person African American golfer to do so. In 2001, he became the youngest player to complete a Grand Slam (winning all top four major professional golf tournaments in a career).

750. **Lance Armstrong** made history by becoming the only person to win seven consecutive Tour de France titles between 1999 to 2005 before being stripped of all his wins due to doping allegations in 2012.

# Military Conflicts Fought by Americans

This chapter will explore **the various military conflicts fought by Americans** throughout history. We'll take a look at thirty facts about conflicts, from the **Revolutionary War** to the ongoing **war in Syria.**

751. **The American Revolutionary War** was fought between Britain and the American colonies from 1775 to 1783. The war was fought after the American colonies declared their independence from Britain and sought to establish a new nation.

752. The war saw a variety of battles fought between the two sides, with the British eventually being defeated by the American forces **at the Battle of Yorktown in 1781**. The war ended with the signing of the Treaty of Paris in 1783, which officially recognized the United States of America as an independent nation.

753. **The Barbary Wars** were a series of conflicts fought between the United States and the Barbary states in North Africa from 1801 to 1815.

754. The wars were fought after **the Barbary states began to attack American merchant ships** in the Mediterranean and demand tribute from the United States. The United States eventually gained control of the region. The First Barbary War ended with the signing of the Treaty of Tripoli in 1805. The Second Barbary War lasted for only three days and also ended in an American victory.

755. **The War of 1812** was a conflict fought between Britain and the United States from 1812 to 1815. The war was triggered by various disputes between the two countries, including American anger over British interference with American shipping and the impressment of American sailors into the British navy.

756. **The British were eventually defeated in the War of 1812**. One of the Americans' greatest victories was the Battle of New Orleans, which happened after the war ended. The conflict officially ended with the signing of the Treaty of Ghent in 1815.

757. **The American Indian Wars** were a series of conflicts fought between Native American tribes and the United States government from the early 17th century to the early 20th century.

758. The wars were fought mainly to gain control of Native American tribal lands and to **push Native Americans from their ancestral homelands**. Many different tribes were involved in the conflicts, but the US eventually gained control of much of the western part of the continent.

759. **The Seminole Wars** were a series of conflicts fought between the United States and the Seminole tribe from 1816 to 1858. The wars were fought after the Seminoles refused to leave their tribal lands in Florida, which the United States wanted to use to expand its territory. The United States eventually gained control of the region.

760. **The Mexican-American War** was fought between the United States and Mexico from 1846 to 1848.

761. The war was triggered by a dispute over the border between the two countries. The United States eventually claimed victory and gained control of much of what is today the southwestern United States. The war ended with the signing of the **Treaty of Guadalupe Hidalgo in 1848.**

762. **The American Civil War** was fought between the Union and the Confederate States of America from 1861 to 1865.

763. **The war was fought after the Confederate States seceded from the Union to establish a new nation**. The war was bloody, with both sides suffering many casualties. The war ended with the surrender of the Confederate Army at Appomattox Court House in 1865.

764. **The Spanish-American War** was fought between Spain and the United States in 1898. The war was triggered by the sinking of the USS Maine in Havana Harbor, Cuba, in February 1898.

765. **The United States claimed victory in the war** and gained control of islands in the Caribbean and Pacific. The war ended with the Treaty of Paris in 1898.

766. **The Philippine-American War** was a conflict fought between the United States and Filipino revolutionaries from 1899 to 1902.

767. **The Filipino revolutionaries'** desire for independence from US control triggered the war. American soldiers were ultimately able to occupy the islands and put down the revolutionaries for the most part.

768. **World War** I was fought between the Allied and Central powers **from 1914 to 1918.** The war was triggered by the assassination of Archduke Franz Ferdinand of Austria-Hungary in June 1914, with the Allied powers eventually claiming victory and gaining control of much of Europe. World War I changed how conflicts were fought and ended with the signing of the Treaty of Versailles in 1919.

769. **World War II** was fought between the Allied and Axis powers **from 1939 to 1945.** The war was triggered by the invasion of Poland by Nazi Germany in September 1939, although the Allied powers eventually claimed victory. The war ended with the surrender of Japan in 1945.

770. **The Korean War** was a conflict fought between North Korea and South Korea from **1950 to 1953**. The war was triggered by North Korea's invasion of South Korea in June 1950.

771. Although North Korea made some gains, Korea did not become united. After the war, Korea remained divided. An armistice agreement was signed, so the war technically never ended.

772. **The Vietnam War** was fought between North Vietnam and South Vietnam from **1955 to 1975**. The war was triggered by the North Vietnamese invasion of South Vietnam in 1955.

773. Other nations entered the Vietnam War, with the United States sending hundreds of thousands of troops to the area. **The Paris Peace Accords was signed in 1973**, and two years later, North Vietnam took over South Vietnam.

774. **The Gulf War** was fought between Iraq and a coalition of forces, including the United States, from 1990 to 1991.

775. **The Iraqi invasion of Kuwait** triggered the First Gulf War in August 1990, with the coalition forces eventually claiming victory and gaining control of the region. The war ended with a ceasefire agreement in 1991.

776. **The Iraq War** was fought between the United States and Iraq **from 2003 to 2011**. The war was triggered by the US invasion of Iraq in 2003.

777. **The United States won the war** and toppled Saddam Hussein's regime. In 2011, the last US troops left Iraq.

778. **The War in Afghanistan** is a conflict that lasted from 2001 to 2021.

779. The war was triggered by the US invasion of Afghanistan in 2001 **after the Taliban refused to hand over Osama bin Laden.** The United States eventually found Osama bin Laden, but it was not successful in the war, as the Taliban took over the country.

780. **The Syrian Civil War** is a conflict that broke out in 2011 between the Syrian government and various rebel groups. The war was triggered by the Syrian government's crackdown on dissidents. As of this writing, the conflict is still ongoing.

# Technology Revolution in the US

This chapter will explore the incredible and groundbreaking technologies that have revolutionized our lives over the past couple of centuries. Through these thirty facts, you'll gain insight into some of **the most significant inventions in history,** such as **telephones, automobiles, and computers!** We'll investigate how these products changed communication and transportation forever. Understanding this fascinating technological revolution is essential for keeping up with a rapidly changing world!

781. **The technological revolution began in the US** in the late 1800s, with new technologies like telephones and cars being developed.

782. **Alexander Graham Bell** is credited with inventing the telephone in 1876. The telephone changed how people communicated.

783. In 1877, **Thomas Edison** invented the phonograph, which could record and play sounds.

784. **Thomas Edison was a prolific American inventor**. He also invented the machine called the Kinetoscope, which could show moving pictures!

785. **The Wright Brothers** are credited with inventing powered human flight after their successful first airplane flight on December 17th, 1903, near Kitty Hawk, North Carolina.

786. **Henry Ford's Model-T car** was released in 1908, revolutionizing transportation around America and making travel easier than ever.

787. **Computers were first introduced into the workplace** in the 1950s and 1960s, making tasks like calculating numbers much faster. Computers really became popular in the 1980s.

788. **German American inventor Ralph Baer** created the first digital video game in 1967 called "Brown Box," which allowed two players to play against each other. The game later morphed into the first console game called Magnavox Odyssey.

789. In 1968, ARPANET **(Advanced Research Projects Agency Network)** sent its first message across computers connected over a network; this is the beginning of what we now know as the internet!

790. **Mobile cell phones** were invented by Martin Cooper in 1973. Cellphones would eventually allow people to make calls on the go without being tied down to landlines or payphones.

791. **Apple released its first personal computer**, the Apple I, in 1976, revolutionizing how people used computers at home and for work.

792. The 1980s saw an explosion of tech products, with companies like **Nintendo** (based in Japan) releasing their iconic gaming console known as NES **(Nintendo Entertainment System).**

793. **IBM introduced the Personal Computer** in 1981, allowing people to use computers for daily tasks and entertainment.

794. In 1994, the popular web browser **Netscape Navigator** was released, which made surfing the internet much easier!

795. **MP3 players** were introduced in 1997 by a South Korean company, drastically changing how people listened to music. We still like to listen to our choice of music today on the go!

796. **Google** became the most used search engine by 2000, becoming a household name worldwide.

797. **Wi-Fi (Wireless Fidelity)** technology was released to consumers in 1997 but didn't become widely available until 2003, when it started appearing in more and more places, like schools, businesses, and homes.

798. **Social media** sites, such as **Facebook**, began popping up in the late 1990s; now, almost everyone has an account on one or more social media platforms.

799. **The Apple iPhone** was released in 2007, bringing revolutionary touchscreen technology into people's lives and making communication even simpler.

800. **Smartphones** with advanced features emerged shortly after the iPhone, revolutionizing how we interact with each other today.

801. Although apps **(applications)** have been around since the late 1990s, they didn't become really popular until around 2008. Today, we use apps to play games and order food.

802. **3D printing** has been around since the 1980s but recently became much more affordable and accessible. People can use 3D printing to print out almost anything they need!

803. **Wearable technology**, such as fitness trackers, has become popular over the past decade. These devices help us monitor our physical activity and health.

804. **Virtual reality (VR)** headsets have been around since 1975, but they didn't become readily available to the public until the mid-2010s. VR puts users into digital environments that look and feel like real life.

805. **Artificial intelligence (AI)** is used in many aspects of our lives today, such as self-driving cars and voice assistants.

806. **Augmented reality (AR)**, which was first experimented with back in 1994, has grown increasingly popular over recent years. Augmented reality combines real life with the virtual world. Pokémon Go is a great example of an augmented reality app.

807. **Autonomous drones** are now being used for delivery services and surveillance tasks due to their increased accuracy and efficiency.

808. **Quantum computing** is a relatively new field of computer science that's pushing the boundaries of what computers can do based on quantum theory.

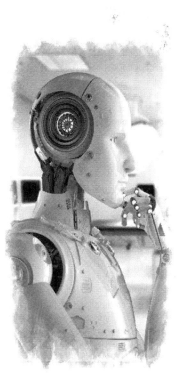

809. **Robotic technologies** have significantly advanced in recent years. Robots are now able to complete complex tasks with precision.

810. **Cloud computing** allows people to store their data online to access it from anywhere without worrying about losing it!

# The Women's Rights Movement in America

This chapter will explore the history and progress of **the women's rights movement in America.** We'll look at thirty facts to discover how influential figures **such as Susan B. Anthony, Alice Paul**, and **Gloria Steinem** helped bring about major changes for women throughout US history.

Discover how organizations like NOW **(National Organization for Women)**, social media platforms, and protests are continuing this struggle today.

811. **The women's rights movement in the United States** took a huge step forward in 1848 at Seneca Falls, New York.

812. **The Seneca Falls Convention** was organized by Elizabeth Cady Stanton and Lucretia Mott, who wanted to gain equal rights for all women.

813. In 1869, **Susan B. Anthony and Elizabeth Cady Stanton** created the National Woman Suffrage Association, which pushed for a constitutional amendment to give women the right to vote.

814. **Wyoming** became the first state to grant full voting rights to women in 1890.

815. A major milestone came in 1920 when Congress ratified **the Nineteenth Amendment**, granting suffrage nationwide after decades of activism from both men and women.

816. In 1960, **the first birth control pill** was approved by the FDA, giving women more freedom in their choices regarding pregnancy and sex.

817. Women gained more freedom in the 1960s when they were able to open bank accounts on their own.

818. In 1963, **Betty Friedan released The Feminine Mystique**, which helped bring awareness to the women's rights movement and sparked a resurgence in the fight for equality.

819. President John F. Kennedy signed **the Equal Pay Act** in 1963, which was designed to stop pay discrimination.

820. **After gaining suffrage, many organizations were formed**. One organization was NOW (National Organization for Women), which was founded in 1966.

821. California became the first state to pass **a no-fault divorce law** in 1969. No-fault divorce laws mean that neither party has to provide an instance of wrongdoing. Divorce rates rose as a result.

822. **Gloria Steinem** became one of the founders of Ms. magazine in 1971. The magazine dealt with women's issues and featured feminist articles.

823. In 1972, **Title IX was passed**, which prohibited discrimination against girls and women in educational programs that receive federal funding.

824. **Roe v. Wade** was ruled on in 1973. The Supreme Court decided that women had the right to decide if they wanted an abortion.

825. In 1974, **the Equal Credit Opportunity Act was passed**. This act made it illegal for creditors to discriminate against applicants based on their sex, race, religion, or marital status.

826. **The Pregnancy Discrimination Act** of 1978 protects pregnant women from being discriminated against in the workplace. The act requires employers to treat pregnant women the same as other employees and not to discriminate against them.

827. **Alice Paul** laid the groundwork for the Equal Rights Amendment (ERA). The amendment was approved by Congress in 1972. However, it failed to gain ratification from enough states for adoption into the Constitution due to strong opposition from conservative groups, such as Phyllis Schlafly's STOP ERA Campaign.

828. Although many women fought for equality, many women didn't want things to change. STOP (**"Stop Taking Our Privileges"**) fought against things like the ERA because they worried it would take away certain privileges like separate restrooms for men and women.

829. In 1981, **Sandra Day O'Connor** became the first woman to sit on the Supreme Court.

830. In 1992, **the US passed the Family and Medical Leave Act** (FMLA), which allows women and men to take up to twelve weeks of unpaid leave per year for certain situations (like taking care of a newborn) without fear of losing their job or health insurance coverage. This was an important milestone in **protecting workers' rights** in the workforce.

831. Another key change came in 1994 when **President Bill Clinton established the Violence Against Women Act**. This office works to end violence against women and girls throughout the United States by supporting victims and holding offenders accountable.

832. **The Lilly Ledbetter Fair Pay Act** was passed in 2009 to strengthen existing equal pay laws. It also allows employees to file discrimination complaints if they have been underpaid due to their gender or race, regardless of how long ago it occurred.

833. In 2012, **the Violence Against Women Act** was passed, which expanded protection for victims of domestic violence and sexual assault. This was a major victory for the women's rights movement in America, as it extended protections to more victims and provided more resources for survivors of abuse.

834. The year 2016 saw the passing of **the Every Student Succeeds Act**, which replaced No Child Left Behind. The act holds schools accountable for the success of all students, regardless of gender, race, or disability.

835. In 2009, **the White House Council on Women and Girls was formed** to advise the president on issues that are important to women and girls throughout America, such as education, economic opportunities, and health care.

836. **The council was disbanded during Trump's presidency**, but President Joe Biden reinstated it, this time calling it the White House Gender Policy Council.

837. **A milestone came in 2020** when Congress passed legislation guaranteeing twelve weeks of paid parental leave to all federal employees, regardless of gender.

838. **The year 2021 saw even further advancements** toward equal pay through legislation introduced at state levels across America to close gender wage gaps within specific industries, such as finance and health care.

839. In 2022, **the US Supreme Court overturned Roe v. Wade**. At the moment, abortion rights reside at the state level. Even conservative states like Kentucky had enough support to defeat state legislation aimed at prohibiting abortion.

840. **Organizations and activists continue to push for changes in women's rights** on a global scale today through protests and social media platforms, such as Twitter and Instagram.

# Music, Art, and Literature Movements during American History

This chapter will explore **the fascinating movements in American music, art, and literature** from 1920 to today. We'll examine thirty facts about these trends, including the Harlem Renaissance, the folk music of the Great Depression, jazz, and abstract expressionism. Learn some interesting facts about punk rock and hip-hop. Discover how **artists have used their work to reflect current events** or express opinions on social issues while challenging traditional conventions.

841. **The Harlem Renaissance** in the 1920s was a time of great African American art, music, and literature.

842. **Folk music,** such as blues and country, was popular during the Great Depression.

843. **Abstract expressionism** was a significant art movement that began in New York City during the 1940s and 1950s. Artists focused on expressing emotion through abstract shapes and colors on canvas or paper without using patterns or recognizable images.

844. **Rock and roll** emerged from rhythm and blues (R&B) music in the late 1940s. The popularity of the genre took off thanks to artists like Chuck Berry.

845. **Jazz musicians**, such as **Miles Davis** and **John Coltrane**, created new sounds in the 1950s, departing from the swing band music that was popular decades prior.

846. **The Beatnik movement** was an artistic subculture of writers, poets, and artists who rebelled against conventional society during the late 1950s and early 1960s.

847. **Pop art began in the 1950s and 1960s** as a reaction to abstract expressionism. These artists used recognizable everyday images from pop culture, such as comics, advertisements, and product packaging.

848. **Minimalist art** became popular in the late 1950s and early 1960s. This style of art features simple geometric shapes that are meant to draw attention away from physical forms toward ideas about space or color instead.

849. **The British Invasion happened** in the mid-1960s, bringing Americans famous bands like the Beatles, the Rolling Stones, and the Who, just to name a few.

850. Protest songs became very popular in the 1960s. Many s**ongwriters spoke out against the Vietnam War.**

851. **The feminist art movement** of the late 1960s sought to create gender equality through artwork by highlighting issues women faced at that time, such as domestic violence and unequal pay for the same work as men.

852. **Postmodern literature** was popular in the 1960s. It uses elements of irony and parody while questioning traditional texts' roles within society.

853. Another popular **type of literature was realism,** which sought to describe reality without embellishments. These texts often involve ordinary people struggling with everyday life problems.

854. **Surrealism literature** uses dreamlike images and symbols to explore complex ideas about life and reality without society's traditional structure or rules.

855. **The black arts movement** lasted from 1965 to 1975. It was an African American literary and artistic movement that sought to create works that addressed themes of racism and oppression.

856. **Punk rock** emerged in the mid-1970s with its driving beats and rebellious lyrics that spoke out against social injustices like racism and poverty.

857. **Punk rockers embraced DIY principles** by encouraging people to make their music instead of relying on major record labels or radio stations for exposure.

858. **Hip-hop was born in New York City** during the 1970s when DJs started mixing samples of different recordings, creating something entirely new in the process.

859. **Postmodern architecture** became popular in the late 1970s. It relies heavily on abstract shapes and curves instead of traditional lines and angles, creating visually stunning buildings!

860. **Poetry slams** became popular in Chicago in the mid-1980s. Poets recite spoken word poetry before crowds and are judged on not only their poems but also their performance.

861. **Grunge music** emerged in Seattle during the mid-1980s. This type of music is known for its loud guitars, distorted sounds, and lyrics about alienation or disaffection from society.

862. **Blues music** enjoyed new popularity in the 1990s, as African American music, literature, and art flourished again after decades of struggle and oppression.

863. **Country music** has been popular since the 1920s but experienced a resurgence in popularity during the 1990s thanks to artists like **Tim McGraw.**

864. **Pop music** has been popular since the mid-1950s and has evolved greatly over the decades.

865. **Latinx writers** have made significant contributions to US literature by writing stories that reflect their culture and experiences living in America.

866. **Many Native American** cultures still practice their traditional arts, including weaving baskets from willow branches or painting images on hides using natural dyes.

867. **Contemporary dance** is a type of performance art that combines different styles, such as modern dance, ballet, and hip-hop.

868. **Street art** is a type of public art that uses graffiti, murals, and stencils to tell stories about current events or express the artist's opinion on social issues.

869. **Street photography** captures everyday moments in public spaces, such as parks, streets, or markets. These photos often depict emotion-filled scenes.

870. **Contemporary art** is an umbrella term used to describe any artwork created today. It includes all kinds of different styles, such as installations, video art, and digital media!

# Major Supreme Court Cases of the 20th Century

This chapter will explore **the major Supreme Court cases of the 20ᵗʰ** century that have shaped America's laws. With these thirty facts, you'll discover how these landmark decisions **protected the freedom of speech and expression**, privacy rights, and criminal justice procedures. We'll also examine the constitutional issues surrounding each case to understand why they were so impactful.

871. ***Lochner v. New York* (1905):** This Supreme Court case struck down a New York law limiting the number of hours a baker could work, ruling that it violated the Due Process Clause of the Fourteenth Amendment. This case established a legal doctrine that was later widely criticized for interfering with the state's power to regulate its citizens.

872. ***Muller v. Oregon* (1908):** In this case, the Supreme Court upheld an Oregon law that imposed maximum working hours for women. The Supreme Court determined that the law was constitutional because it served a legitimate state interest in protecting the health of female workers. This decision established the precedent that states could pass laws regulating the health and safety of their citizens. However, it also hampered the women's rights movement for equality between the sexes.

873. ***Hammer v. Dagenhart* (1918):** This Supreme Court case struck down a federal law prohibiting the interstate shipment of goods produced by child labor. The Supreme Court ruled that the law violated the Constitution's Commerce Clause and was an intrusion on states' rights to regulate their citizens.

874. ***Selective Draft Law Cases* (1918):** In these cases, the Supreme Court upheld the constitutionality of the first peacetime military draft in the United States. The Supreme Court found that Congress had the authority to implement the draft to raise and support armies.

875. ***Schenck v. United States*** (1919): This Supreme Court case upheld the conviction of a man who was charged with violating the Espionage Act of 1917 for distributing literature criticizing the draft. The Supreme Court held that his actions constituted a "clear and present danger" to the nation's security. The case essentially determined that Schenck did not have the right to express his views against the draft, which violates the First Amendment.

876. ***Adkins v. Children's Hospital*** (1923): In this case, the Supreme Court struck down a District of Columbia law establishing a minimum wage for women. The Supreme Court held that the law violated the Due Process Clause of the Fifth Amendment because it interfered with the right to contract freely.

877. ***United States v. Schwimmer*** (1929): In this case, the Supreme Court held that a woman who had applied for citizenship was ineligible because she refused to take an oath of military service. The Supreme Court found that the decision to deny her application was reasonable under the Naturalization Act of 1906.

878. ***Schechter Poultry Corp. v. United States*** (1935): This Supreme Court case struck down a federal law that regulated the sale of poultry and other commodities. The Supreme Court found that the law exceeded Congress's power under the Commerce Clause and was an unconstitutional delegation of power.

879. ***United States v. Miller*** (1939): In this case, the Supreme Court held that a federal law prohibiting the interstate transportation of a sawed-off shotgun was constitutional. The Supreme Court found that the law was within Congress's power under the Commerce Clause to regulate activities that substantially affect interstate commerce.

880. ***United States v. Carolene Products Co.*** (1938): This Supreme Court case established the "footnote four" doctrine, which provides that courts should defer to laws passed by the legislature unless there is a compelling reason to do otherwise. This decision has been widely cited in subsequent cases.

881. ***West Virginia State Board of Education v. Barnette*** **(1943):** In this case, the Supreme Court held that a West Virginia law requiring schoolchildren to salute the American flag violated the First Amendment's protection of freedom of speech and expression. This decision has been widely cited as an example of the Supreme Court's protection of individual liberty.

882. ***Korematsu v. United States*** **(1944):** This Supreme Court case upheld the internment of Japanese Americans during World War II. The Supreme Court found that internment was a reasonable exercise of the government's power to protect national security. This decision has been widely criticized for its violation of civil liberties.

883. ***Brown v. Board of Education*** **(1954):** This Supreme Court case overturned the doctrine of "separate but equal" in public education. The Supreme Court held that racial segregation in public schools violated the Equal Protection Clause of the Fourteenth Amendment. This decision marked a major shift in the court's approach to civil rights.

884. ***Mapp v. Ohio*** **(1961):** In this case, the Supreme Court held that evidence obtained in violation of the Fourth Amendment's protection against unreasonable searches and seizures was inadmissible in criminal proceedings. This decision has been widely cited as an important protection of individual rights against government intrusion.

885. ***Engel v. Vitale*** **(1962):** The Supreme Court held that a New York law requiring public schoolchildren to recite a non-denominational prayer violated the First Amendment's Establishment Clause. This case has been widely cited as an example of the Supreme Court's protection of religious liberty.

886. ***Gideon v. Wainwright*** **(1963):** This Supreme Court case held that state and federal governments must provide legal counsel to those accused of a crime who cannot afford to hire their own lawyer. This decision marked a major shift in the Supreme Court's approach to criminal justice and has been widely cited in subsequent cases.

887. ***Griswold v. Connecticut*** **(1965):** This Supreme Court case struck down a Connecticut law prohibiting the use of contraception, finding that the law violated the right to privacy implied by the Bill of Rights. This decision marked a major shift in the Supreme Court's approach to the protection of individual rights.

888. ***Miranda v. Arizona* (1966)**: In this case, the Supreme Court held that individuals who are taken into police custody must be informed of their right to remain silent and to have an attorney present during questioning. This case has been widely cited as an important protection of individual rights.

889. ***Brandenburg v. Ohio* (1969)**: This Supreme Court case held that the government could not punish individuals for speech unless it is likely to incite imminent violence. This decision has been widely cited as an important protection of the right to freedom of expression.

890. ***New York Times Co. v. United States* (1971)**: The Supreme Court held that the First Amendment's protection of freedom of the press overruled the government's attempt to prevent the publication of classified documents. This decision has been widely cited as an important protection of the press's ability to inform the public.

891. ***Furman v. Georgia* (1972)**: In this case, the Supreme Court held that the existing death penalty laws in the United States were unconstitutional because they were applied in an arbitrary and discriminatory manner. This decision marked a major shift in the Supreme Court's approach to capital punishment.

892. ***Roe v. Wade* (1973)**: This Supreme Court case held that a woman's right to privacy includes the right to terminate a pregnancy. This decision marked a major shift in the Supreme Court's approach to reproductive rights and has been widely cited in subsequent cases.

893. ***United States v. Nixon* (1974)**: In this case, the Supreme Court held that President Richard Nixon had to comply with a subpoena requesting tapes from his White House office. This decision has been widely cited as an important protection of the balance of power between the branches of government.

894. ***Regents of the University of California v. Bakke*** **(1978):** This Supreme Court case struck down a California law that established a separate admissions program for minority applicants, finding that it violated the Equal Protection Clause of the Fourteenth Amendment. This decision has been widely cited in subsequent cases.

895. ***Texas v. Johnson*** **(1989):** In this case, the Supreme Court held that the burning of an American flag was protected by the First Amendment's protection of freedom of speech and expression. This decision has been widely cited as an example of the Supreme Court's protection of individual liberty.

896. ***Webster v. Reproductive Health Services*** **(1989):** The Supreme Court upheld a Missouri law that imposed restrictions on abortion, finding that the law did not violate the right to privacy implied by the Fourteenth Amendment.

897. ***United States v. Williams*** **(1992):** The Supreme Court held that the government's ability to prosecute individuals for conspiracy to commit a crime (in this case, exchanging or selling child pornography) did not violate the First Amendment since the person would be doing something illegal anyway.

898. ***United States v. Lopez*** **(1995):** This Supreme Court case struck down a federal law that prohibited the possession of firearms within a school zone, finding that the law exceeded Congress's power under the Commerce Clause. Schools were deemed to be under the state's jurisdiction, not that of the federal government.

899. ***Reno v. American Civil Liberties Union*** **(1997):** The Supreme Court determined that communications on the internet have First Amendment protection similar to other forms of speech, meaning citizens cannot be censored online without due process.

900. ***Obergefell v. Hodges*** **(2000):** In this case, the Supreme Court stated that same-sex couples had the right to marry under the Due Process Clause and the Equal Protection Clause of the Fourteenth Amendment. This case established the right to same-sex marriage on the federal level.

# African American History and Culture in the US

This chapter will explore the fascinating **history and culture of African Americans** in the United States. Through thirty interesting facts, we'll discover how enslaved Africans arrived in North America, important civil rights reforms, and influential figures like **Martin Luther King Jr**. and **Oprah Winfrey** who broke barriers for future generations.

We'll also **learn about famous African American** inventors, artists, and musicians that made an impact on our culture today. By understanding these elements of African American history, you can better appreciate their immense contributions to this nation.

901. **The first enslaved Africans arrived in Jamestown, Virginia, in 1619** aboard a Dutch trading vessel called the White Lion.

902. **Between 1525 and 1866,** 12.5 million enslaved people were brought to North America, South America, and the Caribbean from Africa.

903. **The Underground Railroad** allowed tens of thousands of African Americans to find freedom via a secret network that connected them with abolitionists willing to help them escape bondage.

904. **The infamous Dred Scott case of 1857** saw the Supreme Court decision that African Americans were not afforded the rights stated in the Constitution.

905. **The Civil War was fought from 1861 to 1865**. Although the Civil War was fought for multiple issues, the most pressing issue was keeping the institution of slavery intact in the South. During the war, President Abraham Lincoln passed the Emancipation Proclamation, freeing enslaved people in the states that had seceded.

906. In 1865, **the Civil War was won by the North**. Several amendments, namely the Thirteenth, Fourteenth, and Fifteenth Amendments, were passed that granted and protected rights to African Americans.

907. **The period of Reconstruction took place after the Civil War**. Reconstruction had several purposes, including reuniting the country and providing a system for African Americans to get on their feet.

908. Although some steps were made in the right direction, **the Jim Crow laws** took a big step backward. Because of the laws, African Americans faced discrimination in housing, education, employment, and public accommodations.

909. **The NAACP was founded** in February 1909 by W. E. B. Du Bois, Ida B. Wells, and other activists to work for civil rights reforms.

910. **The Harlem Renaissance** was a period of artistic, literary, and musical that flourished in the 1920s and 1930s. Langston Hughes, Zora Neale Hurston, and Jacob Lawrence are some of the most renowned figures from this era.

911. **The Tuskegee Airmen** were the first black pilots to serve in the US military. They served during World War II. Their bravery and skill helped redefine the role of African Americans in the US Armed Forces.

912. In 1954, **the Supreme Court ruled that racial segregation** of schools was unconstitutional with Brown v. Board of Education. This case paved the way for the integration of education, eventually leading to more diverse classrooms across America.

913. **The Montgomery bus boycott** occurred after Rosa Parks refused to give up her seat on a bus for white passengers. This event led to the ruling that segregated buses in Alabama were unconstitutional.

914. **The 16th Street Baptist Church in Birmingham**, Alabama, was bombed by KKK members in 1963, killing four girls attending Sunday school. The KKK is a notorious hate group that has gone through multiple iterations. The group is still around today.

915. In 1964, **Martin Luther King Jr. received the Nobel Peace Prize** for his nonviolent protests against racial injustice.

916. In 1965, **President Lyndon Johnson** signed the Voting Rights Act, which outlawed many of the discriminatory voting practices used to prevent African Americans from voting, such as literacy tests and poll taxes.

917. **The Black Panthers was founded in 1966** to protect African American communities from police brutality through militant self-defense tactics. They wanted to ensure African American people could live without fear of police brutality.

918. In 1968, track athletes **John Carlos and Tommie Smith made a protest during their medal ceremony at the Summer Olympics in Mexico City** when they raised black-gloved fists during the US national anthem to show solidarity with the civil rights movement.

919. In 1968, **Martin Luther King Jr.**, a leader in the civil rights movement, was assassinated at the age of thirty-nine while standing on his hotel balcony in Memphis, Tennessee.

920. A holiday celebrating **Dr. King's legacy—Martin Luther King Day**—became an official national holiday throughout America starting in 1983.

921. In 1984, **Byllye Avery**, along with others, started the National Black Women's Health Project to educate women about health disparities in African American communities.

922. **The Million Man March** took place on October 16th, 1995. Nearly a million people from all backgrounds traveled to Washington, DC, to stand against racism and police brutality.

923. The first black president of the United States was **Barack Obama**, who served from 2009 to 2017.

924. **The Black Lives Matter movement** began after the death of Trayvon Martin when his killer, George Zimmerman, was acquitted in July 2013. The movement exploded with the deaths of Michael Brown and Eric Garner in 2014. Since then, the organization has worked toward ending violence inflicted upon black people worldwide.

925. **African American culture** is still very much alive today, with music like jazz, blues, and hip-hop being popular genres among all races.

926. **Famous African American** inventors include **Elijah McCoy** (automatic lubricator for steam engines), **George Washington Carver** (crop rotation), and **Garrett Morgan** (a kind of traffic light).

927. **Famous African Americans** that have broken barriers include **Oprah Winfrey** (media mogul), Colin Powell (the first black US Secretary of State), and **Madam C. J. Walker** (the first female self-made millionaire in America).

928. **African American authors,** such as Toni Morrison, Zora Neale Hurston, and Maya Angelou, have significantly impacted literature.

929. **African Americans** are also known for their artistry and creativity in visual arts, from painting to sculpture to photography.

930. **African American cuisine has evolved** over the years, with dishes like jambalaya, gumbo, and fried chicken being some of the most popular comfort foods.

# Famous Explorers Who Founded Early Settlements in the US

This chapter will explore the fascinating **history of famous explorers** who founded early settlements in the United States. We'll take a look at thirty interesting facts about their voyages, discoveries, and contributions to American history. Furthermore, we'll examine how they utilized nature to survive in harsh conditions and developed complex trade networks between **different tribes across North America.**

931. **Leif Erikson** discovered North America centuries before Columbus, reaching Newfoundland around 1000 CE.

932. **Columbus** kicked off the start of colonization in the New World after stumbling on The Bahamas in 1492.

933. **John Cabot** claimed most of North America for England when he landed in Newfoundland in 1497.

934. **Amerigo Vespucci** explored the New World in the late 15th century and early 16th century. His name is where we get the term "America."

935. **Vasco Nuñez Balboa** crossed Panama and sighted the Pacific Ocean, becoming the first European to see it in 1513.

936. **Ponce de León discovered Florida** while allegedly searching for the Fountain of Youth in 1513. He claimed Florida for Spain and became the first known European explorer to discover what is now the United States.

937. **Giovanni da Verrazzano** sailed from France to eastern North America to search for a route to the Pacific sometime in the 1520s. He explored parts of the eastern coastline and landed near Cape Fear, North Carolina.

938. In 1524, **Estevão Gomes**, a Portuguese explorer, became the first European to discover the Hudson River. Henry Hudson would explore more of this river about ninety years later.

939. **Estevanico** was a Moroccan slave who accompanied Cabeza de Vaca on his expedition to the Southern US in 1527.

940. **Jacques Cartier** explored Canada. He notably traveled the Gulf of Saint Lawrence and the Lawrence River from 1534 to 1542.

941. **Hernando de Soto** became the first European to cross the Mississippi River in 1541.

942. **Francisco Vázquez de Coronado** led an expedition from Mexico to what is now the American Southwest in 1540 and 1542.

943. In 1542 and 1543, **Juan Rodríguez Cabrillo** became the first European to investigate modern-day California.

944. **Pedro Menéndez de Avilés** established St. Augustine as a Spanish settlement on August 28th, 1565. It is the oldest continually inhabited city in the US.

945. **Juan Pardo** established the first European settlement in North Carolina with Fort San Juan, near modern-day Morganton, in the 16th century.

946. **The English** tried to establish a permanent settlement off the coast of North Carolina in 1585. It was called Roanoke.

947. By 1590, the **colony of Roanoke** had been abandoned. To this day, no one is sure what happened to the colonists, although the most likely theory is that they moved to Croatoan Island.

948. **Jamestown, Virginia**, became the first permanent English settlement in America on May 14th, 1607.

949. **Samuel de Champlain** founded Quebec City and other settlements along Lake Ontario and Lake Champlain from 1608 to 1635.

950. **Henry Hudson** explored the area around what is now New York and Canada in 1609 and 1610. Hudson's men were the first Europeans to visit Hudson Bay in 1611.

951. **Hudson** was looking for the Northwest Passage, a waterway that connected the **Atlantic to the Pacific**. The Northwest Passage wouldn't be fully navigated until the early 20th century!

952. **In 1614, the Dutch established New Netherland in what is now New** Jersey and New York. The English took control of this colony sixty years later and renamed it New York.

953. **In 1620, the Pilgrims sailed the Atlantic** on the Mayflower, landing in present-day Massachusetts. They established a small colony there.

954. **Louis Joliet and Jacques Marquette** explored a huge chunk of North America on their 1673 mission. The two went from the Great Lakes region to the Gulf of Mexico.

955. **Marquette and Joliet** were also the first Europeans to explore the northern part of the Mississippi River Valley.

956. **René Robert Cavelier Sieur de La Salle** traveled along the Mississippi River, claiming much of its basin for France during 1682 and 1683.

957. From 1697 to 1702, **Eusebio Kino**, a Jesuit missionary and explorer, investigated Sonora, Mexico, and southern Arizona. He also discovered that Baja California was not an island but a peninsula.

958. In 1773, **the last of the British Thirteen Colonies** would be created. The colony of Georgia was officially established that year. It notably banned slavery and alcohol.

959. **Captain James Cook sailed for England.** He was the first European to find the Hawaiian Islands, doing so in 1778. On his third visit to the islands in 1779, he was killed by the natives.

960. **Alexander Mackenzie was the first European to cross North America** at its widest point, crossing the continent from the Pacific to the Atlantic coast via Canada's northernmost point. He accomplished this feat in 1793.

# Economic Developments in the United States

This chapter will **explore economic developments in the United States**. With these facts, you'll learn how Americans have been able to achieve one of the highest per capita incomes in the world. We'll examine America's burst of economic growth and its downturn due to rising oil prices, unemployment, and inflation.

Finally, we'll discover what caused the bubbles that popped during the 2008-09 recession and look at some of the challenging issues facing the economy today.

961. **The United States has been an economic powerhouse since the late 1800s**, although it had a steady economy, for the most part, since the late 1700s.

962. During the period of 1790 to 1860, manufacturing drove much of **America's economic growth.** More factories opened, and new technologies were developed, such as Eli Whitney's cotton gin and interchangeable parts production system.

963. In the late 1800s, **after the Civil War, America saw its first real burst of economic growth** with a significant expansion of transportation and communication infrastructure, such as railroads and telegraph lines. These helped to link markets across the nation more efficiently.

964. **In 1916, the US GDP passed Britain's** due to America's technological advances in agriculture and industry that allowed for efficient mass production of products like cars and steel. Britain's economy stagnated while America's economy continued to grow.

965. **In the 1920s, the US economy boomed thanks to new inventions and technological advancements.** Assembly lines, radios, the mass production of automobiles, and the beginning of the aviation industry all contributed to the era's economic growth.

966. **After World War II ended in 1945, there was an economic boom** from 1946 through 1959 called the **"Golden Age."** Unemployment reached a record low of 2.5 percent in 1953. Incomes also raised rapidly, and there was a greater demand for consumer goods now that the war was over.

967. **In the 1950s, America's economy continued to expand** with increased manufacturing output and technological advancements. Home appliances, such as refrigerators, became more affordable for middle-class families, leading to a booming consumer market.

968. **The 1970s saw an economic downturn due to rising oil prices**, unemployment, and inflation that caused stagnation in job creation and wages. At the same time, other developed nations caught up technologically, which hurt US exports globally at the time.

969. **In the 1980s, President Ronald Reagan enacted a set of policies called "Reaganomics."** The government focused on lowering taxes for businesses and wealthy individuals and also deregulated many industries (like banking), contributing significantly toward raising economic growth rates by the early 1990s.

970. **The 1990s were considered one of the longest-running periods of uninterrupted economic expansion in American history,** thanks mainly to new technologies, such as the internet, cell phones, and computers. These items allowed people to access markets faster than ever and created tremendous opportunities for wealth.

971. **The early 2000s saw a rapid rise in housing prices**, which was fueled by low interest rates and credit access for people with poor credit histories. This led to the creation of bubbles that popped during the 2008-09 recession. The recession caused unemployment and financial distress.

972. **After the Great Recession, the US economy has been recovering,** but it still faces many problems today. For instance, the US faces income inequality, stagnant wages, rising healthcare costs, and increasing national debt levels, preventing the economy from reaching its full potential.

973. **Today, the US has the eighth-highest per capita income in the world**. On average, people in the US earn around seventy thousand dollars a year.

# Cultural Events That Influenced US History

This chapter will explore **cultural events** that have shaped and **influenced US history**. These fun facts will allow you to gain more insight into **America's first Thanksgiving**, the first **St. Patrick's Day parade in New York**, and much more.

Discover how certain symbols, like the **American flag and the Statue of Liberty**, came to be and examine iconic moments, such as **the first baseball game.**

974. **The first Thanksgiving was celebrated in 1621** between the Wampanoag and English settlers of Plymouth Colony, Massachusetts.

975. **The St. Patrick's Day Parade began in New York City** on March 17th, 1762, as an Irish American celebration. Today, the holiday is celebrated around the world with parades, music, dance performances, and traditional food.

976. **The Declaration of Independence was ratified on July 4th, 1776,** declaring America's independence from Great Britain and forming a new nation. Every July 4th, Americans celebrate Independence Day with food and fireworks.

977. **The iconic American flag, the Stars and Stripes, was allegedly designed by Betsy Ross in 1776** and officially adopted on June 14th, 1777.

978. **The first baseball game played in America** is thought to have occurred between teams from New York's Knickerbocker Club and the New York Baseball Club at Elysian Fields in Hoboken, New Jersey, on June 19th, 1846.

979. **The Transcontinental Railroad connected the East Coast to the West Coast ports. It** was completed on May 10th, 1869, after six years of construction.

980. **The Battle of Gettysburg (July 1–3, 1863) between the Union and Confederate** Army marked a turning point in the Civil War. The war eventually led to the abolishment of slavery in the US.

981. **The first Labor Day Parade was held in New York City** on September 5th, 1882. Today, the first Monday of September is Labor Day, with people celebrating the holiday with parades, concerts, and other events.

982. **The Statue of Liberty is a monumental symbol of freedom and democracy.** It was gifted to the United States by France in 1885. Standing 305 feet tall, it is a reminder of the United Stastes' commitment to liberty, justice, and equality. It has become an icon of hope and inspiration to millions around the world.

983. **The Statue of Liberty was named after Lady Liberty by French sculptor Frederic Auguste Bartholdi,** who designed the statue, which is made out of copper.

984. **Jazz music originated in New Orleans** during the late 19th century as a combination of African American music traditions with influences from European musical styles like ragtime and marching band music.

985. **Ellis Island served as an immigration station** for millions of immigrants entering America from Europe through New York Harbor beginning in 1892. It closed its doors in 1954.

986. **Women's suffrage became law** when the Nineteenth Amendment was ratified on August 18th, 1920.

987. **The National Football League (NFL)** began to play on October 3rd, 1920, making it one of the oldest professional sports leagues in the world (Major League Baseball was the first).

988. **The first American Thanksgiving Day Parade** was held in Philadelphia in 1920. The iconic New York Macy's Thanksgiving Day Parade started in 1924.

989. **The US Navy's first aircraft carrier,** USS Langley, was commissioned in 1922, ushering in a new era of military technology development.

990. **The Harlem Renaissance** was a golden age of African American artistic expression and cultural awakening that started in the 1920s and lasted until the mid-1930s.

991. **The Roaring '20s** was an exciting time in US history. Everything from politics to music and dancing saw changes.

992. On March 3rd, 1932, **President Herbert Hoover** declared **"The Star-Spangled Banner"** by Francis Scott Key to be America's national anthem.

993. **President Franklin D. Roosevelt's** New Deal legislation during the 1930s provided funds for public works projects, welfare reform, and bank regulation, among other measures, to help America recover from the Great Depression.

994. In 1947, **America's first drive-thru** opened: Red's Giant Hamburg in Missouri. Today, there are over 200,000 drive-thrus in the country!

995- In 1955, **Rosa Parks refused to give up her seat on the bus for a white passenger,** sparking the Montgomery bus boycott.

996. **Hawaii became part of the US** on August 21st, 1959. Hawaii became the fiftieth state of the US.

997. On August 28th, 1963, **Martin Luther King Jr. delivered his famous "I Have a Dream"** speech at the end of the March on Washington for Jobs and Freedom. The march and the speech became a defining moment of the civil rights movement, inspiring people all around the globe.

998. On June 28th, 1969, **police raids against members of the LGBTQ community at Stonewall Inn in New York City** triggered protests and riots that launched the modern gay rights movement in US history.

999. In July 1969, **Neil Armstrong became the first man to walk on the moon**, ending the Space Race. This was an incredible feat, and people all over the world tuned in to watch the momentous occasion.

1000. **Woodstock was a three-day concert that promoted peace and love**. Iconic musicians like **Jimi Hendrix, Janis Joplin, Jefferson Airplane**, and more performed near Bethel, New York, in mid-August 1969, attracting almost 500,000 people!

# Conclusion

After reading **one thousand interesting facts about American history**, it should be easy to see how much the country has evolved over the years. Not only have you become more knowledgeable on an array of topics related **to American history**, but hopefully, **this book** has also inspired a newfound appreciation for the events and people that shaped America into **what it is today!**

**To continue your journey and learn** even **more about America's past**, take advantage of the resources listed in the bibliography. Also, make sure to keep an eye out for more **books in this series!**

# Part 2: American History Stories

101 True and Fascinating Tales of Major Events and People from the United States' Past

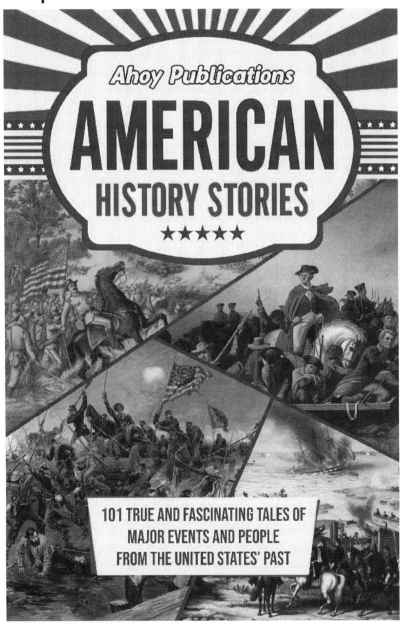

# Introduction

Step into the captivating tapestry of American history, a sweeping chronicle that weaves triumphs, tribulations, moments of explosive change, and quiet courage. From the rugged beginnings in the colonial era to the dawn of a new nation to the unrelenting march toward progress, each chapter in this extraordinary narrative unveils pivotal events that have shaped the United States as we know it today. Delve into riveting tales of exploration, wars that reshaped continents, social movements that challenged the status quo, and groundbreaking advancements that propelled the nation into the modern age.

Get ready for a captivating journey through time as we uncover an intriguing collection of facts, interesting stories, and fascinating characters in the realm of American history.

# Section 1 – From the Mystery of Roanoke to a New Nation: Journey through Early American History

In the late 16<sup>th</sup> and early 17<sup>th</sup> centuries, America witnessed significant historical events that laid the foundation for its future. From the mysterious disappearance of the Roanoke Colony to the establishment of Jamestown in Virginia, these important moments shaped American history.

These fascinating tales about the Thirteen Colonies will shed new light on a part of American history that tends to get written off as dull. Discover why these formative events set a course for America's path to becoming an independent nation.

1. **Roanoke Colony was founded in 1585. It was the first English settlement in North America, but this colony off the coast of North Carolina was short-lived. The people living there mysteriously disappeared when the next ship arrived five years later.**

Led by Governor John White, the colony aimed to become the first permanent English settlement in the New World. White realized the colonists could not survive without additional supplies. In 1587, White returned to England. The trip was hard on his crew, and several men died on the voyage. Once they returned to England, they encountered more problems. England and Spain were at war with each other. White would not be returning to Roanoke anytime soon.

When White returned to Roanoke in 1590, he found the colony completely abandoned. The only clues to their fate were the words "CROATOAN" carved into a tree and "CRO" etched into the fort's gatepost.

What happened to the colony is a mystery to this day. The fate of the Roanoke colonists captivates historians and has fueled speculation for centuries.

Some suggest the colonists relocated to Croatoan Island (present-day Hatteras Island). This hypothesis is supported by the inscriptions left in Roanoke and the existence of a tribe known as the Croatans who inhabited the island at the time. Others propose that the colonists merged with local Native American tribes, assimilating into their cultures and abandoning their English identity. Others believe the colonists were wiped out by Native American attacks. And some of the more far-fetched theories include aliens!

Besides this enduring mystery, the Roanoke Colony is remarkable for another reason. Virginia Dare was born in Roanoke in 1587, the first English-born child. She was the granddaughter of John White. Of course, nothing is known about her life since the colonists mysteriously vanished, but many places in the US, especially in North Carolina, have been named after her.

### 2. Did you know the early colonists of Jamestown had to resort to cannibalism to stay alive?

Jamestown was established in 1607 and became North America's first permanent English settlement. Jamestown was founded in present-day Virginia by the Virginia Company of London, a joint-stock company seeking economic opportunities and a foothold in the New World.

When the colonists arrived in Jamestown, it was too late in the year to plant crops. The region was also seeing one of the worst droughts in its history. It was so severe that it even impacted the local Powhatan tribe. Nevertheless, they made an attempt to eke out an existence. The next year, supply ships arrived with aid and more hungry mouths to feed.

At the beginning of the long winter in 1609, around five hundred settlers were in Jamestown. By the time winter was over, there would only be sixty-one left. What happened? Well, there just was not enough food for all the people. The plan had been to trade food with the Native Americans, so they had grown a small number of crops. Although they made friendly contact with the Native Americans, that ended when John Smith was sent back to England after being injured in a gunpowder accident.

People ate cats, dogs, rats —and even each other – to survive the winter. George Percy, a colonist in Jamestown, stated, "The living dug up and ate corpses, and that a husband killed his wife and then butchered her, preserved her with salt, and ate parts of her before he was caught." Archaeological evidence confirms that cannibalism did indeed take place during what is now known as the Starving Time.

Although that winter was incredibly tough and decimated the colony's population, more people arrived in 1610. Once tobacco began to be exported in 1612, more people flocked to the colony to get it on this profitable venture. Jamestown was the cornerstone of British colonization and was pivotal in shaping American history.

3. **The first enslaved Africans were brought to Virginia in August 1619. A Dutch ship brought about twenty enslaved people to Jamestown, becoming one of the earliest instances of forced labor and slavery within what would become the United States. Slavery would become deeply entrenched in the South's economy, shaping its agricultural practices, social dynamics, and political landscape.**

The Middle Passage was the second leg of the transatlantic slave trade. Africans were forcibly taken from their homes and transported to the Americas. Their journey was characterized by unimaginable cruelty and suffering. Cramped into the holds of slave ships, Africans were subjected to horrendous conditions. They were often chained together, malnourished, and denied basic sanitation. The journey was fraught with disease, overcrowding, and psychological torment, with many perishing before reaching their destination. At least two million Africans died while traveling the Middle Passage.

The brutal reality of the transatlantic slave trade is vividly portrayed in the 1997 historical drama *Amistad*, directed by Steven Spielberg. The film tells the true story of a group of enslaved Africans who mutinied aboard the slave ship *Amistad* and eventually found themselves in a legal battle for their freedom. They won, which helped propel the abolitionist movement.

The 1977 television miniseries *Roots*, based on Alex Haley's novel, provides a broader and more comprehensive look at the experience of slavery. The miniseries follows the life of Kunta Kinte, a young Mandinka man from West Africa who is captured and sold into slavery in the United States. *Roots* depicts the harsh realities of plantation life, including the brutal labor slaves were forced to endure, the separation of families, and the constant threat of violence. It also explores the resilience and strength of the enslaved community, their unbroken spirit, and their determination to maintain their cultural identity.

4. **In 1620, a group known as the Pilgrims sought religious freedom and settled at Plymouth Rock after their journey aboard the Mayflower. While still on board the ship, they signed an agreement for self-governance called the Mayflower Compact. The Mayflower Compact marked a turning point in American history, establishing a foundation for self-rule and democratic ideals that would shape the nation's development.**

However, the initial years for the Pilgrims were anything but smooth sailing. A brutal winter decimated their ranks, leaving them weak and on the brink of starvation. Squanto, a Patuxet man fluent in English who had been kidnapped and returned to his tribe years before, became a vital link, teaching the Pilgrims how to fish, farm, and navigate the unforgiving landscape.

After a grueling harvest season, Governor William Bradford proposed a three-day feast to express gratitude for their newfound survival and to forge a stronger bond with their Wampanoag allies. Chief Massasoit and his people joined the festivities, bringing deer, pumpkins, and dried berries to share alongside the Pilgrims' wild turkey, clams, and homemade sassafras ale. Laughter and shared stories filled the air as games were played and songs sung in both familiar and unfamiliar tongues.

This wasn't just a celebratory feast; it was a strategic move. The shared meal symbolized a fragile peace treaty built on mutual dependence and cautious friendship. While future years would witness conflict and tension, this moment at Plymouth offered a flickering hope for coexistence between two cultures that had collided on foreign shores.

This spirit of shared gratitude and unity resonated with President Abraham Lincoln during the Civil War, leading him to declare the first national Thanksgiving in 1863. Almost two hundred years later, in 1942, President Franklin D. Roosevelt moved Thanksgiving from the last Thursday in November to the fourth Thursday, a change that remains in effect today. These proclamations reflected the evolving significance of Thanksgiving from a local harvest celebration to a national holiday that symbolized unity, gratitude, and the shared values that bind Americans together.

**The First Thanksgiving at Plymouth by Jennie A. Brownscombe (1914).**
*https://commons.wikimedia.org/wiki/File:Thanksgiving-Brownscombe.jpg*

*5.* **In 1630, Puritans led by John Winthrop settled in a new colony called the Massachusetts Bay Colony, with Boston as its center. They aimed to create a "city on a hill," a sort of "guiding light." The colony did indeed become influential during the early colonial era.**

Under Winthrop's leadership, the Puritans established a strict social and religious order based on their interpretation of the Bible. They believed they were chosen by God to create a "New England" that would be a shining example of Christian virtue.

Despite the Puritans leaving England to be able to worship as they pleased, they were not very tolerant of others. As more people arrived, some people disagreed with their beliefs and practices. The Puritans were not happy with this turn of events. One of the most well-known examples is the Puritan attitude and actions toward the Religious Society of Friends, more commonly known as the Quakers.

The arrival of the Quakers in Massachusetts in the 1650s was met with hostility from the Puritan authorities. The Quakers' beliefs, which diverged from the strict Puritan orthodoxy, were seen as a threat to the established order. The Quakers' pacifism, rejection of formal clergy, and emphasis on inner experience were all considered dangerous and subversive.

In response, the Massachusetts Bay Colony passed a series of laws against the Quakers, prohibiting them from entering the colony, attending Quaker meetings, or publishing Quaker literature. Quakers who violated these laws were subject to fines, whippings, and even banishment.

The most severe punishment was reserved for those who entered the colony but did not actually live there. In 1659, four Quakers – Mary Dyer, Marmaduke Stephenson, William Robinson, and William Leddra – were executed by hanging for returning to Massachusetts after being banished. Their deaths marked the climax of Quaker persecution in Massachusetts.

The Toleration Act of 1689 (passed by the English Parliament) brought an end to the persecution of Quakers in Massachusetts. The act granted toleration to all Protestants, including Quakers, and prohibited the Massachusetts government from passing laws that interfered with religious freedom.

**6. You may have noticed that Catholics were not listed when discussing the Toleration Act. The Reformation changed many things in England, including the state religion. In 1632, Maryland was founded as a haven for Catholics, who were being persecuted in England.**

Cecil Calvert – otherwise known as Lord Baltimore – established Maryland as a proprietary colony to create a safe space for Catholics to practice their religion freely. While the Puritans are often cited as pioneers for religious freedom, Plymouth Colony and the Massachusetts Bay Colony were not tolerant of Catholics.

In 1649, the Maryland General Assembly passed the Maryland Toleration Act, which granted religious freedom to all Christians who believed in the Trinity. This was a groundbreaking piece of legislation at the time, as most other colonies in what would become the United States were dominated by Puritans, most of whom were hostile to Catholicism.

The Maryland Toleration Act was not without its limitations. It only applied to Christians and did not guarantee equal rights for all religious groups. However, it was a significant step forward in terms of religious tolerance in the New World.

Many people believe that Maryland, being founded as a safe place for Catholics, was named for the Virgin Mary or even Queen Mary I, but it was not. It was named after the wife of King Charles I, Henrietta Maria, the daughter of King Henry IV of France and Queen Marie de' Medici. Henry IV was well acquainted with religious strife in his own country, having converted to Catholicism to become king during a time of extreme religious tension.

**7. As the years passed, conflict arose between European settlers and Native American tribes over land disputes, competition for resources and trade, and cultural differences. The Pequot War was one of them. This war had profound implications for relations between colonizers and indigenous people in New England.**

On one side were the English colonists, represented by Massachusetts Bay Colony, Plymouth Colony, and Saybrook Colony (an English colony in Connecticut). Led by figures like John Mason and John Endecott, these colonists sought to expand their territory and assert their dominance over the region.

On the other side stood the Pequots, a powerful Native American tribe controlling a vast territory in present-day southeastern Connecticut. Led by sachems (tribal leaders) Sassacus and Wequashcuk – one of the earliest Native American converts to Christianity – the Pequots sought to protect their ancestral lands and resist the expanding colonial presence.

The war began in earnest in 1636 when the Pequots attacked a group of English settlers near Mystic, Connecticut. In response, the colonists launched a series of brutal attacks on Pequot villages, culminating in the infamous Mystic massacre.

The Pequot village, located on Mystic River, only had two exits. The English and their Native American allies, who were upset with the Pequots' actions, blocked the exits and set fire to the village. The only Pequot survivors were the warriors who escaped the burning village. This event, in which hundreds of Pequot men, women, and children were killed, marked a turning point in the war.

By the end of 1637, the Pequots had been largely defeated. Their tribe was decimated. Estimates suggest that around seven hundred Pequots had been killed, while the English suffered around seventy casualties. Hundreds of Pequots were sold into slavery, and some Pequots were given to tribes that had allied with the English.

The war had a profound impact on the relations between the English colonists and the Native American tribes of New England, setting the stage for further conflict and displacement in the region.

This war also demonstrates what happened to many Native American tribes. However, unlike some tribes, the Pequots are still around today. Much of their culture, including their language, had been supplanted by English. Today, the Pequot are making efforts to preserve their culture, including analyzing documents to find clues to their language.

8. **King Philip's War, also known as Metacomet's War, the First Indian War, or the Great Narragansett War, was the deadliest conflict between Europeans and Native Americans during the colonial era. It erupted in 1675 when Metacomet, the Wampanoag sachem, created a broad alliance of Native American tribes to resist the expansionist policies of the English colonists in New England. Metacomet was known as King Philip by the English.**

The war's roots lay in the deep-seated resentment among Native Americans toward the encroachment of English settlers on their ancestral lands. The English settlements disrupted their traditional hunting and fishing grounds, and the imposition of religious and cultural practices clashed with their own.

The war raged for over a year, from 1675 to 1676, and left a trail of death and destruction on both sides. Despite their superior firepower and numbers, the English colonists struggled to subdue the Native American resistance.

The turning point came in December 1675 when the English launched a surprise attack on the Narragansetts' fortified stronghold in the Great Swamp Fight. The settlement's moat had frozen in the cold December weather. The English were able to cross over the moat easily and set fire to the settlement.

Many consider the attack a massacre, with hundreds of Native Americans killed, including many women and children. Many Native Americans ran into the frozen swampland, where hundreds died from their wounds and the cold.

This devastating blow crippled the Native American alliance, and the war gradually turned in favor of the English. By the spring of 1676, most Native American resistance had been crushed.

King Philip's War was one of the deadliest conflicts in American history, with an estimated 3,000 to 6,000 Native Americans and over 2,000 English colonists killed. The war also resulted in the displacement of many Native American tribes and the destruction of their villages and communities.

**An illustration of the Great Swamp Fight.**
*https://commons.wikimedia.org/wiki/File:Capture_of_the_Indian_Fortress.png*

9. **The Elizabeth Key Case was a landmark legal proceeding that took place in the Virginia Colony in the mid-17th century. It had significant implications for the legal status of enslaved individuals and the development of racialized slavery in colonial America.**

Elizabeth Key, also known as Elizabeth Key Grinstead, was born in the Virginia Colony in the 1630s to an Englishman named Thomas Key and an enslaved African woman named Joan. Initially, she was considered an indentured servant. However, her status changed after her father's death. His heirs said that Key was a slave and that she belonged to the estate.

In 1655, Elizabeth Key filed a lawsuit for her freedom. She argued that she should not be enslaved because her father was an Englishman and a free man and because she had been baptized as a Christian. Her case raised complex legal and moral questions about the status of mixed-race individuals and the impact of Christian baptism on enslavement.

In 1656, the Virginia court ruled in favor of Elizabeth Key, declaring that she should be set free. The court recognized the principle of English common law, which did not recognize perpetual servitude. Under English law, the status of a child typically followed that of the father. Since Elizabeth's father was a free Englishman, the court determined that she could not be held in perpetual servitude.

Elizabeth's baptism as a Christian was also considered a factor in her favor. Some legal and moral arguments at the time suggested that Christians should not be held in slavery.

The Elizabeth Key Case set an important legal precedent in the Virginia Colony. It established that the status of children born to enslaved mothers could be influenced by the status of their fathers, especially if their fathers were free Englishmen. This distinction between the children of English fathers and African mothers contributed to the gradual development of a racialized system of slavery in colonial America.

10. **Some of the most interesting stories in history involve pirates. Would you be shocked to know that pirates were a part of colonial American history?**

Edward Teach, commonly known as Blackbeard, was one of the most feared and notorious pirates of the early 18th century. By 1718, he had established a stronghold in the coastal waters of the American colonies, particularly around the Outer Banks and the entrance to Pamlico Sound. Blackbeard's fleet included the *Queen Anne's Revenge*, a former French slave ship he had captured and heavily armed.

The British colonial authorities, led by Lieutenant Governor Alexander Spotswood of Virginia, were determined to put an end to Blackbeard's piracy. Spotswood organized a naval expedition to capture or kill Blackbeard and his crew. He appointed Lieutenant Robert Maynard to lead this mission.

Maynard and his men located Blackbeard's ships anchored at Ocracoke Inlet. On the morning of November 22nd, 1718, the two sides engaged in a fierce battle. Blackbeard and his crew put up a determined defense, and the fight was brutal and intense. During the battle, Blackbeard was shot multiple times and sustained numerous wounds. Ultimately, Blackbeard was finally killed, and his ship, the *Queen Anne's Revenge*, was captured. Maynard's forces took several of Blackbeard's crew members prisoner, while others were killed in the battle or escaped into the nearby swamps.

Blackbeard's death marked a significant victory for the colonial authorities in their efforts to combat piracy in the Atlantic coastal waters. His severed head was later displayed on the bow of Maynard's ship as evidence of his demise. This event had a lasting impact on the perception of piracy and the authority of colonial governments in the New World. Blackbeard's legend and the story of his last battle continue to capture people's imaginations to this day!

# Section 2 – From Wars to Freedom: A Journey through American History from 1754 to 1791

Join us on an exciting adventure through early American history! Discover the important events that shaped the United States, from battles fought in the French and Indian War to the heroic struggles for independence in the Revolutionary War. Witness how a new nation was born with a constitution built on freedom.

11. **George Washington was a veteran of more than just the American Revolution. He also fought in the French and Indian War between 1754 and 1763. Although the French and Indian War is considered a theater of the Seven Years' War, it actually began before that war erupted in continental Europe**

Tensions arose between the British and the French over land in the Ohio Valley. The British Ohio Company of Virginia was granted the land, but the French began to move in. The Virginians were worried that the French would stake a claim. They sent twenty-one-year-old George Washington to tell the French to leave.

Washington delivered the message, but the French refused to leave. He was granted the commission of lieutenant colonel and sent back to the frontier with a company of men.

Meanwhile, the French sent Joseph Coulon de Villiers de Jumonville with a small unit of men to warn Washington to leave the area. Washington and Tanacharison, the leader of the Mingo people, discovered the French camp and decided to attack it.

It is not known what exactly happened in the Battle of Jumonville Glen. The few things that are known are that the battle only lasted around fifteen minutes and that most of the French were either killed or taken prisoner. Jumonville was killed in the action. Several accounts say that Tanacharison killed Jumonville, crushing his skull with a tomahawk.

Washington moved his men to Fort Necessity, where they were attacked by the French. Washington eventually surrendered, which marked the only time he ever surrendered a battle. In the document he was forced to sign, Washington admitted that Jumonville and his men had been assassinated. Jumonville was sent to warn the British to leave, not actually war with them. However, Washington did not know how to read French, and his translator did a poor job explaining what was in the document. Nevertheless, the stage was set for a war.

The French and Indian War also highlighted the increased involvement of Native American tribes in colonial affairs. Various tribes, including the Iroquois Confederacy and the Algonquin Confederacy, aligned themselves with either the British or the French. The tribes were often driven by historical relationships, trade interests, and religious beliefs. These alliances added another layer of complexity to the war, influencing its course and demonstrating the intricate dynamics between European powers and Native American nations.

France would go on to lose the war, which allowed the British to expand their territory in North America. The war would also prove to be troublesome on the economic front for Britain, which was forced to raise taxes on the American colonists. These taxes were not received well, and cries for independence would eventually echo throughout the Thirteen Colonies.

### 12. On March 5th, 1770, the Boston Massacre occurred. British soldiers killed five colonists during a confrontation in Boston; one of the victims, Crispus Attucks, was an African American sailor who became an unwitting symbol of the growing unrest.

On the evening of the incident, a crowd of colonists gathered near the Custom House, where British soldiers stood guard. Several colonists began taunting them and throwing items like stones and snowballs. One soldier eventually fired his weapon, which caused other soldiers to fire theirs. Three people died then; two others later died of their wounds. It is believed Crispus Attucks was the first person to be killed in the massacre. Some consider him the first casualty of the American Revolution.

While the massacre is an interesting story in and of itself, let's take a look at the aftermath of the massacre. John Adams, a young lawyer and an outspoken critic of British policies, found himself defending the British soldiers. Despite the public outcry and the overwhelming evidence against the soldiers, Adams believed these men demanded a fair trial.

Adams argued passionately for the soldiers' right to legal representation, stating that "every person charged with a crime must have the benefit of counsel." Though unpopular at the time, Adams's defense of the British soldiers earned him the respect of both sides and established him as a brilliant legal mind and a champion of justice. His actions during the trial solidified his reputation as a defender of the rights of the accused, a legacy that would continue to resonate throughout his political career.

Of the eight soldiers charged with murder, six were acquitted. Two were convicted of manslaughter and branded on their hands. This outcome, though controversial, demonstrated that even in a time of heightened tensions, the principles of fair justice could prevail. Adams would later sign the Declaration of Independence and become the second president of the United States.

**13. The Boston Tea Party was a protest against the British Tea Act of 1773, which granted the British East India Company a monopoly on tea sales in the American colonies and imposed a tax on tea. In an act of defiance against "taxation without representation," the Patriots boarded British tea ships and threw the tea into Boston Harbor. Over three hundred chests of tea were thrown into the water, with the losses amounting to almost two million dollars today.**

Most people are familiar with the Boston Tea Party. It was a famous event in American history that played a pivotal role in the lead-up to the American Revolution. However, many people may be unfamiliar with a woman named Sarah Bradlee Fulton.

Sarah Bradlee Fulton was the wife of John Fulton, a member of the Sons of Liberty, a secret organization that played a key role in the protest against British taxation and policies in the American colonies. On the night of December 16th, 1773, when the Boston Tea Party took place, Sarah Bradlee Fulton supported the cause by assisting the Patriots in their protest against the British Tea Act. It is believed Sarah came up with the idea of having the protesters disguise themselves as Mohawks. Sarah and other women helped prepare for the event by making the disguises for the men. They sewed these disguises using blankets and feathers. They also helped paint the men's faces. This brilliant idea ensured that the Patriots could carry out their act of defiance without being easily recognized.

Sarah Bradlee Fulton's involvement in supporting the protest by creating disguises for the participants highlights the significant contributions of women to the American Revolution and the cause of colonial independence. Their roles extended beyond traditional domestic spheres and played a crucial part in the events leading up to the American Revolution.

**A lithograph of the Boston Tea Party.**
*https://commons.wikimedia.org/wiki/File:Boston_Tea_Party_Currier_colored.jpg*

**14. On April 19th, 1775, fighting erupted at Lexington and Concord in Massachusetts, marking the start of armed conflict between American militiamen, called Minutemen, and British troops. Famed writer Ralph Waldo Emerson would later describe the fighting. He called the opening shots of the battle "the shot heard 'round the world." The phrase is meant to convey the idea that these shots were not just some random skirmish but rather a momentous event that would have far-reaching consequences.**

The Battles of Lexington and Concord were not mere skirmishes; they were the opening salvos of the American Revolutionary War. Under General Thomas Gage's command, the British sought to seize military supplies from the colonists in Concord. However, they were met with fierce resistance from the Minutemen, a group of armed colonists prepared to fight for their independence.

The fighting at Lexington and Concord was intense and bloody. The British suffered heavy casualties, with 73 soldiers killed and 174 wounded. Though outnumbered and outgunned, the colonists fought valiantly, suffering forty-nine deaths and thirty-nine wounded.

To this day, no one is quite sure who took that "shot heard 'round the world." The British told the American militias to disband. John Parker, the captain of the militia, told his men to go home. However, there was so much confusion, with people yelling at each other, that some men didn't leave or left very slowly. Eventually, a shot rang out, and the rest was history.

These battles dealt a significant blow to British morale. The British underestimated the colonists' resolve, expecting to quell the uprising quickly. However, the Minutemen's resistance demonstrated that the colonists would not be easily subdued, shaking British confidence.

The Battles of Lexington and Concord stand as a testament to the courage and determination of the American colonists in their fight for independence. They were not just military engagements; they were the opening chapter in the struggle for a new nation.

15. **On July 4th, 1776, the Second Continental Congress adopted the Declaration of Independence, a document that had been drafted by Thomas Jefferson and had been altered slightly by Benjamin Franklin and John Adams. As you may have guessed, the Declaration of Independence formally proclaimed the colonies' independence from Great Britain.**

The Declaration of Independence outlined the grievances of the American colonists against the British Crown, including taxation without representation, the quartering of British troops in the colonies, and the denial of trial by jury. About a quarter of the fifty-six signers of the Declaration of Independence were imprisoned, exiled, or otherwise persecuted by the British during the Revolutionary War. Three signers lost their lives during or because of the war.

Thomas Jefferson was the man most responsible for the content and actual writing of the Declaration of Independence. Jefferson was the poet/philosopher of the American Revolution. His eloquent pen penned the immortal lines of the Declaration of Independence, forever etching the ideals of liberty and equality into the American consciousness.

However, Jefferson wasn't just a wordsmith. He was a complex figure. He was a slave owner who grappled with the contradictions of his own beliefs. Even though he was a passionate advocate for democracy, he also harbored aristocratic tendencies. He and John Adams, who were at times political rivals, were also fast friends later in life, and their letters to each other provide important insights into the founding of America and its political ideas. Both men died on the same day – July 4th, 1826 – fifty years to the day after the new nation was announced with the Declaration of Independence!

**Jefferson's official presidential portrait.**
*https://commons.wikimedia.org/wiki/File:Official_Presidential_portrait_of_Thomas_Jefferson_(by_Rembrandt_Peale,_1800)(cropped).jpg*

**16. Perhaps the most famous battle of the Revolutionary War was the Battle of Trenton. The battle resulted in an astounding American victory, but it is also famous because of the painting Washington Crossing the Delaware, which was actually painted seventy-five years later by a German painter who had never been to America.**

Under a biting December wind, General George Washington undertook a daring gamble on the banks of the Delaware. The Continental Army, dwindling and demoralized, faced winter's unforgiving grip and whispers of disbandment. Yet, on Christmas night, 1776, Washington led a ragged force across the icy river, aiming for a surprise attack on Hessian troops garrisoned in Trenton.

The plan was audacious. Crossing in treacherous conditions, the American column marched ten miles through the frigid night, arriving at Trenton before dawn. Hessian forces, lulled by Christmas festivities, were caught unprepared. The assault, led by Washington himself, proved swift and decisive. The Hessian ranks crumbled under the surprise American assault, and their commander fell in the opening volleys. Nearly two-thirds of the Hessian force surrendered within an hour, delivering a much-needed victory for the beleaguered colonists.

The Battle of Trenton was a strategic masterpiece. It rekindled hope within the Continental Army, stemming the tide of desertion. Washington's decisive leadership and the army's unexpected success shattered the British aura of invincibility, bolstering morale and demonstrating American resilience. Though a small engagement, the Battle of Trenton reverberated across the colonies, proving the nascent nation's ability to strike back and reigniting the flames of revolution.

**17. In September 1781, the tide of the American Revolution culminated in the pivotal Battle of Yorktown in Virginia. Trapped on a peninsula and cut off by relentless Franco-American forces under General Washington and General Rochambeau, British General Lord Cornwallis faced a dire predicament.**

The siege itself was a meticulous orchestration of firepower and strategy. American and French engineers constructed a ring of fortifications that steadily constricted the British defensive perimeter. Heavy cannons pounded the British positions relentlessly, while French naval superiority ensured no escape route by sea. Facing imminent assault and lacking reinforcements, Cornwallis attempted a desperate breakout, only to be repelled. On October 19th, with dwindling supplies and mounting casualties, he surrendered his entire army, effectively ending major land operations in the American Revolution.

Adding another layer of intrigue to this pivotal moment is the story of "The World Turned Upside Down." According to historical accounts, the British band, as customary, played a march to honor the victors after the formal surrender. However, instead of a traditional British tune, they surprisingly struck up the melody of "The World Turned Upside Down," a ballad often associated with English social unrest and upheaval.

While the exact motivation behind this choice remains shrouded in speculation, it resonated with the gravity of the situation. For the newly formed American nation, it mirrored the realization of their revolutionary goals; the colonists' world, formerly dominated by British rule, had indeed turned upside down. For the defeated British, it was a bittersweet acknowledgment of their altered fortunes.

On September 3rd, 1783, the Treaty of Paris was signed, and the Revolutionary War was brought to a close. The treaty formally recognized the United States as an independent nation. This momentous agreement marked a turning point in world history, establishing a new balance of power and ushering in the era of American democracy.

**18. On September 17th, 1787, the Constitutional Convention in Philadelphia concluded with delegates signing the United States Constitution, a landmark document that established the framework for a new federal government. The Constitution, with its system of checks and balances, separation of powers, and emphasis on individual rights, stands as a cornerstone of American democracy and a testament to the power of collective wisdom.**

While the American Constitution is a unique document, many of its ideas came to the Founding Fathers through English constitutional history and the Enlightenment thinkers of France and Great Britain in the early 1700s. However, some historians contend the Constitution was inspired by another group of people: the Native American Iroquois Confederation in the border areas of the United States and Canada.

It must be emphasized that the Iroquois Confederacy's direct influence on the Articles of Confederation and the Constitution is debated among historians. However, it is possible that their political structure offered an intriguing model for the nascent American government.

The Iroquois Confederacy comprised six independent nations united by a common council, the *Grand Council*. They practiced a form of confederation that balanced individual tribal autonomy with collective decision-making. This might have resonated with the American colonists, who sought unity against British rule while cherishing their own sovereignty. The Articles of Confederation, the first governing document of the United States, reflected this influence, creating a weak central government reliant on unanimous consent from independent states.

However, the Iroquois Confederacy's inherent limitations became evident. As individual Iroquois nations prioritized their needs, unified action often faltered, ultimately contributing to their vulnerability against European encroachment. This served as a cautionary tale for the American framers. When drafting the Constitution, they sought to strengthen the central government while still honoring state autonomy. The bicameral Congress, with its House of Representatives reflecting individual states and the Senate representing equal representation for all, mirrored the Iroquois approach to balancing local and national interests.

19. **On April 30th, 1789, George Washington was elected as the first president of the United States. Washington's presidency, from 1789 to 1797, was paramount in shaping the early United States. His leadership during this critical formative period established precedents for the presidency, fostered national unity, and laid the foundation for a strong and stable government.**

Many stories and legends have sprung up about George Washington. Let's go over three of the most popular.

**The Cherry Tree:** The image of young George chopping down a cherry tree and confessing his deed to his stern father, declaring, "I cannot tell a lie," is ingrained in American legend. However, the story, first published in Parson Mason Weems's 1806 biography, likely originated as a morality tale aimed at children rather than a historical account. While Washington was undoubtedly known for his integrity, the cherry tree myth, with its idealized portrayal, paints an unrealistic picture of Washington's life and downplays the complex motivations governing his actions.

**Wooden Teeth:** Perhaps one of the most enduring and bizarre myths revolves around Washington's teeth. Images often depict him with wooden dentures. While Washington suffered from severe dental problems throughout his life and experimented with various dentures made from diverse materials, including hippopotamus ivory and human teeth, there's no evidence he ever utilized wooden ones. This myth likely arose from misinterpretations of historical descriptions and was fueled by caricatures depicting him with an exaggerated, wooden grin.

**Throwing a Silver Dollar across the Potomac:** For many years, American grade-school students were taught a story about Washington throwing a coin across the wide Potomac River. It's a captivating image, but it is false. The truth, like many historical narratives, is nuanced. While there's mention of Washington hurling an object (not a silver dollar) as a teen across the Rappahannock, not the much wider Potomac, primary sources remain elusive. The iconic silver dollar and majestic river are later embellishments, making Washington a larger-than-life legend.

This myth, though factually shaky, served a purpose. It cemented perceptions of Washington as an exceptional figure, capable of extraordinary feats even before his presidential ascent. But it's a reminder to critically examine historical narratives and separate romanticized portrayals from documented facts.

**20. John Leland was a prominent Baptist preacher in Virginia during the late 18th century. He fervently advocated for religious liberty and separation of church and state. At the time, Virginia had an established state church, the Anglican Church (Church of England), which received government support and privileges. Leland, as a Baptist, experienced religious discrimination and believed in the importance of protecting religious freedom for all.**

During the debate over the ratification of the US Constitution, Leland was initially skeptical of the document because it lacked explicit protections for individual rights, including religious freedom. He was concerned that without such protections, the federal government might interfere with religious practices and beliefs.

James Madison, a key figure in drafting the Constitution, was running for a seat in the first US Congress. Leland, along with other Baptists and religious minorities, sought assurances from Madison that he would support amendments to the Constitution that would protect individual liberties. In 1788, Leland met with Madison in Orange County, Virginia, and presented him with a list of proposed amendments, including those focused on religious freedom. Madison listened to Leland's concerns and promised to support amendments safeguarding these rights.

When Madison was elected to the first Congress, he followed through on his promise by introducing a series of amendments to the Constitution, which would later become the Bill of Rights. Among these amendments was the First Amendment, which includes the Establishment Clause and the Free Exercise Clause, guaranteeing religious freedom and prohibiting the establishment of a state religion.

John Leland's advocacy for religious freedom and his meeting with James Madison played a significant role in shaping the inclusion of religious liberty protections in the Bill of Rights. His dedication to the principle of religious freedom helped ensure that it became a fundamental part of the US Constitution, protecting the rights of all citizens to practice their religion freely.

# Section 3 – The Expansion of America and the Reform Era

Next, we will explore the fascinating period of expansion and reform in US history. Discover how America grew both geographically and socially through westward expansion, the Trail of Tears, and the women's suffrage movement. This was a pivotal time in US history; *these fascinating stories will show why.*

**21. In 1803, President Thomas Jefferson commissioned Meriwether Lewis and William Clark to lead an expedition into the newly acquired Louisiana Territory. Their primary mission was to explore and map the western part of the continent and seek a water route to the Pacific Ocean. At the time, there was a belief that the Northwest Passage might exist – a passage that would greatly facilitate trade and transportation.**

During their journey westward, Lewis and Clark's expedition encountered numerous challenges, including harsh weather, difficult terrain, and encounters with Native American tribes. However, one of the most memorable incidents occurred when they encountered a grizzly bear in what is now North Dakota in 1805.

On May 14th, 1805, Meriwether Lewis was hunting alone when he encountered a massive grizzly bear. The bear charged at Lewis, who was armed only with a small caliber weapon. Lewis shot the bear, but it didn't stop. He fired several more shots, and eventually, the bear fell only feet away from him.

Lewis and his men estimated the bear's weight at over six hundred pounds. It was a massive grizzly, and its size and aggression were unlike anything they had encountered before. The encounter with the grizzly bear highlighted the dangers and challenges faced by the expedition as they ventured into uncharted territory. It also illustrated the need for keen marksmanship and resourcefulness in surviving the wilderness.

Despite the hardships and dangers, Lewis and Clark's expedition was a remarkable success. They mapped vast stretches of land, made contact with indigenous peoples, documented new plant and animal species, and disproved the existence of a continuous

US water route to the Pacific. Their journey helped expand America's understanding of the western part of the continent and paved the way for future westward expansion.

22. **The War of 1812 erupted amid trade disputes and British interference in American shipping. Britain, which was embroiled in its own struggle in the Napoleonic Wars, saw the young American republic as a thorn in its side, as America was a competitor on the seas and a haven for British deserters. The tipping point came when the British Royal Navy seized American ships and impressed sailors into their service, a blatant affront to American sovereignty.**

*Did you know that future President Andrew Jackson fought in the War of 1812? Or that his most famous moment in the war occurred after the war had ended?*

At the time of the Battle of New Orleans, Major General Andrew Jackson was in command of American forces in the city. Jackson's forces consisted of a diverse mix of regular soldiers, local militia, free African Americans, and even pirates, such as Jean Lafitte and his privateers. The British, led by General Edward Pakenham, launched a major assault on the American position on January 8th, 1815.

Despite being outnumbered, Jackson's troops, fortified behind earthworks, inflicted heavy casualties on the British. The British suffered over two thousand casualties, including the death of General Pakenham, while the American forces sustained only a few dozen casualties. The Battle of New Orleans was a resounding American victory and is often regarded as one of the most decisive battles of the War of 1812.

What makes this battle particularly interesting is that it was fought after the Treaty of Ghent had been signed on December 24th, 1814, in Belgium, officially ending the war. However, due to the slow pace of communications in the early 19th century, news of the treaty's ratification did not reach the United States until after the battle had been fought.

The Battle of New Orleans bolstered American morale and national pride, as it was seen as a significant victory over a well-trained British force. It also had political implications, as Andrew Jackson's success in defending New Orleans contributed to his rise as a national hero and eventually played a role in his successful presidential campaign in 1828.

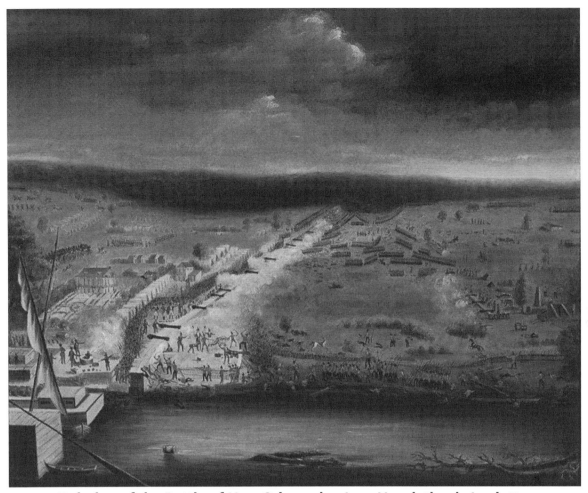

**Painting of the Battle of New Orleans by Jean Hyacinthe de Laclotte.**
*https://commons.wikimedia.org/wiki/File:Battle_of_New_Orleans,_Jean_Hyacinthe_de_Laclotte.jpg*

23. **In the early 1830s, tensions were rising between American settlers and Mexican authorities in the Mexican province of Texas. The Mexican government, under President Antonio López de Santa Anna, began to assert greater control over Texas, leading to discontent among the American settlers.**

In 1831, the Mexican government provided a small cannon to the settlement of Gonzales for defense against local Native American tribes. The cannon was small, often referred to as a "six-pounder," and it had limited military significance. In September 1835, as tensions between Texans and Mexican authorities grew, a detachment of Mexican soldiers was sent to Gonzales to retrieve the cannon. They demanded its return, fearing that it could be used against Mexican forces in a potential uprising.

The Texans in Gonzales, led by George W. Collingsworth and supported by other settlers, responded defiantly to the Mexican demand. They refused to return the cannon and instead raised a homemade flag featuring a black cannon, a star, and the words "Come and Take It."

This flag and the Texan response essentially became a declaration of defiance. The Mexican detachment and the Texans exchanged shots on October 2nd, 1835, marking the beginning of the Texas Revolution. The Battle of Gonzales was a small skirmish but had profound symbolic significance.

Despite the limited military importance of the cannon, the Texans managed to drive off the Mexican forces. They retained the cannon as a symbol of their determination to resist Mexican authority. The phrase "Come and Take It" became a rallying cry for Texian forces throughout the Texas Revolution. It symbolized their resolve to fight for their independence and resist Mexican control.

The "Come and Take It" flag and the cannon remain enduring symbols of Texan pride and resistance to oppression. The cannon is preserved and displayed at the Gonzales Memorial Museum, and the flag's imagery is still associated with the spirit of Texan independence.

**24. The Indian Removal Act was signed into law by President Andrew Jackson in 1830. The act led to the forced relocation of thousands of Cherokee, Creek, Seminole, and other indigenous tribes from their ancestral lands. Mainstream historians believe anywhere between four and ten thousand people died or were killed on the Trail of Tears.**

Cherokee leader John Ross played a prominent role in resisting the forced removal of the Cherokee Nation. John Ross, born in 1790, was of mixed Cherokee and Scottish ancestry. He became a leader within the Cherokee Nation and served as the principal chief from 1828 to 1866.

As the president of the Cherokee Nation, Ross worked tirelessly to use legal means to resist removal. The Cherokee people established a written constitution modeled after that of the United States in 1827. The following year, Georgia determined that the constitution was invalid and that the Cherokee were subject to Georgia laws.

John Ross brought the landmark case *Cherokee Nation v. Georgia* (1831) to the Supreme Court. The court ruled that it had no jurisdiction to listen to the case. In *Worcester v. Georgia* (1832), the court ruled that the state of Georgia had no authority over Cherokee lands, declaring the Cherokee Nation a sovereign nation. However, President Andrew Jackson refused to enforce the court's decision.

In 1838, federal troops were sent to forcibly relocate the Cherokee to Indian Territory (present-day Oklahoma). John Ross led his people on the arduous journey westward, but the conditions were deplorable. Thousands of Cherokees died from exposure, disease, and lack of resources during the forced migration. Despite Ross's efforts, the Cherokee Nation could not prevent the tragedy of the Trail of Tears.

A popular legend says that Ross's wife, known as Quatie, became ill after giving her coat to a crying child. While this story can't be verified, Quatie did die of pneumonia on the Trail of Tears.

Ross continued to advocate for the rights of the Cherokee people in Indian Territory, negotiating with the US government for compensation and the establishment of a new homeland. John Ross's leadership and dedication to his people's well-being during this tumultuous period make him a significant figure in American history.

**25. The Mountain Men were rugged frontiersmen who roamed the American wilderness during the early 19th century, primarily in the Rocky Mountains and other western regions. Hugh Glass was a mountain man and fur trapper who operated in the wilderness of the American West. His story is perhaps one of the most incredible survival tales of the American frontier.**

In 1823, while on an expedition along the Grand River in South Dakota, Glass encountered a grizzly bear while hunting. The bear attacked him, severely mauling him and leaving him with life-threatening injuries. Despite his dire condition, Glass somehow managed to kill the bear with his flintlock rifle.

However, he was left alone and gravely wounded in the wilderness by his fellow trappers, who believed he had no chance of survival. With incredible determination, Glass crawled and dragged himself through the wilderness. He fashioned a makeshift stretcher from a broken rifle, and using it, he covered over two hundred miles over a period of six weeks, surviving on meager food and water.

Along his journey, Glass encountered various dangers, including encounters with Native American tribes. At one point, he was forced to fend off hostile Arikara, who had attacked him.

Ultimately, Glass reached the safety of Fort Kiowa, a trading post on the Missouri River, where he received medical attention. His story of survival became legendary in the American West and served as a testament to the indomitable spirit of the mountain men.

Although Hugh Glass's story has likely been embellished over the years, his tale of survival has inspired books, movies, and folklore, including the 2015 film *The Revenant*, which starred Leonardo DiCaprio in the role of Hugh Glass.

**An illustration of Hugh Glass being attacked by a bear.**
*https://commons.wikimedia.org/wiki/File:Hugh_Glass_Illustration.jpeg*

26. **The Oregon Trail is one of American history's most iconic routes during the westward expansion. It was a challenging and arduous journey taken by thousands of pioneers in the mid-19th century as they sought new opportunities and a better life in the Oregon Territory.**

The Oregon Trail was a roughly two-thousand-mile-long wagon route that began in Missouri and extended to the fertile valleys of Oregon. It was a grueling journey that often took several months, crossing challenging terrain, including deserts, mountains, and rivers.

One of the most tragic stories associated with westward expansion involves the Donner Party, a group of pioneers led by George and Jacob Donner. In the spring of 1846, they set out for California along a new route known as the Hastings Cutoff, which was supposed to be a shortcut. Unfortunately, the Hastings Cutoff turned out to be longer and more treacherous than expected. The Donner Party faced numerous hardships, including delays, dwindling supplies, and harsh weather in the Sierra Nevada Mountains.

When they reached the Sierra Nevada in late October 1846, the Donner Party was ill-prepared for the harsh winter conditions. Trapped by deep snow, they were forced to camp at what is now known as Donner Lake.

As the winter wore on, the pioneers faced extreme hunger and starvation. Some members of the party resorted to cannibalism to survive. Rescue parties eventually reached the stranded pioneers in early 1847, but many had already perished.

The Oregon Trail and the Donner Party story are emblematic of the trials and tribulations faced by those who ventured west in pursuit of new opportunities and a better future during the era of westward expansion in the United States.

### 27. Frederick Douglass was born into slavery in Maryland around 1818 (his exact birthdate is not known). As a young boy, he endured the harsh conditions of slavery and the brutality of his masters.

At the age of around twenty, Douglass decided to escape from slavery. He devised a daring plan that involved borrowing the identification papers of a free African American sailor. With these papers, he disguised himself as a sailor and even wore a sailor's uniform while making his way to the train station in Baltimore.

Douglass's escape was filled with danger and uncertainty. He had to navigate various checkpoints and encounters with authorities who could have discovered his true identity at any moment. His courage and resourcefulness played a crucial role in his successful escape.

Eventually, he arrived in the free state of Pennsylvania and settled in New Bedford, Massachusetts. There, he adopted the name Frederick Douglass to avoid being recaptured.

Once free, Douglass became deeply involved in the abolitionist movement. He began attending anti-slavery meetings and soon became a powerful and captivating speaker, sharing his own experiences as a former slave and advocating for the abolition of slavery.

In 1845, he published his first autobiography, *Narrative of the Life of Frederick Douglass, an American Slave*. The book was a sensation and garnered attention both in the United States and abroad. However, its publication put Douglass at risk of being recaptured by slaveholders. To evade recapture, Douglass embarked on a tour of Ireland and the United Kingdom, where he continued to speak out against slavery. During this time, supporters raised money to purchase his freedom from his former owner, allowing him to return to the United States as a free man.

Frederick Douglass went on to become a prominent abolitionist leader, a staunch advocate for women's suffrage, and a distinguished writer and orator. His life story, from enslavement to freedom, remains a powerful and inspiring testament to the indomitable human spirit and the fight for justice.

**28. The Seneca Falls Convention in 1848 marked a pivotal turning point in the history of women's rights, igniting a movement that would revolutionize the social and political landscape of the United States. At the heart of this movement were two remarkable women: Elizabeth Cady Stanton and Lucretia Mott.**

Elizabeth Cady Stanton was a fiery orator and social reformer. She emerged as a leading voice for women's rights. Her impassioned speeches and written works challenged the prevailing notion that women were intellectually inferior and incapable of self-governance. Stanton believed that women possessed the same inherent rights as men and deserved equal opportunities in all aspects of life, including the right to vote.

Elizabeth married a prominent abolitionist, Henry Brewster Stanton. She took the word "obey" out of the marriage vows, later writing, "I obstinately refused to obey one whom I supposed I was entering into an equal relation." Although she took her husband's last name, she never referred to herself as Mrs. Henry Stanton, as was the custom at the time.

Alongside Stanton stood Lucretia Mott, a Quaker minister and abolitionist who brought her unwavering commitment to social justice to the women's rights movement. Mott's eloquence and moral authority resonated with the convention's attendees, inspiring them to demand a fundamental transformation of gender relations.

In 1840, Mott traveled to London to attend the World's Anti-Slavery Convention. Mott was a well-known advocate for the abolition of slavery and a firm believer in equal rights for all, regardless of gender. However, she faced a significant setback when she arrived at the convention. The male delegates at the World's Anti-Slavery Convention, despite their shared commitment to the abolitionist cause, refused to allow female delegates to participate. Mott was barred from speaking or participating in the proceedings solely based on her gender. Her experiences here led to the Seneca Falls Convention.

Together, Stanton and Mott crafted the Declaration of Sentiments, a bold manifesto that challenged the prevailing legal and social structure that subjugated women. The declaration boldly proclaimed, "All men and women are created equal," a radical assertion that defied the deeply entrenched patriarchal norms of the time.

29. **In the early 19th century, educational opportunities for women in the United States were limited, with few options beyond elementary schooling. Mary Lyon, born in 1797 in Massachusetts, recognized the need for higher education for women. Lyon was deeply committed to the idea of providing women with access to a rigorous and comprehensive education. She was a dedicated teacher and worked to save money for her educational endeavors.**

In 1834, Mary Lyon founded Mount Holyoke Female Seminary (now Mount Holyoke College) in South Hadley, Massachusetts. It was one of the first institutions of higher education exclusively for women in the United States.

What made Mount Holyoke particularly groundbreaking was its commitment to providing women with a rigorous curriculum that included advanced studies in subjects like mathematics, science, literature, and history. Lyon's vision was to prepare women not only for domestic roles but also for professions and careers.

Lyon was deeply involved in the seminary's day-to-day operations, serving as its founder and first principal. She was known for her dedication to the students and her high standards for education.

One of Mary Lyon's innovative ideas was to have students participate in the operation of the school as a way to reduce costs and make education more accessible. Students took on responsibilities such as cooking, cleaning, and farming as part of their education.

Mount Holyoke Female Seminary was successful and became a model for women's education. It inspired the founding of other women's colleges and played a crucial role in advancing women's access to higher education.

Mary Lyon's commitment to women's education and her pioneering efforts made her a trailblazer in the field. Her legacy lives on through Mount Holyoke College and the countless women who have benefited from the educational opportunities she championed.

30. **The Mexican-American War lasted from 1846 to 1848. The US victory in the war expanded American territory significantly, with Mexico ceding present-day California, Nevada, Arizona, and more, setting the stage for further westward expansion and sparking debates over whether newly acquired territories would allow slavery or be free states.**

Several prominent figures participated in the Mexican-American War, including Zachary Taylor, Winfield Scott, Ulysses S. Grant, Robert E. Lee, and "Stonewall" Jackson. *However, one group of people isn't as well known.*

A group of US Army soldiers known as the Saint Patrick's Battalion or the San Patricios fought in the Mexican-American War. This unit was largely composed of Irish and other European immigrants who had enlisted in the United States Army. During the Mexican-American War, some of these soldiers became disillusioned with the conflict, viewing it as an unjust invasion of Mexican territory. Motivated by a combination of anti-Catholic sentiment, mistreatment by their officers, and sympathy for the Mexican cause, a significant number of Irish soldiers defected from the US Army and joined the Mexican forces.

Under the leadership of John Riley (a deserter from the US military), the group fought against their former comrades. One notable engagement involving the San Patricios occurred during the Battle of Churubusco in August 1847. The San Patricios fought bravely against overwhelming odds but ultimately faced defeat. Many were captured, and a significant number were subsequently court-martialed and executed for desertion.

Despite the controversial nature of their actions, the San Patricios are remembered in both Mexican and Irish history as a group of individuals who found themselves torn between loyalties and ideologies during a turbulent period. The story of the Saint Patrick's Battalion serves as a reminder of the complex motivations and consequences of war, as well as the diverse backgrounds of those who participate in conflicts.

# Section 4 – Forging a United Nation: The Crucible of 1850– 1877

From 1850 to 1877, several significant events shaped the nation, including the Dred Scott decision and the secession of the Southern states, which started the Civil War.

This section looks at the lead-up to the Civil War, the war itself, and what happened afterward.

**31. The Missouri Compromise of 1820 was an attempt to maintain a precarious balance between the slave and free states following Maine's petition for statehood. While it temporarily resolved the issue of statehood, the compromise inadvertently exacerbated sectional tensions and foreshadowed the looming Civil War.**

The admission of Missouri as a slave state and Maine as a free state was a delicate balancing act intended to preserve the equilibrium between the two factions. However, this perceived balance was deceptive, as the addition of Missouri further strengthened the South's political power and representation in Congress.

In 1854, the Kansas-Nebraska Act was passed, which repealed the Missouri Compromise and allowed residents of those territories to decide the issue of slavery through popular vote. This decision sparked fierce clashes between pro-slavery and anti-slavery factions in Kansas. These clashes were aptly known as "Bleeding Kansas."

One battle of Bleeding Kansas saw only one accidental death. The sacking of Lawrence, Kansas, happened in 1856. Sheriff Samuel Jones went to Lawrence, which had been established by those who supported the end of slavery, to arrest settlers who supported abolition and were involved in a nearby conflict. Jones was driven out of the town, with people firing their guns at him.

As a result of this "assassination" attempt, a pro-slavery force attacked Lawrence. The pro-slavery forces ransacked the town, looting homes, destroying businesses, and setting fire to the Free State Hotel. One of the men from the pro-slavery faction died when a piece of the hotel fell on his head.

The sacking of Lawrence intensified the animosity between pro-slavery and anti-slavery factions in Kansas. It also contributed to the wider national tensions that eventually led to the outbreak of the American Civil War. The events in Lawrence underscored the bitter and violent nature of the struggle over the future of Kansas and the issue of slavery, foreshadowing the conflicts that would follow in the years leading up to the Civil War.

### 32. In 1857, Dred Scott, an enslaved man, ignited a national firestorm over slavery when he sued for his freedom after residing in free territories.

Dred Scott was born into slavery around 1795 in Virginia and later taken to the free state of Illinois and the Wisconsin Territory by his owner, Dr. John Emerson. In these regions, slavery was prohibited by the Missouri Compromise of 1820. After returning to Missouri, a slave state, Dred Scott and his wife Harriet filed lawsuits for their freedom based on the fact they had been living in territories where they were considered free.

The legal battle culminated in the infamous Supreme Court case *Dred Scott v. Sandford*. The Supreme Court, led by Chief Justice Roger B. Taney, delivered a controversial decision with far-reaching consequences. The Supreme Court ruled that enslaved individuals, even if taken to free territories, remained property and were not entitled to freedom or citizenship. Chief Justice Taney's opinion also declared the Missouri Compromise unconstitutional, arguing that Congress had no authority to prohibit slavery in the territories.

This decision heightened tensions and contributed to the growing divisions between the North and the South over the issue of slavery. The Dred Scott decision profoundly affected American society, exacerbating tensions that eventually led to the Civil War. It also played a role in the election of 1860, as the Republican Party, led by Abraham Lincoln, opposed the expansion of slavery into new territories.

The legacy of the Dred Scott case persisted even after the Civil War, influencing the drafting of the Fourteenth Amendment, which granted citizenship to all persons born or naturalized in the United States, regardless of race or previous condition of servitude. Today, the Dred Scott decision is considered one of the worst Supreme Court decisions in American history.

33. **On October 16th, 1859, John Brown, an abolitionist, led a raid on the federal armory at Harpers Ferry, Virginia, in an attempt to spark a slave uprising. He attempted to get several renowned abolitionists to join him, such as Frederick Douglass and Harriet Tubman, but both declined.**

Brown believed hundreds of slaves would join his cause. However, he had no way of contacting slaves on nearby plantations. He wasn't willing to give up the cause, though.

The first casualty of the raid was a freed Black man who had been shot from behind by one of the raiders on October 17th. The Lost Cause movement, which arose in 1866 and focused on the Confederacy fighting for states' rights, not slavery, claimed the man who had been shot was for slavery remaining in the states.

Brown and his men would go on to capture several hostages and hold them in the armory's fire engine house. The raid was quickly suppressed by a combined force of local militia and US Marines led by Colonel Robert E. Lee. Stonewall Jackson and Jeb Stuart, talented military officials on the Confederacy's side during the Civil War, also helped put down the raid.

Brown and his men were captured on October 18th. Brown was tried for treason and murder and was executed on December 2nd, 1859. John Wilkes Booth, who would go on to kill President Abraham Lincoln, witnessed Brown's death by hanging.

In the North, Brown's raid was considered a heroic act of defiance against slavery. Abolitionists
hailed Brown as a martyr, and his actions inspired many to join the anti-slavery movement. However, others in the North were horrified by the violence and condemned Brown's actions.

In the South, Brown's raid fueled fears of a slave insurrection and intensified Southern resentment toward the North. Many Southerners believed the raid was part of a larger plot by abolitionists to destroy their way of life. This belief further solidified Southern determination to protect slavery, even if it came to war.

34. **Fort Sumter is located in the harbor of Charleston, South Carolina. In 1860, it was one of the last remaining federal military installations in the South under Union control. In December 1860, South Carolina seceded from the Union, followed by several other Southern states. However, Fort Sumter remained under Union control – a clear source of tension between the North and the South.**

President James Buchanan's administration tried to resupply and reinforce the fort peacefully. However, negotiations with South Carolinian authorities stalled, and the situation became increasingly volatile. On April 6th, 1861, Confederate Brigadier General

P. G. T. Beauregard, in command of Confederate forces in Charleston, was ordered by the Confederate government to demand the surrender of Fort Sumter. Major Robert Anderson, the Union commander of the fort, refused to surrender, but he was running low on supplies and ammunition.

On April 12th, 1861, Confederate forces opened fire on Fort Sumter, beginning a thirty-four-hour bombardment. This marked the start of the American Civil War. The Union garrison at Fort Sumter fought back, but they were outmatched, and the fort suffered significant damage.

On April 13th, Major Anderson and his men surrendered. Remarkably, there were no fatalities during the bombardment, although one Union soldier died and three were injured while firing a salute during the Union's evacuation.

The fall of Fort Sumter galvanized both the North and the South. President Abraham Lincoln called for seventy-five thousand volunteers to suppress the rebellion, leading to the mobilization of Union forces and the escalation of the Civil War. Fort Sumter remained in Confederate hands for most of the war but was eventually recaptured by Union forces in 1865.

*35.* **The Civil War has many interesting stories. One of them involves a general named Benjamin Butler. In May 1861, three enslaved men – Frank Baker, James Townsend, and Shepard Mallory – escaped from Confederate-held territory in Virginia and sought refuge at Fort Monroe, a Union stronghold in Virginia commanded by General Butler. When their owner, Colonel Charles Mallory, demanded the return of his "property," General Butler faced a dilemma.**

Butler had been a lawyer before the war and recognized that returning the escaped men to the Confederate forces would essentially mean aiding the enemy. So, he deemed the three men "contraband of war," arguing they were being used by the Confederacy to support its war effort.

This decision set a precedent for the Union's treatment of escaped slaves. The term "contraband" became widely used, and other Union commanders adopted Butler's approach. As more enslaved individuals sought refuge behind Union lines, the North's policy evolved, setting the stage for a shift in the Union's stance on slavery.

While the Emancipation Proclamation had not been issued at that point, the contraband policy marked a significant step toward the eventual emancipation of enslaved people. President Abraham Lincoln issued the Emancipation Proclamation on January 1st, 1863, declaring all enslaved individuals in Confederate-held territory to be free. Four states (Delaware, Maryland, Kentucky, and Missouri) retained slavery until the end of the war and the passage of the Thirteenth Amendment in 1865.

President Abraham Lincoln sought to preserve the unity of the Union and prevent further secession by not challenging slavery in these border states. He believed that emancipation in these states would alienate them and push them into the Confederacy. These border states were also situated between the Union and the Confederacy, making them crucial for controlling the flow of goods, troops, and information.

While the Emancipation Proclamation didn't immediately free all enslaved people, it changed the character of the Civil War by making the abolition of slavery a central war aim. The story of the contraband policy at Fort Monroe illustrates how individual actions and decisions by military commanders, such as General Benjamin Butler, can play a role in shaping the broader trajectory of a war.

### 36. The Battle of Gettysburg is known for several key moments, one of which is Pickett's Charge, a Confederate assault led by General George Pickett on the final day of the battle, July 3rd, 1863.

General George Pickett was a Confederate division commander known for his distinctive appearance, including his long, jet-black beard. He was tasked with leading a desperate and ill-fated assault against the center of the Union lines on Cemetery Ridge. Pickett's Charge involved approximately twelve thousand Confederate soldiers who marched across an open field toward the Union positions while enduring devastating artillery and rifle fire.

The charge was a valiant but ultimately unsuccessful effort to break the Union lines. Confederate forces suffered heavy casualties, and the charge is often considered the high-water mark of the Confederacy.

General Pickett himself narrowly escaped death during the charge. As he rode his horse toward the front lines, he was injured when his horse was shot out from under him. Pickett was knocked unconscious but survived, though he was deeply affected by the loss of his men.

After the failed charge, General Pickett reportedly met with General Robert E. Lee, the Confederate commander, who took responsibility for the defeat and expressed his regret for ordering the ill-fated assault.

General George Pickett's name became forever associated with the charge, and he would carry the weight of that association for the rest of his life. He later referred to the charge as "the slaughter pen." The Union victory at Gettysburg is often seen as a turning point in the war.

**37. On April 9th, 1865, General Robert E. Lee surrendered to General Ulysses S. Grant, effectively ending the Civil War and beginning the process of rebuilding and reconciliation.**

The owner of the home where Grant and Lee met, Wilmer McLean, had moved to Appomattox after his first house was partially destroyed in the war's first major battle, the First Battle of Bull Run, in 1861. McLean allegedly said, "The war began in my front yard and ended in my front parlor."

The Union forces would take several objects from the home, such as the table used to sign the surrender. They paid McLean hundreds of dollars for these priceless artifacts. However, some items were simply stolen.

Grant was overcome with emotion when he saw Lee at the surrendering table. The two talked of the Mexican-American War, which they had fought together on the same side. General Grant would give Lee generous terms of surrender. Lee's men would not be imprisoned for treason. They could keep their sidearms and horses, and Grant gave them food.

General Grant's decision to grant generous terms of surrender to Lee and his army was a strategic move aimed at minimizing further bloodshed and promoting reconciliation. He instructed his troops to treat the Confederates with respect and dignity, avoiding any acts of retribution. Grant's magnanimous treatment of Lee extended to the personal interactions between the two generals.

During their meeting at the McLean House in Appomattox, Grant allowed Lee to retain his sword, a symbol of his military rank and honor. While seemingly insignificant, Lee deeply appreciated this gesture, and served as a powerful symbol of respect and reconciliation.

The treatment of Lee at Appomattox was not merely an act of military courtesy; it was a conscious decision to promote healing and unity in a nation torn apart by war.

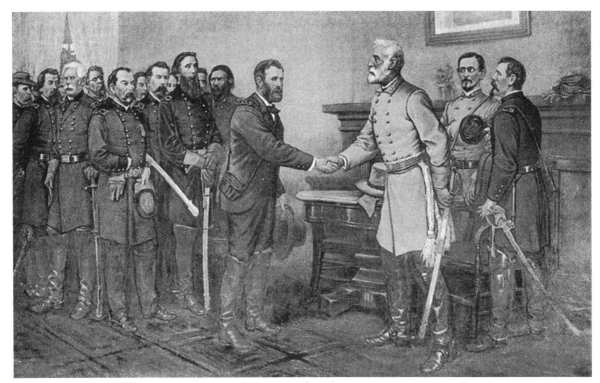

**Lee surrendering to Grant at the Appomattox Court House.**

38. **The Thirteenth Amendment abolished slavery in the United States. Its passage marked a decisive turning point in the nation's history, ending the legalized institution of slavery that had entrenched itself for centuries. The amendment's impact extended beyond the immediate liberation of enslaved people, setting the stage for further advancements in civil rights and equality.**

Thaddeus Stevens, a fiery congressman from Pennsylvania, played a crucial role in abolishing slavery in the United States. His sharp tongue and political maneuvering earned him the title "The Old Commoner," and his influence in the Republican Party proved critical in pushing through the Thirteenth Amendment.

Stevens's personal life was complex, and his relationship with his Black housekeeper, Lydia Hamilton, added further layers to his legacy. While Stevens never publicly declared their status, some historians believe they maintained a long-term, loving relationship. They lived together for decades, and Stevens financially supported her and their daughter.

However, speculating on the intimate nature of their relationship risks historical overreach. Instead, it's crucial to recognize the ambiguity surrounding their bond while acknowledging Stevens's unwavering commitment to racial equality. He openly challenged racial prejudice, championed voting rights for Black Americans, and fiercely condemned Jim Crow laws.

Stevens's dedication to abolition wasn't solely fueled by political expediency. He genuinely believed in human equality, a conviction honed over decades of fighting injustice. While his personal life remains shrouded in some mystery, his contribution to ending slavery in the United States remains undeniable.

### 39. Most people have heard of John Wilkes Booth. But have you ever heard of a woman named Mary Surratt?

During the American Civil War, Mary Surratt was a boarding house owner in Washington, DC. She became linked to the assassination of President Abraham Lincoln through her son, John Surratt, and her boarding house's association with John Wilkes Booth, the assassin.

John Wilkes Booth, a Confederate sympathizer and actor, hatched a plot to assassinate President Lincoln, Vice President Andrew Johnson, and Secretary of State William H. Seward. On the evening of April 14th, 1865, Booth shot President Lincoln at Ford's Theatre while the president was attending a play.

Mary Surratt's son, John Surratt, was involved in the conspiracy and had connections to Booth. He had participated in earlier discussions about kidnapping President Lincoln but was not directly involved in the assassination itself.

After the assassination, Booth fled Washington, DC, and a massive manhunt was launched to capture him and his co-conspirators. Mary Surratt and others were suspected of conspiring with Booth. On April 17th, 1865, Mary Surratt was arrested at her boarding house. During the subsequent trial by a military commission, she was accused of providing aid and shelter to Booth and his co-conspirators, even though she maintained her innocence.

Mary Surratt's trial was controversial. On June 30th, 1865, she was found guilty and sentenced to death. Mary Surratt was hanged alongside three other convicted conspirators on July 7th, 1865. She was the first woman in US history to be executed by the federal government.

Her execution was met with mixed reactions, with some believing she was a willing participant in the plot and others sympathizing with her as a mother who may have been unaware of her son's activities. Her conviction and execution remain the subject of historical debate, as some argue that her role in the conspiracy may not have warranted the death penalty.

**40.** **Hiram Revels was born in Fayetteville, North Carolina, in 1827 to free parents of African and Native American descent. In 1866, during the Reconstruction era following the Civil War, Revels became a minister in the African Methodist Episcopal Church. Soon after, he entered politics. He was appointed an alderman in Natchez, Mississippi, becoming one of the first African Americans to hold a public office in the South.**

In 1867, Mississippi was readmitted to the Union under the Reconstruction Acts, and the state's legislature elected Hiram Revels to the US Senate in 1870. Revels became the first African American to serve in the US Senate and the US Congress.

Revels served as a US senator from Mississippi from February 25th, 1870, to March 3rd, 1871. While in the Senate, he advocated for civil rights, education, and equality for African Americans. One of Revels' most notable speeches in the Senate was his response to a speech by Senator Charles Sumner of Massachusetts. Sumner argued for the desegregation of public schools, and Revels supported his position by sharing the progress made toward racial equality in Mississippi.

Revels's service in the Senate was met with both praise and hostility, with some of his fellow senators opposing his presence due to his race. Despite the challenges, he conducted himself with dignity and integrity.

After his term in the Senate, Revels continued to be involved in education and ministry. He became the first president of Alcorn Agricultural and Mechanical College (now Alcorn State University) in Mississippi, a historically Black institution.

Hiram Revels's legacy extends beyond his time in office. He paved the way for other African Americans to serve in Congress and contributed to advancing civil rights and education during the Reconstruction era. Although the Reconstruction era did not end positively for Black Americans, with the Jim Crow laws being passed in the South, his legacy as a pioneering figure in American history continues to be celebrated today.

# Section 5 – From Rails to Rights: Transformative Events in the Late 19th and Early 20th Centuries

Important events unfolded in America during the late 19th and early 20th centuries. Explore events like the Great Railroad Strike, the Spanish-American War, and the Triangle Shirtwaist Factory fire. The Progressive era brought sociopolitical changes, and the suffrage movement culminated in the Nineteenth Amendment.

There is a lot to uncover from this period, so let's get started!

**41. The Great Railroad Strike of 1877 began in Martinsburg, West Virginia, when workers for the Baltimore and Ohio Railroad (B&O) went on strike on July 16th, 1877. The strike was sparked by a wage cut for B&O railroad workers, who were already facing challenging working conditions and low pay.**

Frustration among the workers had been building for years. As the strike in Martinsburg escalated, it quickly spread to other cities and railroad hubs along the B&O line, including Baltimore, Maryland, and Pittsburgh, Pennsylvania. Soon, railroad workers from other companies joined the strike as well.

The strike became one of the largest and most violent labor uprisings in US history. Striking workers blocked rail lines, sabotaged equipment, and clashed with police and state militias. In Baltimore, the strike took a particularly violent turn. Rioting erupted as striking workers clashed with the Maryland National Guard. Troops fired into the crowd, resulting in numerous deaths and injuries. The strike continued to spread to other states, including Illinois and Missouri, where additional railroads were affected, leading to further confrontations and violence.

President Rutherford B. Hayes eventually intervened, sending federal troops to quell the unrest. The use of federal troops marked one of the earliest instances of federal military intervention in a labor dispute in the United States. The strike gradually subsided as federal troops and state militias gained control of the situation. By early August 1877, the strike had effectively ended.

While the strike did not achieve its immediate goals of wage increases and improved working conditions for railroad workers, it did bring attention to labor issues and set the stage for future labor movements and the growth of labor unions in the United States.

**42. The Dawes Act of 1887 authorized the US government to break up Native American tribal lands into individual allotments, with the goal of assimilating Native Americans into mainstream American society. Its consequences included the loss of traditional lands and cultural identity among Native American communities.**

Prior to the Dawes Act, the Osage Nation had negotiated treaties that secured their territory in what is now Oklahoma. However, the discovery of oil on Osage lands in the late 19th century intensified pressure for assimilation and land division. Under the Dawes Act, the Osage Reservation was allotted to individual tribal members, and the surplus land was opened to non-native settlers.

What makes the Osage story particularly significant is the oil found in their lands. The Dawes Act inadvertently made the Osage among the wealthiest people per capita in the world at the time due to the discovery of oil reserves. Each tribal member received an allotment, including mineral rights, which led to lucrative oil leases.

In response to this wealth from oil, the US government implemented a system whereby non-indigenous guardians were appointed to manage the financial affairs of some of the Osage, especially those deemed "incompetent" to handle their wealth. This system led to widespread corruption and exploitation, with some guardians siphoning off the Osage people's wealth.

The Osage became victims of a series of murders. Several Osage women were killed by their White husbands for money. Most of the murders from this period were never solved.

This tragic series of events highlighted the vulnerability of indigenous communities in the face of external exploitation. Eventually, in the 1920s, the Osage Nation and the federal government worked together to address the corruption and injustice. The Osage murders became the FBI's first major homicide investigation.

**43. Rising tensions between the US and Spain, fueled by newspaper sensationalism and the explosion of the USS Maine, led to the Spanish-American War. Although the explosion of the USS Maine is an interesting story, we are going to take a look at what future President Theodore Roosevelt was up to.**

The Rough Riders was a volunteer cavalry regiment led by Colonel Theodore Roosevelt. The regiment was a diverse mix of cowboys, miners, lawmen, and college athletes, and it also included a notable contingent of African American soldiers. The Rough Riders gained fame for their role in the Battle of San Juan Hill, which took place on July 1st, 1898, near Santiago de Cuba.

During the battle, the Rough Riders and other US forces faced well-entrenched Spanish positions on San Juan Hill. The attack was intense, with heavy fire from Spanish troops positioned in blockhouses and trenches. The Rough Riders, led by Roosevelt, and the Buffalo Soldiers, an African American regiment, played key roles in the uphill assault. One of the most iconic moments of the battle was the charge up Kettle Hill and San Juan Hill.

As the Rough Riders and other US forces advanced, Roosevelt led the charge on horseback, becoming a symbol of American courage and determination. Contrary to the name, the Rough Riders, for the most part, didn't use horses. The horses had been left behind in the US due to some confusion.

Nevertheless, the Rough Riders fought valiantly. Their involvement in the Battle of San Juan Hill received extensive media coverage, and their exploits were celebrated back in the United States. Theodore Roosevelt's leadership during the battle significantly contributed to his political rise, and he later became the vice president and then president of the United States.

The Spanish-American War had far-reaching consequences. The US emerged victorious, gaining Puerto Rico, Guam, and the Philippines. The acquisition of territories propelled the United States onto the global stage, expanding its influence beyond its borders and establishing it as a major power. This newfound status ushered in a period of increased involvement in international affairs, with the United States taking on a more assertive role in shaping the world order.

**44. "Soapy" Smith, whose real name was Jefferson Randolph Smith II, was a notorious American con artist and crime boss who operated during the late 19th and early 20th centuries. He became infamous for his schemes and criminal activities in various parts of the United States, including the Klondike Gold Rush in Alaska and the frontier town of Skagway, Alaska.**

Soapy Smith was born in Coweta County, Georgia, on November 2nd, 1860. He grew up in a family of con artists and learned the tricks of the trade from a young age. Soapy was a master of confidence tricks, shell games, and other forms of deception.

He often operated in towns that were experiencing rapid growth due to the Klondike Gold Rush, where newcomers were eager for entertainment and opportunities but also vulnerable to scams. Soapy Smith is perhaps best known for his activities in Skagway, Alaska, during the Klondike Gold Rush. He and his gang established a criminal empire in the town, a major gateway for prospectors heading to the goldfields of the Yukon.

Soapy and his gang controlled Skagway through a combination of fraud, intimidation, and violence. He established a telegraph office and used it to intercept messages – gaining valuable information about newcomers and their wealth. Soapy's gang, known as the "Soap Gang," engaged in various illegal activities, including rigged gambling games, fake lotteries, and extortion. He and his henchmen would often target vulnerable newcomers, swindling them out of their money.

Soapy Smith's reign in Skagway eventually drew the attention of law enforcement and vigilantes who were determined to clean up the town. In July 1898, a confrontation known as the "Shootout on Juneau Wharf" occurred between Soapy's gang and a group of vigilantes led by Frank Reid. Soapy Smith was fatally wounded in the shootout and died the next day.

Soapy Smith's life and criminal activities have been the subject of numerous books, articles, and even a few films. His name is often associated with the era of frontier lawlessness and the challenges of maintaining order in rapidly growing, lawless towns.

**An image of Soapy Smith.**
*https://commons.wikimedia.org/wiki/File:Soapy_Smith_1898c.jpg*

**45. Before Upton Sinclair's 1906 novel The Jungle shed searing light on the American meatpacking industry, darkness reigned in the nation's stockyards. Chicago's Packingtown, a sprawling complex of slaughterhouses and processing plants, hummed with the unglamorous industry churning out meat for a hungry nation. Yet, beneath the surface of economic prosperity lurked a grim reality for the men and women who kept the gears turning.**

These workers, drawn by the promise of steady wages, predominantly hailed from countries like Lithuania, Poland, and Germany. Their diverse languages and backgrounds collided in the cacophony of the kill floor. But shared hardships forged a grim camaraderie. Their days were brutal: long hours in damp, fetid conditions amidst the constant thud of cleavers, the stench of blood and offal, and the ever-present threat of injury from unforgiving machinery.

Safety was a fleeting privilege, sacrificed for expediency. Fingers were lost to unguarded saws, limbs became tangled in gears, and exhaustion blurred vision, leading to countless cuts and gashes. Illness bloomed from the filth and fumes, affecting the health of workers already weakened by malnutrition and meager pay.

Greed dictated every corner of the operation. Meat deemed unfit for human consumption was repackaged and sold, tainted products disguised with chemicals and preservatives. The workers, deemed replaceable cogs in the machine, lived in cramped, squalid housing, preyed upon by landlords and saloon keepers.

Sinclair, posing as a Lithuanian immigrant, plunged into this world for seven weeks. His fictional protagonist, Jurgis Rudkus, became a vessel for the collective suffering he witnessed. Jurgis's descent from hopeful newcomer to broken man mirrored the fate of countless real-life workers. Through him, Sinclair exposed the industry's gruesome underbelly – the callous disregard for worker safety, the rampant adulteration of food, and the exploitation of vulnerable immigrants.

The book's impact was immediate and visceral. Public outcry forced President Theodore Roosevelt to launch an investigation, leading to the passage of the Pure Food and Drug Act and the Meat Inspection Act of 1906. While these reforms didn't eradicate all problems, they marked a turning point, forcing the industry to acknowledge its responsibility for worker safety and food quality.

**46. On March 25th, 1911, a devastating fire broke out at the Triangle Shirtwaist Factory in New York City. The factory was located on the eighth, ninth, and tenth floors of the Asch Building in Manhattan.**

The Triangle Shirtwaist Factory was a clothing sweatshop where predominantly immigrant women and girls worked long hours in unsafe conditions. The workers produced shirtwaists (blouses) for women.

The fire started on the eighth floor, likely due to a discarded cigarette or a faulty sewing machine, and quickly spread. The factory's doors were locked to prevent theft and unauthorized breaks, trapping workers inside. The lack of fire safety measures, such as sprinklers and fire escapes, made it difficult for workers to escape the rapidly advancing fire. The fire department's ladders could not reach the upper floors of the building.

In a desperate attempt to escape the flames, some workers jumped from the windows to their deaths on the pavement below. Others were burned alive or asphyxiated in the smoke-filled rooms. The fire lasted only about 18 minutes but resulted in the deaths of 146 people, the majority of whom were young immigrant women, many of them Jewish and Italian.

The Triangle Shirtwaist Factory fire shocked the nation. It galvanized the labor reform movement and led to increased awareness of workers' rights and the need for improved safety conditions in factories. In the aftermath of the fire, public outcry and increased activism for workers' rights and safety reforms led to legislative changes in New York State and eventually nationwide. These reforms included improved fire safety regulations, worker compensation laws, and the establishment of factory inspection agencies.

**47. The women's suffrage movement gained momentum during the Progressive era, with women demanding the right to vote. The efforts of suffragettes and other organizations led to the passage and enactment of the Nineteenth Amendment in 1919 and 1920, respectively, granting women the right to vote.**

However, it was not smooth sailing. At the forefront of the women's suffrage movement were activists known as the Silent Sentinels. They picketed the White House, demanding the right to vote for women. Many of these suffragists were arrested and, following their arrests, endured harsh conditions in prison.

On November 14th, 1917 (also known as the Night of Terror), a group of thirty-three suffragists, including Lucy Burns and Alice Paul, were transferred to the Occoquan Work House, where they were subjected to brutal treatment by prison guards. The women were beaten, verbally abused, and force-fed when they went on hunger strikes to protest their imprisonment.

One of the most infamous incidents involved the treatment of Alice Paul, who was placed in a straitjacket, tied to her cell bars, and left for hours. Other suffragists faced similar brutality, with some being thrown into cold, unsanitary cells and denied basic necessities.

News of the Night of Terror spread rapidly, drawing attention to the suffragists' cause and intensifying public support for women's suffrage. The harsh treatment faced by these activists helped expose the brutality of the authorities and contributed to a shift in public opinion.

All of the suffragists involved in the Night of Terror were released by November 27th. It would only take two months for President Woodrow Wilson – who was blamed for the cruelty – to announce a bill on women's suffrage.

**An image of the Silent Sentinels protesting outside the White House**

*https://commons.wikimedia.org/wiki/File:Women_suffragists_picketing_in_front_of_the_White_house.jpg*

**48. President Theodore Roosevelt is well known for his reforms in office. However, let's break up our stories of the reforms made during the Progressive era and focus on something a little different.**

In November 1902, President Theodore Roosevelt embarked on a hunting expedition in Mississippi, guided by a famous Mississippi bear hunter named Holt Collier. The expedition aimed to hunt black bears, which were prevalent in the area. After days of hunting, the party had little success, and President Roosevelt was eager to find a bear to shoot.

On November 14th, the hunting dogs cornered a black bear. Roosevelt approached the bear but was troubled by its exhausted and defenseless condition. He considered it unsportsmanlike to shoot the bear in such a state. Instead of shooting the bear, Roosevelt ordered that it be put out of its misery with a knife, ending the hunt without shooting the bear.

News of President Roosevelt's act of compassion spread quickly, and it captured the public's imagination. A political cartoonist named Clifford Berryman depicted the scene in a cartoon titled "Drawing the Line in Mississippi," published in *The Washington Post* on November 16th, 1902. The cartoon portrayed Roosevelt refusing to shoot the bear, and this image soon became iconic.

The bear in the cartoon was depicted as a small, cuddly bear cub, which later inspired a Brooklyn candy shop owner named Morris Michtom. Morris Michtom's wife, Rose, had the idea to create a stuffed bear toy based on the cartoon. They called it the teddy bear, combining Roosevelt's nickname, "Teddy," with "bear."

The teddy bear became a sensation and quickly gained popularity. The teddy bear's popularity led to the establishment of the Ideal Novelty and Toy Company by the Michtoms, and it became a beloved children's toy.

The compassion displayed by Theodore Roosevelt during the bear hunt inspired the creation of the teddy bear and cemented his reputation as a compassionate leader.

**49. In the early 20th century, the United States faced a series of financial panics and banking crises. One of the most significant of these crises occurred in 1907, known as the Panic of 1907. The Panic of 1907 was characterized by a severe financial downturn, bank runs, and a lack of centralized control over the nation's monetary system. The absence of a central bank made it challenging to respond effectively to the crisis.**

The panic was largely triggered by the attempt to manipulate the stock price of the United Copper Company, leading to a chain reaction of bank runs and financial instability. Prominent banker and financier J. P. Morgan played a key role in stemming the panic. Morgan personally organized a group of fellow bankers who pooled their resources to support troubled banks and restore confidence in the financial system.

While Morgan's efforts helped stabilize the situation, they also highlighted the need for a more systematic and permanent solution to financial crises and the regulation of the banking system. In the wake of the Panic of 1907, there was a growing consensus that the United States needed a central banking system to provide stability, regulate the money supply, and act as a lender of last resort during financial crises.

In 1913, President Woodrow Wilson signed the Federal Reserve Act into law, creating the Federal Reserve System. The Fed was established as a decentralized central bank with twelve regional banks and a Board of Governors in Washington, DC. The Federal

Reserve was given the authority to issue currency, set interest rates, regulate banks, and provide a safety net during financial emergencies.

It became the cornerstone of the United States' modern monetary and financial system. Over the years, the Federal Reserve has played a crucial role in managing the country's monetary policy, responding to financial crises, and fostering economic stability.

**50. The construction of the Panama Canal, a monumental engineering feat, was completed in 1914. This waterway connected the Atlantic and Pacific Oceans, significantly reducing ship travel time and enhancing international trade and transportation. The canal facilitated global trade and commerce and projected American engineering prowess and strategic dominance on the world stage. This engineering marvel solidified America's position as a major player in international affairs, ushering in an era of American dominance for most of the 20th century.**

One interesting story related to the Panama Canal involves the successful efforts to combat and eradicate mosquito-borne diseases during its construction. Malaria and yellow fever were major health threats to workers during the early attempts to build the Panama Canal, particularly during the French construction efforts in the late 19th century. The French project, led by Ferdinand de Lesseps, faced significant challenges, including high worker mortality rates due to these diseases.

When the United States took over canal construction in the early 20th century, Chief Engineer John F. Stevens and later Chief Engineer George W. Goethals implemented a comprehensive public health campaign to address mosquito-borne diseases. The campaign was led by Dr. William C. Gorgas, a US Army surgeon and sanitation expert. Gorgas and his team focused on controlling the mosquito population, which transmitted diseases like malaria and yellow fever. They implemented measures such as draining standing water, fumigating buildings, and introducing larvicide to kill mosquito larvae.

One of the most significant breakthroughs was the discovery that the *Aedes aegypti*, also known as the yellow fever mosquito, was the primary vector for yellow fever. By eliminating the breeding grounds of this specific mosquito, Gorgas and his team drastically reduced the incidence of yellow fever.

The successful control of mosquito-borne diseases was crucial for completing the Panama Canal. The improved public health conditions allowed for a steady and efficient workforce. The canal was officially opened on August 15th, 1914. The efforts to combat disease during the construction of the Panama Canal were pioneering in the field of tropical medicine and contributed to advancements in public health practices worldwide.

# Section 6 – From Victories to Superpower: The Transformative Years of 1914–1945 in American History

From 1914 to 1945, important events shaped American history. The Roaring Twenties brought economic growth, but the Great Depression brought economic decline. The US entered World War II after the attack on Pearl Harbor, ultimately dropping atomic bombs on Hiroshima and Nagasaki, setting the stage for the Cold War.

Let's look at some interesting stories from American history during this pivotal era in the modern age.

**51. As Europe geared up for the cataclysm of World War I, a different conflict simmered across the Rio Grande. The years leading to America's 1917 entry into the global war were marked by escalating tensions with Mexico, a turbulent mix of revolutionary unrest, border skirmishes, and clashing personalities.**

The embers of this tension were ignited by the Mexican Revolution, a bloody struggle for social justice that erupted in 1910. American interests, particularly mining and oil companies, found themselves caught in the crossfire. Raids across the border by revolutionary factions led by charismatic figures like Pancho Villa became commonplace, stoking fears of instability and threats to American lives and property.

President Woodrow Wilson, a pacifist at heart, navigated this volatile landscape with cautious neutrality. He recognized the legitimacy of Mexican aspirations for reform but worried about escalating violence and safeguarding American interests. This balancing act proved increasingly difficult as border attacks, particularly Villa's raid on Columbus, New Mexico, in 1916, became bolder and more brazen.

Enter General John Pershing, a rising star in the US Army. Wilson, pressured by public outrage and congressional demands for action, sent Pershing across the border with a mission to capture Villa and restore order. The "Punitive Expedition," as it was called, became a frustrating exercise in cat-and-mouse pursuit. Pershing, a meticulous planner, struggled to track down the elusive Villa in the vast Mexican desert, while Mexican President Venustiano Carranza vehemently opposed the incursion of his nation's sovereignty.

Meanwhile, a young George Patton, serving under Pershing, honed his tactical skills and thirst for action. Though the expedition failed to capture Villa, it served as a training ground for the American military, preparing them for the larger conflict to come.

Ultimately, America's entry into World War I in 1917 drew focus away from the Mexican border. The Punitive Expedition was withdrawn, leaving behind a simmering discontent and a reminder of the complex and often fraught relationship between the two nations.

**52. During World War I, the United States remained neutral for the initial years of the conflict while Germany waged unrestricted submarine warfare against Allied shipping. In January 1917, British intelligence intercepted a coded telegram sent by the German foreign minister Arthur Zimmermann to the German ambassador in Mexico, Heinrich von Eckardt.**

The Zimmermann Telegram proposed a military alliance between Germany and Mexico in the event that the United States entered World War I on the side of the Allies (Britain, France, and Russia, among others). Germany promised Mexico financial support and the return of territory lost to the United States, specifically Texas, New Mexico, and Arizona.

British codebreakers successfully decrypted the telegram and shared its contents with the United States in late February 1917. The revelation of the Zimmermann Telegram had a profound impact on the United States. It aroused public outrage and significantly influenced public opinion regarding the war.

On April 2nd, 1917, President Woodrow Wilson asked Congress for a declaration of war against Germany, stating that the world must be made safe for democracy. The United States officially entered World War I on April 6th, 1917.

American involvement in the war played a critical role in tipping the balance in favor of the Allies and ultimately contributed to their victory. The Zimmermann Telegram is often cited as a pivotal event that led to the United States' entry into World War I.

After the war, German officials confirmed the authenticity of the Zimmermann Telegram, further cementing its historical significance. The Zimmermann Telegram is a compelling example of how intelligence and diplomacy intersected during World War I. Its interception and disclosure demonstrated the power of codebreaking in warfare.

**53. The Roaring Twenties was a period of economic prosperity and cultural change, characterized by the introduction of new technologies, jazz music, and social liberation. However, this era was also marred by the passage of the Eighteenth Amendment, which prohibited the production, sale, and transportation of liquor.**

While intended to promote temperance, Prohibition had the unintended consequence of giving rise to a thriving illegal alcohol trade and the emergence of powerful criminal organizations. One of the most notorious figures of this era was Al Capone, also known as "Scarface." Capone rose to prominence as a gangster and bootlegger in Chicago, where he controlled a significant portion of the illegal alcohol trade. His criminal empire included speakeasies, breweries, and a network of corrupt officials. Capone's operation was highly organized, and he became known for his ruthlessness in eliminating rivals and maintaining control over his territory. His criminal activities extended beyond alcohol, involving racketeering, gambling, and other illicit enterprises.

Despite the violence associated with Capone and his gang, he managed to cultivate a public image as a charismatic and generous figure. For instance, in response to the economic hardships faced by many Americans during the Great Depression, Al Capone decided to establish soup kitchens to provide free meals to those in need. These soup kitchens, often organized by Capone's associates, distributed food to Chicago's unemployed and impoverished individuals.

Capone's motivations for these charitable efforts were likely complex. Some speculate that he saw this as a way to improve his public image, especially given the negative attention he received for his criminal activities. Additionally, the economic hardships of the Great Depression presented an opportunity for Capone to gain favor among the public.

The story of Al Capone and the Prohibition era provides a window into the complex and often contradictory dynamics of a transformative period in American history. To this day, the Eighteenth Amendment is the only amendment in the US Constitution to be repealed. Prohibition ended in 1933.

**Al Capone in 1930.**
*https://commons.wikimedia.org/wiki/File:Al_Capone_in_1930.jpg*

**54. In 1927, Charles Lindbergh achieved one of the greatest feats in aviation history when he became the first person to fly solo nonstop across the Atlantic Ocean. This historic flight earned him international acclaim and forever marked his place in the annals of aviation.**

On May 20th, 1927, Lindbergh took off from Roosevelt Field in New York on his solo journey to Paris, France. Lindbergh's flight covered a distance of approximately 3,600 miles (5,800 kilometers). He navigated primarily using dead reckoning and celestial navigation. The flight lasted thirty-three hours and thirty minutes.

Lindbergh landed at Le Bourget Field in Paris on May 21st, 1927, to a hero's welcome. A crowd of 100,000 people gathered to greet him, and he became an instant international sensation. Lindbergh received numerous awards and honors for his achievement, including the Orteig Prize, which offered a $25,000 reward for the first nonstop transatlantic flight.

Charles Lindbergh's life took a dark turn in 1932. Charles Lindbergh Jr., the twenty-month-old son of Charles Lindbergh and his wife, Anne Morrow Lindbergh, was kidnapped from the family's home in Hopewell, New Jersey. The Lindbergh baby abduction became a sensational and high-profile case, ultimately leading to one of the most famous criminal investigations in American history.

On the night of March 1st, 1932, the Lindbergh baby was taken from his nursery through an open window. A handwritten ransom note demanding $50,000 was left behind.

The Lindberghs complied with the ransom demands and initiated negotiations with the kidnapper, who used a series of coded letters and phone calls to communicate. The ransom was paid, but the baby was not returned.

Tragically, in May 1932, the baby's remains were found in a wooded area about 4.5 miles from the Lindbergh home. An autopsy determined that the child had died from a fractured skull.

The investigation led to the arrest of Bruno Hauptmann, a German immigrant who had some of the ransom money in his possession. Hauptmann was tried, found guilty of kidnapping and murder, and subsequently executed in the electric chair in 1936. To this day, people are unsure if Hauptmann was guilty.

The Lindbergh baby kidnapping case had a profound impact on American law, leading to the Federal Kidnapping Act, also known as the "Lindbergh Law," which made kidnapping a federal offense if the victim was taken across state lines. It also heightened security measures and awareness surrounding child safety.

*55.* **On October 29th, 1929, the stock market crashed, marking the beginning of the Great Depression, the worst economic downturn in American history. The Great Depression, which spanned from 1929 to the late 1930s, was a period of unprecedented economic hardship in the United States. The stock market crash of 1929 triggered a devastating domino effect, leading to widespread unemployment, business failures, and financial ruin. The nation's industrial heartland was particularly hard-hit, as factories shuttered and workers lost their jobs. Farmers struggled with plummeting crop prices and harsh weather conditions while poverty and hunger became rampant.**

After World War I, Congress passed legislation promising a bonus to veterans, but the payment was not scheduled until 1945. As the Great Depression deepened, many veterans found themselves in dire economic circumstances. In response, a group of approximately 20,000 veterans, known as the *Bonus Expeditionary Force* or *Bonus Army*, marched to the nation's capital in the summer of 1932 to demand immediate payment of their bonuses. The veterans set up makeshift camps in and around Washington, DC, hoping to draw attention to their cause. They occupied government buildings, including abandoned federal buildings and an area across from the Capitol known as Anacostia Flats. The Bonus Army hoped to influence Congress to pass legislation for early payment of their bonuses.

As the summer progressed, tensions rose, and the situation became more contentious. The veterans faced resistance from local authorities. President Herbert Hoover ordered the evacuation of the Bonus Army's camps. On July 28th, 1932, the US Army, led by General

Douglas MacArthur and Major Dwight D. Eisenhower, both of whom would play important roles in World War II, forcibly removed the veterans from their camps. Tear gas and military force were used to disperse the protesters.

The eviction of the Bonus Army was a highly publicized and controversial event. The images of the US military confronting World War I veterans garnered widespread attention and contributed to the negative public perception of President Hoover's handling of the economic crisis.

**The Bonus Army clash with the police in 1932.**
*https://commons.wikimedia.org/wiki/File:Bonus_marchers_05510_2004_001_a.gif*

**56. During the Great Depression of the 1930s, Hoovervilles – makeshift shantytowns that housed homeless and unemployed Americans – sprang up in various cities across the United States. One of the most well-known Hoovervilles was located in New York City, right in the heart of Manhattan's Central Park.**

This Hooverville, often called the "Central Park Hooverville," was established in the early 1930s. Central Park's Hooverville was home to hundreds of homeless individuals and families who had lost their jobs, homes, and savings due to the economic hardships of the Great Depression. Residents of Central Park Hooverville constructed their homes from whatever materials they could find, such as cardboard, wood scraps, and metal. The shacks and tents were densely packed into the area, forming a makeshift community.

Life in Central Park Hooverville was challenging, with residents lacking access to basic amenities like running water and sanitation facilities. The community faced overcrowding, poor hygiene, and inadequate shelter, but it provided a sense of community and support for its inhabitants.

In addition to the dire living conditions, residents faced the constant threat of eviction. City officials and park authorities often attempted to clear Hooverville, viewing it as an eyesore and a violation of park regulations.

Central Park Hooverville became a symbol of the economic suffering and homelessness caused by the Great Depression. Photographers and journalists documented life in Hooverville, bringing attention to the plight of the homeless during this challenging period.

As the country slowly emerged from the Great Depression and implemented relief programs under President Franklin D. Roosevelt's New Deal, conditions in Hoovervilles gradually improved. Central Park Hooverville was eventually dismantled in the mid-1930s, but its existence serves as a lasting reminder of the economic hardship and social challenges faced by Americans during the Great Depression.

*57.* **On December 29th, 1940, Roosevelt announced that the United States would be the "Arsenal of Democracy," pledging to provide military aid and support to countries fighting against the Axis powers in World War II. The US became a major supplier of war material, contributing significantly to the eventual victory of the Allies. The USA gave the USSR over 400,000 trucks alone.**

Yes, although the US and Russia are often at odds today, the two were allies during World War II. As part of the Lend-Lease program, the United States provided military aid to the Soviet Union, which was a crucial partner on the Eastern Front against Nazi Germany.

One remarkable aspect of the Lend-Lease program was the aircraft deliveries to the Soviet Union through the use of a route known as the Alaska-Siberia (ALSIB) airway. This airway allowed American-made aircraft to be flown from the United States to the Soviet Union, crossing over Alaska and Siberia.

Pilots, many of whom were civilian aviators, played a crucial role in delivering the aircraft. They flew the planes across the treacherous terrain of Alaska and the vast distances of Siberia, facing extreme weather conditions, long flights, and challenging navigation.

One of the notable aircraft delivered through the ALSIB route was the Bell P-39 Airacobra. This single-engine fighter aircraft, equipped with a unique mid-mounted cannon, became an important asset for the Soviet Air Force on the Eastern Front.

The ALSIB route witnessed hundreds of successful deliveries of American aircraft to the Soviet Union during the war. The cooperation through the Lend-Lease program, including the daring flights of the ALSIB route, strengthened the Allied effort against the Axis powers and showcased the global scale of collaboration during World War II.

**58. On December 7th, 1941, Pearl Harbor was attacked by the Japanese, prompting the United States to enter World War II. Needless to say, the attack on Pearl Harbor was a pivotal moment in American history, marking the nation's entry into World War II and shaping its foreign policy for decades to come. The immediate ramifications of the attack were devastating, with over two thousand Americans killed, hundreds wounded, and seven ships sinking.**

During the surprise attack by the Japanese, the USS *Nevada* was moored at Battleship Row on the southern side of Ford Island. The ship was one of the primary targets and suffered several bomb hits and torpedo strikes. Despite being heavily damaged, the crew of the USS *Nevada*, under the command of Captain Francis W. Scanland, managed to get the ship underway.

Realizing that the battleship was in danger of sinking and blocking the harbor entrance, Captain Scanland ordered the USS *Nevada* to head for the open sea. Under intense enemy fire, the ship made a daring attempt to escape the harbor. Despite sustaining further damage and being targeted by Japanese aircraft, the USS *Nevada* successfully navigated the harbor channel. The crew intentionally beached the battleship on Hospital Point to prevent it from sinking in the harbor entrance.

The grounding of the USS *Nevada* had strategic implications. It allowed the ship to avoid obstructing the harbor and allowed the US to salvage and eventually repair it. In the aftermath of the attack, the USS *Nevada* was repaired, modernized, and returned to active service in the Pacific theater later in the war.

The story of the USS *Nevada*'s attempt to escape during the attack on Pearl Harbor showcases the determination, resourcefulness, and bravery of the Americans under challenging circumstances. The ship's successful grounding and subsequent recovery became a symbol of resilience in the face of adversity during one of the darkest days in American military history.

**The USS Nevada in 1944.**
*https://commons.wikimedia.org/wiki/File:Uss_nevada.jpg*

**59. The United States dropped atomic bombs on the Japanese cities of Hiroshima and Nagasaki in early August 1945, leading to Japan's surrender and the end of World War II.**

While it is difficult to know for sure, it is believed the atomic bombings of Hiroshima and Nagasaki resulted in an estimated 129,000 to 226,000 Japanese deaths, with the majority of the casualties occurring in the immediate aftermath of the explosions. The bombings also caused widespread injuries and long-term health effects, including radiation sickness and cancer.

In 1955, ten years after the bombing, a group of twenty-five Japanese women who had survived the atomic blast sought medical help in the United States to address severe disfigurements and scars caused by the radiation. The Japanese women were victims of the long-term effects of the atomic bomb, facing physical and social challenges due to their appearance.

A humanitarian effort was launched to bring these women to the United States for medical treatment and reconstructive surgery. The initiative was led by Dr. Tatsuo

Yamada, a Japanese plastic surgeon, and journalist Norman Cousins, who helped coordinate the project. The undertaking was named the Hiroshima Maidens program.

The Hiroshima Maidens arrived in the United States in 1955, where they received medical care, surgeries, and rehabilitation at Mount Sinai Hospital in New York City. The treatment aimed to improve both their physical health and their social well-being by addressing the visible effects of the atomic bomb.

The story of the Hiroshima Maidens gained significant media attention, and the women became symbols of the long-term consequences of nuclear warfare. The program provided medical care and facilitated cultural exchange and understanding between the Japanese survivors and the American medical community.

**60. In the late 1940s, after the successful testing of atomic bombs in the New Mexico desert, the Manhattan Project continued its research to improve the design and efficiency of these weapons. One critical component of the atomic bomb was a sphere of fissile material, usually plutonium or uranium, that could sustain a nuclear chain reaction when brought to a critical mass. This core was often referred to as the "pit."**

In August 1945, a few days before the bombing of Nagasaki, physicist Harry Daghlian was conducting experiments at the Los Alamos Laboratory in New Mexico. He was working with a plutonium core, later known as the "demon core." Daghlian was performing a critical experiment to measure the effects of placing tungsten carbide bricks around the plutonium core, essentially testing how close the core could come to achieving a critical mass without causing a nuclear chain reaction. Daghlian accidentally dropped a brick onto the plutonium core during the experiment, causing it to go *supercritical*.

Neutron radiation flooded the room, and Daghlian quickly realized the danger he was in. With heroic effort, Daghlian removed the brick and attempted to limit his radiation exposure, but it was late; he had received a lethal dose of radiation during the incident.

Daghlian was rushed to the hospital, and despite the best efforts of medical staff, he died twenty-five days later on September 15th, 1945, becoming the first known fatality directly attributed to radiation exposure from a criticality accident.

The "demon core" was involved in another criticality accident less than a year later when physicist Louis Slotin conducted a similar experiment. Slotin also died from radiation exposure, further emphasizing the dangers of working with fissile materials.

These incidents contributed to increased awareness of the hazards of nuclear research and the need for strict safety protocols in nuclear facilities. They also played a role in the development of safety measures and procedures for handling fissile materials.

# Section 7 –America's Journey from 1946 to 1980

From 1946 to 1980, various pivotal events shaped American history. The Cold War tensions between the US and the Soviet Union set the stage with proxy wars like the Korean War and the Vietnam War. *Brown v. Board of Education* deemed school segregation unconstitutional, fueling the civil rights movement. The Watergate scandal and Nixon's resignation exposed corruption.

Explore this period with a look at some interesting stories!

**61. The Marshall Plan was a US program that provided aid to Western Europe following the devastation of World War II. Enacted in 1948, it provided over fifteen billion dollars to help finance rebuilding efforts in Europe. The plan aimed to restore economic stability, prevent the spread of communism, and foster economic interdependence between Europe and the United States.**

After World War II, France faced severe economic challenges, including a crippled industrial base, food shortages, and a struggling economy. The Marshall Plan played a crucial role in helping France rebuild and revitalize its economy. One notable example is the transformation of the French city of Le Havre.

Le Havre had suffered extensive damage during the war, and its port - critical for trade and economic activity, was in ruins. The city was selected as a recipient of Marshall Plan aid. Under the leadership of Auguste Perret, a French architect, Le Havre underwent a remarkable reconstruction project. Perret adopted innovative urban planning and architectural techniques, including the use of reinforced concrete, to rebuild the city quickly and efficiently. The reconstruction of Le Havre became a showcase for modern urban design and post-war recovery.

In 1950, Le Havre was officially unveiled as a shining example of the successful implementation of the Marshall Plan. The rebuilt city featured wide streets, modern buildings, and a revitalized port. The transformation of Le Havre symbolized not only the physical reconstruction of war-torn Europe but also the economic and social revival made possible by the Marshall Plan.

**62. In 1950, North Korean forces invaded South Korea, leading to a three-year conflict. The US and other allies intervened to support South Korea against communist aggression. The Korean War was a proxy war between the United States and the Soviet Union, contributing to the Cold War tensions.**

One notable battle from this war took place in Inchon. Inchon is a port city on the west coast of Korea. During the war, it was heavily fortified and considered an unlikely location for an amphibious invasion due to its challenging tidal conditions. The tides in Inchon were among the highest in the world, with a range of up to thirty-six feet, making it a risky and unconventional choice for an amphibious assault.

Against the advice of many military advisors, General Douglas MacArthur, the Supreme Commander of the United Nations Command, devised a plan to launch a surprise attack on Inchon. The operation, codenamed Operation Chromite, aimed to cut off North Korean forces and relieve the pressure on United Nations forces, which had been pushed to the Pusan Perimeter in the southeastern part of the Korean Peninsula.

On September 15th, 1950, UN forces launched a bold amphibious assault on Inchon. The operation's success relied on precise timing to take advantage of the narrow window when the tides were at their highest. The element of surprise, combined with the audacity of attacking such a challenging location, caught the North Korean forces off-guard.

The amphibious assault at Inchon proved to be a masterstroke, as the UN forces quickly secured the city and began to turn the tide of the war. The successful operation is often credited with altering the course of the Korean War in favor of the UN forces.

Ultimately, the Korean War would end in a stalemate. Some believe the two sides remained in a frozen conflict since no peace treaty that marked the end of the war was ever signed. Nevertheless, the Battle of Inchon remains a remarkable example of military strategy and bold decision-making, showcasing General MacArthur's leadership and the effectiveness of well-executed amphibious operations in unconventional environments.

**63. Linda Brown was a third-grader in Topeka, Kansas. She had to walk a considerable distance to her segregated Black school, even though there was a white school much closer to her home. Her father, Oliver Brown, became frustrated with the unequal educational opportunities available to his daughter and decided to take action. In 1950, Oliver Brown, along with several other African American parents, filed a class-action lawsuit against the Board of Education of Topeka, Kansas.**

Their case, combined with other cases from Delaware, South Carolina, Virginia, and Washington, DC, was consolidated into what became known as *Brown v. Board of Education*. The plaintiffs argued that racial segregation in public schools was a violation of the Fourteenth Amendment, which guarantees equal rights to all citizens.

The case was argued before the Supreme Court in 1952 and 1953. In 1954, the Supreme Court, in a unanimous decision, ruled in favor of the plaintiffs, declaring that state laws establishing separate public schools for Black and White students were unconstitutional. The landmark decision in *Brown v. Board of Education* overturned the precedent set by the 1896 case *Plessy v. Ferguson*, which upheld the concept of "separate but equal" facilities for different races.

Linda Brown, though just a child at the time of the case, became a symbol of the fight against racial segregation in education. The *Brown v. Board of Education* decision marked a pivotal moment in the civil rights movement and set the stage for dismantling segregation in all areas of public life in the United States. The legacy of this case continues to influence discussions about equal access to education and civil rights.

**64. On December 1st, 1955, Rosa Parks, a seamstress and civil rights activist, was riding a bus in Montgomery, Alabama, after a long day of work. She was seated in the "colored" section of the bus, which was the racially segregated seating arrangement enforced in the city.**

As the bus continued its route, it became crowded, and some White passengers were left standing. The bus driver, James F. Blake, demanded that Rosa Parks and three other African American passengers give up their seats to White passengers. Rosa Parks made a courageous decision to refuse to give up her seat to a White man, which was against the city's segregation laws.

Parks's act of civil disobedience led to her arrest and subsequent charges of violating segregation laws. She was taken into custody by the police and spent the night in jail. News of her arrest spread quickly, sparking outrage and mobilizing the African American community in Montgomery.

Leaders of the Montgomery Improvement Association (MIA), including a young minister named Martin Luther King Jr., organized a boycott of the city's buses in protest of Parks's arrest and racial segregation on public transportation. The Montgomery bus boycott, as it became known, lasted for 381 days. African Americans in Montgomery refused to ride the city's buses, causing a significant financial strain on the transportation system. The boycott's success caught the attention of the nation and the world, drawing support from civil rights activists, sympathizers, and leaders across the country.

In 1956, the United States Supreme Court ruled in the case of *Browder v. Gayle* that racial segregation on Montgomery buses was unconstitutional, effectively ending segregation on public transportation in the city. Rosa Parks's courage and the Montgomery bus boycott marked a turning point in the civil rights movement. Her actions and the subsequent legal victory demonstrated the power of nonviolent protest and grassroots activism.

**Rosa Parks in 1955. You can see Martin Luther King Jr. in the background.**
*https://commons.wikimedia.org/wiki/File:Rosaparks.jpg*

**65. During the height of the Cold War, the United States conducted extensive surveillance missions over the Soviet Union to gather intelligence. The U-2 spy plane was a crucial tool in these efforts due to its high-altitude capabilities.**

On May 1st, 1960, a U-2 spy plane piloted by Francis Gary Powers took off from Pakistan on a reconnaissance mission to photograph Soviet military installations. The mission, codenamed Operation Grand Slam, aimed to gather valuable intelligence about the Soviet Union's nuclear capabilities.

While flying over Soviet airspace, Powers's U-2 plane was detected and tracked by Soviet radar. Despite the aircraft's high altitude, it was eventually hit by a surface-to-air missile. Powers's U-2 was brought down, and he was captured by Soviet authorities.

Powers survived the crash and was taken into custody. Initially, the US government claimed that the U-2 was a weather reconnaissance plane that had gone off course and inadvertently strayed into Soviet territory. However, the Soviet Union presented evidence of the espionage mission, including photos taken by Powers's camera equipment.

The U-2 incident caused a major diplomatic crisis between the United States and the Soviet Union. The Soviets accused the US of conducting espionage flights, which the US initially denied but later admitted.

Powers was put on trial in the Soviet Union and sentenced to ten years in prison for espionage. He spent over a year in captivity before being exchanged for Soviet spy Rudolf Abel in a high-profile prisoner exchange on the Glienicke Bridge in Berlin in 1962.

The U-2 incident prompted increased scrutiny of US reconnaissance efforts and the development of alternative surveillance methods. However, the U-2 spy plane remained in service and played a role in subsequent intelligence-gathering missions during the Cold War and beyond.

### 66. The Cuban Missile Crisis of 1962 was a tense standoff between the United States and the Soviet Union over the presence of Soviet nuclear missiles in Cuba, which is just ninety miles off the coast of Florida.

To gather crucial intelligence about the missile installations in Cuba, the United States conducted reconnaissance flights using U-2 spy planes. These high-altitude flights allowed the US to monitor the situation and provide photographic evidence to the world.

On October 27th, 1962, during the height of the crisis, U-2 pilot Major Rudolf Anderson Jr. was on a reconnaissance mission over Cuba. He was flying at an altitude of 70,500 feet, well above the range of Soviet surface-to-air missiles. Despite the altitude, Soviet generals ordered a surface-to-air missile to be fired at Anderson's U-2 plane. The missile struck the aircraft, causing it to disintegrate and killing Anderson. He became the only combat casualty of the Cuban Missile Crisis.

Rudolf Anderson's tragic death underscored the extremely high stakes of the Cuban Missile Crisis and the dangers faced by those involved in intelligence-gathering missions. His sacrifice served as a poignant reminder of the need for accurate information and diplomacy during times of international crisis. It also contributed to the resolution of the crisis, as it became clear that a peaceful solution was preferable to the potentially catastrophic consequences of nuclear war.

The Cuban Missile Crisis was eventually resolved through negotiations, with the US agreeing to remove its missiles from Turkey and the Soviets agreeing to dismantle their missile installations in Cuba.

**67. Dr. Martin Luther King Jr. was a central figure in the civil rights movement and played a crucial role in advocating for the passage of the Civil Rights Act of 1964.**

In the early 1960s, Dr. King and other civil rights leaders organized a series of nonviolent protests, including sit-ins, marches, and voter registration drives, to challenge segregation and discrimination in the United States. These protests, particularly the Birmingham campaign in 1963, drew national attention and placed immense pressure on the federal government to address civil rights issues.

On August 28th, 1963, Dr. King delivered his iconic "I Have a Dream" speech during the March on Washington for Jobs and Freedom, which took place at the Lincoln Memorial in Washington, DC. His powerful and inspiring words resonated with millions of Americans and helped galvanize support for civil rights legislation.

President John F. Kennedy was initially cautious about pushing for comprehensive civil rights legislation, fearing backlash from Southern segregationist lawmakers. However, the momentum of the civil rights movement and the moral imperative became increasingly evident.

Tragically, President Kennedy was assassinated on November 22nd, 1963. His successor, President Lyndon B. Johnson, recognized the need to honor Kennedy's legacy and moved forward with civil rights legislation.

President Johnson, who had served in the Senate and understood how to navigate the legislative process, used his political skills to push for the Civil Rights Act of 1964. He also used his relationship with lawmakers to secure their support for the bill. On July 2nd, 1964, President Johnson signed the Civil Rights Act into law. The act prohibited discrimination on the basis of race, color, religion, sex, or national origin, and it ended segregation in public places and banned employment discrimination.

Dr. Martin Luther King Jr.'s leadership and the grassroots efforts of countless activists nationwide played a significant role in creating the public demand for the Civil Rights Act. The passage of the Civil Rights Act of 1964 marked a historic step toward dismantling institutional racism and advancing civil rights in the United States. It remains a landmark piece of legislation in American history.

**68. On July 20th, 1969, NASA's Apollo 11 mission achieved the historic feat of landing two astronauts, Neil Armstrong and Edwin "Buzz" Aldrin, on the lunar surface. Michael Collins remained in orbit around the moon aboard the command module.**

As the lunar module *Eagle* descended to the moon's surface, Neil Armstrong, the mission's commander, took control of the spacecraft. The situation became tense as they encountered a rocky and uneven landing site with only seconds of fuel remaining. Armstrong's exceptional piloting skills allowed him to manually maneuver the spacecraft, avoiding a potentially catastrophic landing. With just twenty-five seconds of fuel left, Armstrong safely touched down on the moon's surface.

The historic moment occurred when Neil Armstrong descended the lunar module's ladder and became the first human to set foot on the moon. He famously said, "That's one small step for man, one giant leap for mankind." The quote was intended to convey the significance of this achievement for all of humanity. However, it is often misquoted as "That's one small step for a man," with the "a" making the sentence grammatically complete. Armstrong maintained that he had said "a" during the transmission but acknowledged that it might not have been clearly audible due to radio static.

Regardless of the exact wording, Armstrong's first step on the moon was an extraordinary moment that captivated the world and marked a historic milestone in space exploration. Buzz Aldrin joined Armstrong on the lunar surface, and together, they conducted experiments, planted the American flag, and collected lunar samples during their two-and-a-half hours outside the lunar module.

The successful return of Apollo 11's astronauts to Earth on July 24th, 1969, marked the conclusion of this historic mission and a monumental achievement in human exploration. The Apollo 11 moon landing remains one of the most iconic events in human history, representing the pinnacle of human achievement in space exploration. Neil Armstrong's famous words as he stepped onto the lunar surface continue to inspire generations and remind us of the incredible capabilities of science and technology.

**Buzz Aldrin salutes the American flag.**
*https://en.wikipedia.org/wiki/File:Buzz_salutes_the_U.S._Flag.jpg*

**69. The Vietnam War, spanning from 1955 to 1975, marked a tumultuous period in American history, characterized by escalating US involvement in a highly controversial conflict that ignited widespread protests and demonstrations. This divisive war, rooted in the Cold War struggle between communism and democracy, saw the US embroiled in a protracted and costly military effort to support South Vietnam against communist North Vietnam and its allies.**

In December 1972, the United States was engaged in negotiations with North Vietnam to end the war. However, peace talks had reached an impasse, and President Richard Nixon decided to take drastic measures to push for a resolution. On December 18th, 1972, Operation Linebacker II began, later called the "Christmas Bombing."

Over the course of eleven days, from December 18th to December 29th, the US conducted an intensive bombing campaign targeting Hanoi and Haiphong in North Vietnam. The objective was to force North Vietnam back to the negotiating table by inflicting significant damage on its infrastructure and military capabilities. The bombing campaign involved the use of B-52 Stratofortress bombers and other aircraft, dropping a massive number of bombs on the designated targets. The scale and intensity of the bombings were unprecedented, with the US dropping over twenty thousand tons of bombs during this period.

The Christmas Bombing had a profound impact on both North Vietnam and the international community. It caused widespread destruction and civilian casualties, drawing criticism from around the world. The intense public reaction and diplomatic pressure contributed to the resumption of peace talks.

Remarkably, despite the devastation caused by the bombings, peace talks resumed in January 1973, leading to the signing of the Paris Peace Accords later that month. The accords paved the way for the withdrawal of US forces from Vietnam and established a ceasefire. The Christmas Bombing, while controversial and heavily criticized, played a role in ultimately bringing about a negotiated end to the Vietnam War.

**70. The Watergate scandal began with a break-in at the Democratic National Committee headquarters in the Watergate complex in Washington, DC, on June 17th, 1972. The burglars were caught, leading to an investigation.**

Two investigative reporters, Bob Woodward and Carl Bernstein of *The Washington Post*, played a crucial role in uncovering the scandal. Their reporting exposed a series of illegal activities, including the break-in and a subsequent cover-up by the Nixon administration.

What made their investigation even more intriguing was the mysterious source known as "Deep Throat." Deep Throat was a high-ranking official within the US government who provided Woodward and Bernstein with crucial information, guidance, and leads related to the Watergate scandal. Deep Throat insisted on remaining anonymous and communicated with the reporters in secret meetings in parking garages. His information was instrumental in connecting the dots and unraveling the extent of the scandal.

For more than thirty years, Deep Throat's identity remained one of the greatest mysteries in American journalism and politics. Speculation and theories about his identity persisted. In 2005, it was revealed that W. Mark Felt, an associate director of the FBI during the Watergate era, was Deep Throat. Felt's decision to provide confidential information to the reporters was driven by his concern for the integrity of the FBI and his belief that the truth about Watergate needed to be exposed. The revelation of Deep Throat's identity added a new layer of historical significance to the Watergate scandal and solidified his place in American political history.

The Watergate scandal ultimately led to the resignation of President Richard Nixon on August 8th, 1974, as he faced imminent impeachment by Congress. Vice President Gerald Ford succeeded Nixon as president. Ford would go on to pardon Nixon, ending any chance of an indictment.

# Section 8 – Shaping the Nation: From Reaganomics to the Oklahoma City Bombing

From 1981 to the early 2000s, several important events and developments shaped American history. Technological advancements, such as the introduction of personal computers, revolutionized the way people lived and worked. The fall of the Berlin Wall in 1989 marked the end of the Cold War and signified a major shift in global dynamics. Cultural shifts and tragic incidents like the Los Angeles riots and the Oklahoma City bombing highlighted the ongoing challenges and complexities faced by the United States during this period.

Let's see how the nation was shaped during this era.

**71. President Ronald Reagan, often dubbed the "Great Communicator," wove humor into his speeches and debates with the ease of a seasoned storyteller. His quips weren't fiery punchlines but rather gentle nudges, disarming audiences with self-deprecating wit and playful jabs at opponents.**

In a debate about his age, Reagan chuckled, "I have no intention of running for President of the United States when I'm 73. My current plan is to be Governor of California for four more years, then go do some movies, or maybe write a book, then retire and watch all the ball games I want." This self-aware deflection deflected potential age concerns with a dose of charm. He eventually did go on to run for president– *a race he won!*

Reagan reveled in poking fun at himself. Describing the arduous budget process, he once joked, "The budget process is much like a pregnant elephant. All the excitement happens in the dark, and the result is rather large and ungainly." This down-to-earth humor resonated with audiences, painting him as relatable and approachable.

Reagan's humor wasn't just a sideshow; it served a purpose. It disarmed tension, endeared him to audiences, and helped him articulate complex ideas in memorable ways. His gentle wit became a signature style that cemented his image as a folksy leader with a twinkle in his eye and a mischievous grin.

Unfortunately, Reagan's sense of humor sometimes got him into trouble. For instance, on August 11ᵗʰ, 1984, during a radio address preparation session at his California ranch, while testing the microphone, Reagan said, "My fellow Americans, I'm pleased to tell you today that I've signed legislation that will outlaw Russia forever. We begin bombing in five minutes."

Though intended as a lighthearted joke, this off-the-cuff remark was picked up by the microphone and later leaked to the public. It caused a stir on both sides of the Iron Curtain, with the Soviet Union condemning the statement as irresponsible and Reagan's opponents in the upcoming presidential election criticizing it as a sign of poor judgment.

**72. On March 30th, 1981, President Ronald Reagan was leaving the Washington Hilton Hotel after delivering a speech. As he exited the hotel and approached his limousine, shots were fired. John Hinckley Jr., a mentally unstable individual, fired six shots in an attempt to assassinate President Reagan. Hinckley was armed with a .22 caliber revolver and had a history of stalking actress Jodie Foster, which played a role in his motivation for the attack.**

President Reagan was hit by one of the bullets, which punctured his left lung and came close to his heart. White House Press Secretary James Brady, a Secret Service agent, and a District of Columbia police officer were also injured in the shooting. In the chaos that followed, Secret Service agents quickly reacted to protect the president and rushed him to the hospital. The swift medical response and surgery saved Reagan's life.

Reagan's famous humor and resilience emerged even amid a life-threatening situation. As he was wheeled into the operating room, he reportedly joked to the medical team, "I hope you're all Republicans."

The assassination attempt prompted a nationwide outpouring of support for President Reagan. He received thousands of get-well messages and letters from people across the country. John Hinckley Jr. was arrested at the scene and later found not guilty by reason of insanity during his trial. The verdict led to significant changes in laws regarding the insanity defense.

President Reagan recovered from his injuries and continued to serve as president of the United States for the remainder of his two terms, from 1981 to 1989. The attempted assassination had a lasting impact on presidential security procedures, leading to increased security measures for future presidents.

**A picture of Reagan just before he was shot.**

**73. Have you ever wondered how computers began to impact our lives? On August 12th, 1981, IBM unveiled the IBM 5150, the first personal computer (PC) to gain widespread adoption. This groundbreaking innovation marked the dawn of the PC revolution, transforming how people worked, communicated, and entertained themselves. The IBM PC's open architecture and compatibility with a vast array of software applications fueled its popularity, paving the way for the creation of a thriving personal computing industry.**

In 1984, Apple launched the Macintosh computer, a revolutionary product that marked a significant departure from the text-based interfaces of earlier computers. The Macintosh featured a graphical user interface with icons, windows, and a mouse – a design inspired by the work done at Xerox PARC (Palo Alto Research Center) in the 1970s.

The story begins with Xerox PARC, where researchers developed a revolutionary graphical user interface, *Alto*. This system incorporated the use of a mouse and graphical elements, allowing users to interact with the computer more intuitively. Xerox, however, failed to capitalize on the potential of this groundbreaking technology.

In a twist of fate, Steve Jobs, co-founder of Apple, visited Xerox PARC in 1979 and saw the Alto in action. Recognizing the immense potential of the graphical user interface, Jobs initiated the development of a similar system for Apple's upcoming computer, the Macintosh.

The Macintosh, introduced in January 1984, featured a 9-inch monochrome display, a 3.5-inch floppy disk drive, and an affordable price tag compared to other graphical systems at the time. The Macintosh's graphical user interface, combined with its marketing campaign, which included the famous *1984* Super Bowl commercial, made it a standout product.

The Macintosh's release had a profound impact on the personal computer industry. It set new standards for user-friendly designs and influenced the development of future operating systems. Computers were made more accessible to a broader audience, shaping how people interact with technology. The legacy of the Macintosh continues to influence computing and user interface design to this day.

**74. The Space Shuttle Challenger was a part of NASA's Space Shuttle program and made its maiden flight on April 4th, 1983. It was designed to carry astronauts and payloads into space.**

On January 28th, 1986, the Challenger was set to launch from the Kennedy Space Center in Florida on mission STS-51-L. This mission was significant because it included the first private citizen selected to fly in space. Christa McAuliffe, a high school social studies teacher from New Hampshire, was chosen from thousands of applicants to be the first private citizen and teacher in space as part of NASA's Teacher in Space Project. Her selection was intended to promote the importance of education and space exploration.

Millions of Americans and people worldwide watched the Challenger launch live on television. However, just seventy-three seconds after liftoff, the shuttle broke apart, resulting in the tragic deaths of all seven crew members. The disaster was caused by the failure of an O-ring seal in one of the solid rocket boosters, which led to the explosion of the external fuel tank.

The Challenger explosion had a profound impact on the space program and raised questions about the safety of the Space Shuttle fleet. NASA suspended the Space Shuttle program for over two years while investigations were conducted and safety improvements were implemented.

Christa McAuliffe's dream of becoming the first teacher in space was tragically cut short, but her legacy endured. Her memory inspired further dedication to space exploration and education. In 1998, NASA launched the Christa McAuliffe Fellowship Program to honor her legacy and support teachers in their professional development.

The Challenger explosion remains a somber and significant chapter in the history of space exploration. It serves as a reminder of the risks and challenges associated with human spaceflight and the dedication of those who pursue the frontiers of science and discovery.

**75. On June 12th, 1987, during a visit to West Berlin, President Ronald Reagan delivered a historic and memorable speech at the Brandenburg Gate, a prominent location near the Berlin Wall. President Reagan addressed the divided city of Berlin in his speech, directly challenging the Soviet leader, Mikhail Gorbachev, and the East German government. He declared, "Mr. Gorbachev, open this gate! Mr. Gorbachev, tear down this wall!"**

President Reagan's words were a clear and unequivocal call for the removal of the Berlin Wall, a powerful symbol of the division between East and West Germany. At the time, some advisors had urged Reagan to avoid making such a direct and confrontational statement, fearing it might harm relations with the Soviet Union. However, Reagan insisted on including these iconic words in his speech.

The speech was received with enthusiasm by West Berliners, who saw it as a powerful expression of Western solidarity and a message of hope for reunification. While the Berlin Wall did not come down immediately following Reagan's speech, it added pressure and brought international attention to the issue of the wall's existence.

Two years later, in 1989, a series of events, including peaceful protests, led to the fall of the Berlin Wall. The removal of the wall marked a pivotal moment in history, and the subsequent reunification of East and West Germany followed in 1990.

President Reagan's "Tear Down This Wall" speech is remembered as a powerful statement of American leadership, principles, and commitment to the cause of freedom. It remains an iconic moment in the history of the Cold War.

**76. Operation Desert Storm was the US-led military campaign that aimed to liberate Kuwait from Iraqi occupation during the Gulf War (1990–1991). On January 16th, 1991, the US and its coalition allies launched a massive air campaign against Iraq, targeting military installations, communication centers, and strategic targets. This marked the beginning of the aerial phase of Operation Desert Storm. The coalition included countries such as the United Kingdom, France, Saudi Arabia, and many others, with the United States providing the bulk of the military forces.**

One of the most iconic moments of the Gulf War was the live coverage of the conflict by CNN. Journalist Peter Arnett, reporting from Baghdad, provided real-time updates and images of the airstrikes, bringing the war into living rooms worldwide.

On February 24th, 1991, the coalition launched a ground offensive to retake Kuwait. US Army General H. Norman Schwarzkopf, the commander of the coalition forces, orchestrated the campaign. The US military employed innovative tactics during the ground offensive, including the "left hook" strategy, which involved a flanking maneuver by the US and coalition forces to encircle and defeat the Iraqi Army.

The ground offensive was highly successful, and within a few days, Kuwait was liberated from Iraqi forces. The coalition had achieved its primary objective.

Following a hundred hours of ground combat, the Gulf War ended with a ceasefire on February 28th, 1991. Iraq's military capabilities were significantly degraded, but Saddam Hussein remained in power.

The US and its coalition allies demonstrated the effectiveness of a coordinated, multinational military force in addressing international conflicts. The Gulf War had a lasting impact on US military doctrine and operations, influencing future strategies and military engagements.

**77. On March 3rd, 1991, Rodney King, an African American man, was brutally beaten by four Los Angeles Police Department officers after a high-speed chase. The incident was captured on amateur video by a witness and later widely broadcast on television. The footage showed King being repeatedly struck with batons, kicked, and subjected to other forms of excessive force, even though he appeared to offer no resistance.**

The video ignited outrage and brought attention to issues of police brutality and racial injustice. When the officers involved were acquitted in a state criminal trial in April 1992, it sparked widespread protests and civil unrest in Los Angeles. The riots, which began on April 29th, 1992, lasted for several days and resulted in significant property damage, injuries, and loss of life.

Reginald Denny, a White truck driver, became another focal point of the riots after he was pulled from his truck and severely beaten by a group of individuals. The unrest highlighted long-standing racial tensions and socio-economic disparities in Los Angeles.

In the aftermath of the riots, federal charges were brought against the officers involved in the beating of Rodney King. In 1993, two of the officers were found guilty of violating King's civil rights, while the other two were acquitted.

Rodney King became a symbol of police misconduct and the need for reform in law enforcement. The incident and its aftermath contributed to increased scrutiny of police practices, discussions about racial profiling, and calls for reform in the criminal justice system. Rodney King's story became a powerful symbol of the ongoing struggle for civil rights and justice in the United States.

**Aftermath of the riots.**

**78. In 1994, Paula Jones, a former Arkansas state employee, filed a sexual harassment lawsuit against Bill Clinton, then the governor of Arkansas. Jones alleged that Clinton had made unwanted sexual advances toward her in 1991. Clinton denied the allegations, but the lawsuit led to a series of investigations that would eventually culminate in his impeachment by the House of Representatives.**

In 1996, Kenneth Starr, an independent counsel appointed by the attorney general, was tasked with investigating the Whitewater controversy, a scandal involving Clinton's investment in a failed real estate venture in Arkansas. During his investigation, Starr uncovered evidence of a sexual relationship between Clinton and White House intern Monica Lewinsky. In 1998, Starr began investigating whether Clinton had committed perjury by denying the relationship with Lewinsky under oath. Clinton also testified before a grand jury about the Lewinsky matter and was questioned about his efforts to have Lewinsky deny the relationship.

In December 1998, the House of Representatives impeached Clinton on charges of perjury and obstruction of justice. The perjury charge related to his testimony about the Lewinsky affair, while the obstruction of justice charge arose from his attempts to influence Lewinsky's testimony and conceal evidence. Clinton's trial in the Senate began in January 1999.

After weeks of testimony and debate, the Senate acquitted Clinton on both charges. He remained in office and completed his second term as president. While the Senate ultimately acquitted him, the impeachment process left a lasting stain on his legacy and further polarized the American political landscape.

**79. In August 1992, Randy Weaver, his wife Vicki, and their children were living on Ruby Ridge, a remote mountainous area in northern Idaho. The Weavers held anti-government and White supremacist views. Randy became a target of investigation by the Bureau of Alcohol, Tobacco, and Firearms (ATF) for selling illegal firearms.**

The situation escalated on August 21st, 1992, when federal agents attempted to arrest Randy Weaver for his firearms violations. The Weavers resisted arrest, and a shootout ensued. During the exchange of gunfire, Deputy US Marshal William Degan and Weaver's teenage son, Samuel, were killed.

The FBI became involved, and a standoff developed. The standoff lasted eleven days, during which negotiations between the Weavers and federal authorities took place. The situation further escalated when FBI sniper Lon Horiuchi shot and killed Vicki Weaver while she was inside the family's cabin.

The Ruby Ridge standoff drew widespread attention and criticism, with concerns raised about the use of force by federal agents and questions about the tactics employed during the standoff. The incident also fueled anti-government sentiments and became a rallying point for various militia and extremist groups.

The subsequent trials of Randy Weaver and Kevin Harris (a family friend involved in the shootout) ended with Weaver acquitted of most charges and Harris acquitted of all charges except for one count of aiding and abetting the voluntary manslaughter of a federal officer.

The Ruby Ridge standoff had a lasting impact on public perception of government actions and the use of force, contributing to debates about the appropriate role of law enforcement in dealing with individuals holding anti-government views. It remains a significant and controversial chapter in the history of law enforcement and the interactions between the government and citizens.

80. **On April 19th, 1995, the Alfred P. Murrah Federal Building in Oklahoma City burst into a monstrous plume of dust and debris. Timothy McVeigh, a veteran consumed by a toxic mix of anti-government anger and extremist beliefs, chose that building as his target, aiming to strike a blow against what he saw as a tyrannical state.**

Disillusioned with the military after Waco and Ruby Ridge, McVeigh embraced radical anti-government ideologies and was fueled by conspiracy theories and a deep distrust of authority. He found like-minded individuals in the fringes of the militia movement, where his simmering rage found validation and twisted purpose.

Driven by this concoction of anger and warped ideals, McVeigh planned his act with chilling precision. A Ryder truck packed with fertilizer and fuel became his weapon, the Murrah building, housing a daycare center and government offices, his chosen battlefield. On that fateful morning, he detonated the bomb, shattering lives and the tranquility of Oklahoma City.

Baylee Almon was just one year old at the time of the bombing. She was in the second-floor daycare center of the Murrah Federal Building when the explosion occurred. The blast caused a portion of the building to collapse, including the daycare area.

In the aftermath of the bombing, a powerful and heart-wrenching photograph was captured by Charles H. Porter IV, a photojournalist who happened to be at the scene. The photograph showed Oklahoma City firefighter Chris Fields holding Baylee Almon, who was covered in dust and debris, as he carried her to safety. Baylee was limp, and her tiny body was a stark contrast to the strength and determination shown by the firefighter.

Tragically, Baylee Almon did not survive the bombing and was one of the 168 people who lost their lives that day. She had just celebrated her first birthday the day before the explosion. The image of her rescue became an iconic symbol of the tragedy and the heroism displayed by first responders and ordinary citizens who rushed to help in the explosion's aftermath.

81. **On July 27th, 1996, during the Centennial Olympic Games in Atlanta, a bomb exploded in Centennial Olympic Park, a popular gathering place for spectators and athletes. The explosion occurred in the early morning hours during a concert attended by thousands of people. The blast resulted in two fatalities and injured over one hundred people, some of them critically.**

The immediate response to the bombing was characterized by the heroism of first responders, medical personnel, and volunteers who provided assistance to the injured. Security guard Richard Jewell discovered the suspicious backpack containing the bomb before it exploded. His quick thinking and evacuation efforts likely saved many lives.

Initially, Richard Jewell was hailed as a hero for his actions, but he later became a suspect in the investigation due to a profiling analysis conducted by the FBI. His life was profoundly impacted by the media frenzy and suspicion surrounding him.

In 1997, Eric Robert Rudolph, a domestic terrorist, was arrested and subsequently pleaded guilty to the Centennial Olympic Park bombing, as well as other bombings. He was motivated by anti-abortion and anti-gay beliefs.

The bombing at the 1996 Summer Olympics underscored the need for enhanced security measures at major sporting events and public gatherings. Richard Jewell, who was wrongly accused in the initial stages of the investigation, later cleared his name, but the experience profoundly affected his life. He became an advocate for civil liberties and privacy rights.

The Centennial Olympic Park bombing was a tragic event that marred the 1996 Summer Olympics but also highlighted the resilience and heroism of those who responded to the crisis. It remains an important chapter in the history of both the Olympic Games and domestic terrorism in the United States.

# Section 9 – A Defining Era: Transformative Events in American History from 2001 to 2021

In the years spanning from 2001 to 2021, America experienced a series of transformative events. The devastating 9/11 terrorist attacks reshaped the nation's foreign policy, leading to the War on Terror and military interventions in Afghanistan and Iraq. The financial crisis of 2008 provoked economic turmoil. The rise of social media also left a lasting impact on American society.

In this section, discover some interesting stories from America's not-so-distant past.

**82. On September 11th, 2001, nineteen militants associated with the Islamic extremist group al-Qaeda hijacked four commercial airplanes and carried out suicide attacks against targets in the United States.**

The hijackers, most of whom were citizens of Saudi Arabia, boarded the planes armed with box cutters and knives. Once airborne, they took control of the cockpits and diverted the planes from their original destinations. At 8:46 a.m., American Airlines Flight 11 crashed into the north tower of the World Trade Center, followed by United Airlines Flight 175 at 9:03 a.m., which struck the south tower. Both towers collapsed within two hours, destroying surrounding buildings and damaging others.

At 9:37 a.m., American Airlines Flight 77 crashed into the western side of the Pentagon, causing a partial collapse of the building. Passengers and crew members aboard United Airlines Flight 93, which was headed for Washington, DC, fought back against the hijackers and regained control of the plane. The plane crashed in a field near Shanksville, Pennsylvania, at 10:03 a.m., killing all forty-four people on board.

Nearly three thousand people were killed in the attacks, which triggered major US initiatives to combat terrorism and defined the presidency of George W. Bush. The Bush administration argued that the threat of terrorism required the use of enhanced interrogation techniques, which critics labeled as torture. The administration also expanded domestic and international surveillance programs, raising concerns about privacy rights.

The 9/11 attacks were the deadliest terrorist attack in human history and had a profound impact on the United States and the world. The attacks led to the launch of the War on Terror, which included the invasion of Afghanistan and the overthrow of the Taliban government. The attacks also led to increased security measures at airports and other public places worldwide.

**The explosion after the plane hit the South Tower.**

*https://commons.wikimedia.org/wiki/File:Explosion_following_the_plane_impact_into_the_South_Tower_(WTC_2)_-_B6019~11.jpg*

**83. In response to 9/11, the United States began military operations in Afghanistan, marking the beginning of the War on Terror. The United States' involvement in Afghanistan began on October 7th, 2001, with the launch of Operation Enduring Freedom, a military operation aimed at dismantling the al-Qaeda terrorist network and overthrowing the Taliban regime that had harbored them. The US-led coalition quickly achieved its initial objectives, removing the Taliban from power and establishing a new Afghan government. However, the US and its allies remained bogged down in Afghanistan for nearly two decades, facing a persistent insurgency and struggling to stabilize the country.**

The US military went to other places as well. For years, intelligence agencies and special operations units worked to locate and apprehend Osama bin Laden, who had been evading capture since the attacks on September 11th, 2001. The search involved complex intelligence gathering, surveillance, and collaboration among various agencies.

The breakthrough in locating bin Laden came through years of tireless efforts and intelligence work. The Central Intelligence Agency (CIA) gradually pieced together information about a compound in Abbottabad, Pakistan, where they suspected bin Laden might be hiding. The compound, situated in a residential area near a military academy, raised suspicions due to its high walls, limited access, and lack of communication with the outside world.

In May 2011, President Barack Obama authorized a covert operation to raid the compound. On May 2nd, US Navy SEAL Team Six conducted a daring nighttime raid, penetrating Pakistani airspace without prior notification. The SEALs engaged in a firefight with those inside the compound, resulting in the death of Osama bin Laden.

The successful operation was a significant moment in the War on Terror, marking the end of a nearly decade-long hunt for the mastermind of the 9/11 attacks. The news of bin Laden's death was met with widespread relief and a sense of closure for many who had lost loved ones in the 2001 attacks.

The story of the hunt for Osama bin Laden and the operation that led to his death is a testament to the perseverance of intelligence and military professionals in pursuing justice and responding to acts of terrorism. The operation showcased the capabilities of special forces and highlighted the complex nature of counterterrorism efforts in the modern era.

**84.** **The Iraq War, also known as Operation Iraqi Freedom, was a conflict that began in 2003 when a US-led coalition invaded Iraq to remove President Saddam Hussein from power. The war was primarily driven by concerns about Iraq's alleged possession of weapons of mass destruction (WMDs) and its links to terrorism. After Saddam Hussein's regime was toppled, Iraq faced a prolonged period of insurgency and instability, ultimately leading to the withdrawal of US troops in 2011.**

During the Iraq War, an extraordinary act of bravery involved Private First Class Ross McGinnis, a US Army soldier. On December 4th, 2006, in Baghdad, Iraq, McGinnis was manning the machine gun turret of a Humvee while on patrol with his fellow soldiers. As the patrol moved through a crowded marketplace, an insurgent on a nearby rooftop threw a hand grenade into their Humvee.

McGinnis had a split-second decision to make. He could have jumped out of the turret to save himself, but instead, he selflessly sacrificed his life to protect his fellow soldiers. With incredible courage, McGinnis shouted a warning to his comrades and then used his own body to cover the live grenade, absorbing the full force of the explosion. His heroic actions saved the lives of four other soldiers in the vehicle, who survived the blast with only minor injuries.

Private First Class Ross McGinnis posthumously received the Medal of Honor, the highest military decoration in the United States, for his extraordinary bravery and sacrifice. His story serves as a powerful reminder of the selflessness and valor displayed by many individuals in the face of danger during times of conflict.

**85.** **In September 2008, the global financial crisis peaked with Lehman Brothers' bankruptcy, causing widespread economic turmoil, job losses, and a severe recession in the United States and much of Europe.**

Lehman Brothers was a venerable Wall Street investment bank with a history dating back to the mid-19th century. However, by 2008, it found itself heavily exposed to the subprime mortgage market, which was in the midst of a significant downturn. The bank had invested heavily in mortgage-backed securities and faced mounting losses as the housing market declined. As Lehman Brothers faced severe financial distress in September 2008, the US government was reluctant to provide a bailout, unlike the interventions that had occurred with other financial institutions.

On September 15th, 2008, Lehman Brothers filed for Chapter 11 bankruptcy, marking one of the largest bankruptcies in US history. The collapse of Lehman Brothers had profound and far-reaching consequences. The interconnectedness of financial institutions meant that Lehman's bankruptcy had a domino effect, spreading fear and uncertainty throughout the financial system. The crisis prompted unprecedented government interventions, including the Troubled Asset Relief Program (TARP) in the United States, aimed to stabilize the financial sector.

The events of 2008 ultimately led to a severe economic recession with global repercussions, impacting individuals, businesses, and economies around the world. Lehman Brothers' downfall became a symbol of the excesses and risks within the financial industry, and the crisis highlighted the need for regulatory reforms to prevent a similar meltdown in the future. The 2008 financial crisis remains a significant chapter in economic history, influencing financial regulations and shaping perceptions of risk and responsibility in the financial sector.

**86. On January 15th, 2009, US Airways Flight 1549, an Airbus A320, struck a flock of Canada geese shortly after takeoff from New York City's LaGuardia Airport. Both engines lost power, and Captain Chesley "Sully" Sullenberger and First Officer Jeffrey Skiles faced a dire situation.**

With no engine power and limited options, Captain Sullenberger made the quick and daring decision to perform an emergency water landing in the frigid waters of the Hudson River. Remarkably, all 155 passengers and crew on board survived the emergency landing and were able to evacuate the aircraft onto the wings and into nearby rescue boats.

Captain Sullenberger and First Officer Skiles were hailed as heroes for their cool-headed and skillful response to the crisis. Their experience and training played a critical role in the safe outcome.

The incident became a global media sensation, with the rescue efforts and interviews with passengers and crew members capturing the public's attention. The National Transportation Safety Board (NTSB) conducted an investigation, which confirmed the bird strike as the cause of the engine failure.

Both Captain Sullenberger and First Officer Skiles received numerous awards and recognition for their actions. The "Miracle on the Hudson" is a captivating and heartwarming story of heroism and quick thinking in the face of a life-threatening emergency. It demonstrated the importance of well-trained and experienced flight crews and showcased the potential for positive outcomes even in the most challenging situations.

**The evacuation of the plane after landing in the Hudson River.**

*Greg L, CC BY 2.0 <https://creativecommons.org/licenses/by/2.0>, via Wikimedia Commons;*
https://commons.wikimedia.org/wiki/File:US_Airways_Flight_1549_(N106US)_after_crashing_into_the_Hudson_River_(crop_2).jpg)

**87. Jim Obergefell and John Arthur were a same-sex couple from Cincinnati, Ohio, who had been together for over two decades. However, their relationship faced significant legal and societal challenges due to the lack of marriage equality in Ohio at the time. John was terminally ill with ALS (amyotrophic lateral sclerosis), and the couple's greatest wish was to have their marriage legally recognized before John's health deteriorated further.**

In 2013, with the help of friends and family, Jim and John chartered a medical plane and flew to Maryland, where same-sex marriage was legal. They were married on the tarmac of Baltimore-Washington International Airport while John was lying on a gurney inside the plane.

After their wedding, Jim Obergefell and John Arthur filed a lawsuit challenging Ohio's refusal to recognize their marriage on John's death certificate. This case was consolidated with similar cases from other states and became known as *Obergefell v. Hodges*.

John Arthur died in 2013, but that didn't stop Obergefell; in fact, he became even more determined to see same-sex marriage be legalized.

On June 26th, 2015, the US Supreme Court issued a historic ruling in favor of marriage equality, declaring that same-sex marriage was a constitutional right nationwide. The decision meant that Jim Obergefell's marriage to John Arthur was legally recognized, allowing him to be listed as the surviving spouse on John's death certificate.

Jim Obergefell's personal journey to ensure that his marriage was recognized, even in the face of tragedy, became a powerful symbol of the fight for marriage equality in the United States. His dedication to love, justice, and civil rights played a significant role in the Supreme Court's landmark decision in *Obergefell v. Hodges*.

**88. The Great Recession of 2008, triggered by the financial crisis, cast a long shadow on American society. Beyond the economic hardship, it severely affected public trust in key institutions, particularly banks and government agencies.**

At its core, Occupy Wall Street wasn't simply a protest against the immediate economic crisis; it was a reaction to a perceived wider systemic injustice. Average Americans struggling with job losses, foreclosures, and dwindling savings witnessed a financial elite who were seemingly unscathed, their wealth protected by bailouts and regulations that appeared skewed in their favor. The image of Wall Street profiting from the wreckage while Main Street bore the brunt of the pain fueled a potent combination of anger and resentment.

Occupy Wall Street, with its diverse mix of participants, became a platform for expressing this collective disillusionment. The iconic "We are the 99%" slogan resonated deeply, uniting individuals under a shared sense of being wronged by a system that favored the privileged. Their encampments, such as the one at Zuccotti Park in New York City, became physical shelters and symbolic displays of dissent, challenging the power dynamics of the financial system and demanding greater accountability.

Many of the protesters showed a keen knowledge of history. During the 1929 stock market crash, several stockbrokers were said to have jumped from office windows on Wall Street since their entire fortune had been destroyed in just one or two days. Outside many of the large brokerage houses in 2008, some protesters held large signs saying "JUMP!" showing the anger many felt for the greed, mismanagement, and lack of government oversight that caused the financial crisis.

While Occupy Wall Street didn't directly alter the financial landscape, its impact extended beyond the immediate protests. It sparked important conversations about income inequality, corporate accountability, and the need for financial reform. It injected a dose of skepticism into public discourse, forcing institutions to acknowledge and address the concerns of ordinary citizens. Moreover, it demonstrated the power of collective action, proving that even a disparate group of individuals bound by shared frustration could raise their voices and make their concerns heard.

**89. The emergence of social media gained significant traction in the 2000s, with platforms like Facebook and Twitter becoming increasingly popular. Social media revolutionized communication, information sharing, activism, and how people connect and interact globally.**

But how did it start? Facebook gets the credit for making social media popular and accessible. Mark Zuckerberg and his college roommates Andrew McCollum, Eduardo Saverin, Chris Hughes, and Dustin Moskovitz launched Facebook from their dormitory at Harvard University in February 2004. Originally called "The Facebook," the platform was initially created as a way for Harvard students to connect with each other online. The site quickly gained popularity within the Harvard community, and expansion to other universities and colleges followed.

The turning point for Facebook's rapid expansion came in September 2006 when it opened its doors to the general public, allowing anyone with a valid email address to join. This move marked a significant departure from its earlier exclusivity to college students. The decision to open up the platform was driven by the desire to reach a broader audience and increase user engagement.

As Facebook continued to grow, it introduced new features, such as the news feed in 2006 and the like button in 2009, further enhancing the user experience. The platform's user base expanded globally, and by 2012, Facebook had reached one billion active users.

Facebook's success has had a profound impact on the way people communicate, share information, and connect online. It has also played a role in shaping the broader landscape of social media, influencing the development of other platforms, and contributing to the rise of a social media-centric culture in the 21st century.

**90. In December 2019, President Trump signed the National Defense Authorization Act (NDAA) into law for the fiscal year of 2020. While the NDAA is a routine piece of legislation that funds the US military, this particular signing had a unique aspect that drew attention.**

The John S. McCain National Defense Authorization Act for fiscal year 2019 included a provision requiring the US Navy to name a warship after Senator John McCain, who had served as a naval aviator during the Vietnam War. Senator McCain was known for his distinguished military service and later as a prominent politician.

During the signing ceremony for the NDAA in December 2019, President Trump did not mention Senator McCain by name nor acknowledge the ship naming provision. However, the story garnered attention when it was reported that a Navy destroyer, the USS *John S.*

*McCain*, had been stationed in Japan, and a tarp had been placed over the ship's name to obscure it during President Trump's visit to a US Navy base in Yokosuka, Japan.

The incident sparked a debate about whether the tarp was placed intentionally to avoid mentioning Senator McCain's name in the president's presence or if it was for routine maintenance reasons. President Trump later tweeted that he was unaware of the tarp and had not requested it.

The tarp incident became a topic of discussion and scrutiny, reflecting the complex relationship between President Trump and Senator McCain, who had been a vocal critic of the president's policies and leadership style. It also highlighted the broader conversations around the intersection of politics, the military, and the recognition of public figures.

### 91. The United States maintained a military presence in Afghanistan from 2001 to 2021. Its presence in the country began after the 9/11 attacks. The mission initially aimed to dismantle al-Qaeda and remove the Taliban regime from power.

In February 2020, the Trump administration reached an agreement with the Taliban, setting a timeline for the withdrawal of US and NATO forces in exchange for Taliban commitments, including not harboring terrorists. In April 2021, President Joe Biden announced that the US would complete its withdrawal by August 31st, 2021, ending nearly two decades of military involvement. The decision faced both support and criticism.

As the US withdrawal accelerated in 2021, the Taliban made rapid territorial gains. By August, they captured Kabul, leading to the collapse of the Afghan government.

The US and its allies initiated an emergency evacuation operation from Kabul airport to evacuate US citizens, Afghan allies, and vulnerable populations. The evacuation faced challenges due to the security situation and the sheer number of people needing assistance.

The US completed its military withdrawal by August 31st, 2021, marking the end of its combat mission in Afghanistan. The situation raised concerns about the fate of Afghan women, girls, and minorities under Taliban rule, as well as potential humanitarian crises.

Despite the military withdrawal, diplomatic efforts continued to address Afghanistan's future, including negotiations and international discussions. The withdrawal from Afghanistan was a complex and controversial process with significant implications for US foreign policy, regional stability, and the Afghan people. It marked the end of a lengthy military engagement and raised questions about the future of Afghanistan and the fight against terrorism in the region.

# Section 10 – American Pop Culture: A World of Entertainment

Today, people are obsessed with celebrities, TV shows, movies, sports, and video games. That is not surprising. People have been invested in the lives of famous people, sports games, and media for millennia.

In this section, we will take a look at some interesting stories about American celebrities and pop culture.

**92. In the early 20th century, during the height of the silent film era, one of the most iconic and enduring cinematic characters was created – Charlie Chaplin's "Tramp." The character was known for his distinctive appearance, featuring a bowler hat, a toothbrush mustache, a cane, and oversized shoes.**

In 1914, when Chaplin was working at Keystone Studios, he was tasked with creating a new character for his next film. He quickly put together the Tramp's signature look using wardrobe items from the studio's costume department with just a few minutes to spare before shooting. Chaplin's Tramp character made its debut in the film *Kid Auto Races at Venice* (1914), and it was an instant success with audiences. The character's universal appeal and relatability transcended language barriers, making Chaplin an international superstar.

Over the years, the Tramp appeared in numerous silent films, including classics like *The Kid* (1921), *City Lights* (1931), and *Modern Times* (1936). The character was a symbol of resilience and optimism in the face of adversity, reflecting the challenges and hopes of the Great Depression era.

Charlie Chaplin's creation of the Tramp character remains an enduring and iconic contribution to the history of cinema. The character's influence can still be seen in popular culture today, and it serves as a testament to the power of silent films to convey emotion and connect with audiences worldwide.

**Charlie Chaplin as the Tramp.**
*https://en.wikipedia.org/wiki/File:Charlie_Chaplin.jpg*

**93. In the 1920s, Jack Dempsey, known as the "Manassa Mauler," was one of the world's most celebrated and feared boxers. His famous bout against Luis Ángel Firpo on September 14th, 1923, became a historic moment in boxing history.**

The fight took place at the Polo Grounds in New York City. Dempsey was the reigning World Heavyweight Champion, while Firpo was a hard-hitting Argentine heavyweight contender. What made this fight particularly memorable was the incredible first round.

The first round of the fight was nothing short of chaotic and exhilarating. Firpo, known for his aggressive style, unleashed a series of powerful punches that had Dempsey on the ropes. At one point in the round, Firpo landed a massive right hand that sent Dempsey crashing through the ropes and out of the ring. Dempsey's head narrowly missed hitting a typewriter on press row.

Dempsey's trainer, Jack Kearns, and the fight's referee, Johnny Gallagher, helped him back into the ring. According to the rules at the time, Dempsey had twenty seconds to return to the ring after being knocked out. He made it back just in time.

Despite the dramatic knockdown, Dempsey eventually regained his composure and fought back. He knocked Firpo down multiple times during the second round, and the fight was finally stopped, with Dempsey declared the winner.

Jack Dempsey's victory in his fight against Firpo was a testament to his resilience and punching power. It remains one of the most iconic moments in boxing history, showcasing the unpredictability and drama of the sport. The fight solidified Dempsey's status as a legendary figure in the world of boxing.

**94. Bob Hope was one of the most iconic and beloved entertainers of the 20th century, known for his career in vaudeville, radio, film, and television. He became especially renowned for his decades-long commitment to entertaining American military personnel serving overseas.**

Bob Hope's involvement with the USO (United Service Organizations) began during World War II when he performed his first show for servicemen and women in 1941. Throughout his career, he went on to entertain troops during World War II, the Korean War, the Vietnam War, and other conflicts. Hope's USO tours were extensive and covered various war zones and military bases worldwide. He traveled to places in the Pacific, Europe, the Middle East, and Southeast Asia, bringing laughter and a touch of home to American troops stationed far from their families.

Bob Hope's performances were more than just entertainment; they were a source of comfort and morale-boosting for servicemen and women in challenging and often dangerous circumstances. His shows provided a brief respite from the rigors of military life.

In addition to his performances, Bob Hope and his wife, Dolores, worked tirelessly to support military causes and raise funds for veterans. They were dedicated advocates for veterans' rights and welfare.

Bob Hope's dedication to the USO and the troops left a lasting legacy. He made his last USO tour in 1991, at the age of eighty-eight, making him one of the longest-serving supporters of the organization. The Bob Hope Airport in Burbank, California, was named in his honor, and he received numerous awards and recognitions for his contributions to the military and entertainment.

Bob Hope's commitment to bringing joy and laughter to the men and women serving in the armed forces exemplifies the power of entertainment to uplift spirits during challenging times. His USO tours remain a shining example of the positive impact that celebrities and entertainers can have on the lives of military personnel and their families.

**95. In 1958, at the height of his music career, Elvis Presley received his draft notice to serve in the United States Army. Despite his fame and success, he didn't seek special treatment and chose to fulfill his military obligations like any other draftee.**

Elvis joined the US Army on March 24th, 1958, and completed basic training at Fort Hood, Texas. During training, he endured the rigors of military life, including marching drills, physical fitness training, and marksmanship. Elvis's service didn't go unnoticed by the media and the public. His military service became major news stories, and it was widely reported that he had cut his famous sideburns and received a regulation military haircut.

While stationed in Germany from 1958 to 1960, Elvis served as a member of the 3rd Armored Division and continued to perform music during his off-duty hours. He also met his future wife, Priscilla Beaulieu, who lived in Germany at the time.

Despite his celebrity status, Elvis was treated like any other soldier and not given special privileges. He was often seen socializing with fellow soldiers and participating in military activities.

In 1960, after completing his two-year service, Elvis received an honorable discharge from the Army. He returned to his music career and went on to achieve even greater success in the entertainment industry. Elvis's military service is remembered not only for his willingness to serve his country but also for its impact on his personal life and career. It demonstrated his commitment to fulfilling his citizen duties and ability to adapt to different circumstances.

**96. In the early 1950s, Walt Disney had a vision of creating a groundbreaking amusement park that would revolutionize the world of entertainment. He envisioned a place where both children and adults could enjoy attractions and entertainment and be able to immerse themselves in the magic of storytelling.**

Walt's dream of a theme park was met with skepticism from many investors and industry experts. They believed amusement parks were dirty, chaotic, and unsuitable for families. Undeterred, Walt Disney was determined to turn his dream into a reality. He embarked on a mission to secure financing for his ambitious project.

Walt Disney faced numerous rejections from banks and potential investors. Many dismissed his idea as too risky. This period of his life became known as "Walt's Folly." However, Walt Disney's determination paid off when he successfully convinced ABC, the television network, to partner with him. In exchange for providing ABC with a weekly television show, Walt received financial support for Disneyland.

On July 17th, 1955, Disneyland opened its doors in Anaheim, California. Although it faced a rough opening day (known as "Black Sunday"), the park became a smash hit. The park featured various themed lands, including Adventureland, Fantasyland, and Tomorrowland, along with iconic attractions like Sleeping Beauty's Castle and the Jungle Cruise.

Disneyland became the prototype for future theme parks worldwide and solidified Walt Disney's reputation as an entertainment visionary. Today, Disneyland has expanded into a global brand, with multiple parks and resorts in different countries, each offering its own unique attractions and experiences.

**97. In the late 1950s, Ruth Handler, co-founder of the toy company Mattel, noticed that her daughter, Barbara, often played with paper dolls and gave them adult roles. Handler envisioned creating a three-dimensional adult-like doll that could serve as a role model for young girls.**

Inspired by a German doll called Bild Lilli, Handler and her husband Elliot set out to create a doll that was both fashionable and adult in appearance. They named the doll "Barbie" after their daughter.

In 1959, Mattel introduced the Barbie doll at the American International Toy Fair in New York City. The doll's official full name was Barbie Millicent Roberts, and she was marketed as a teenage fashion model.

Barbie quickly became a sensation. Her first outfits included a black-and-white striped swimsuit, sunglasses, and high heels, reflecting the fashion trends of the time. Over the years, Barbie has undergone numerous transformations and taken on various careers, fashion styles, and interests. She became a doctor, astronaut, teacher, athlete, and more, reflecting evolving societal roles for women.

Barbie's success extended beyond the toy industry. She became a cultural icon and inspired countless collectors, artists, and even fashion designers. Barbie dolls have been featured in various forms of media, including movies, TV shows, and books.

Despite occasional controversies related to body image and diversity, Barbie remains one of the world's most recognizable and enduring toy brands. In recent years, efforts have been made to diversify the Barbie line by introducing dolls of different ethnicities, body types, and careers.

The invention of the Barbie doll and its enduring impact on American pop culture is a fascinating story that highlights the influence of toys and fashion on society and the evolving representation of women in media and playtime. A movie about Barbie was made in 2023; it was a hit — a record-breaking box office success earning over $1.4 billion worldwide.

**98. In the 1960s, during the height of the Vietnam War, Muhammad Ali, then known as Cassius Clay, became not only a boxing champion but also a prominent figure in the civil rights and anti-war movements.**

In 1966, Ali received a notice for the military draft, which required him to serve in the US Army and potentially be deployed to Vietnam. At the time, Ali was the reigning World Heavyweight Champion. However, Ali refused to comply with the draft, citing his religious beliefs as a member of the Nation of Islam and his opposition to the war in Vietnam. He famously declared, "I ain't got no quarrel with them Viet Cong."

Ali's refusal to be drafted into the military led to a legal battle and significant controversy. During his prime years, he was stripped of his boxing titles and banned from the sport. Despite facing imprisonment and the loss of his boxing career, Ali stood firm in his convictions. He continued to speak out against the war and racial injustice in America.

In 1971, the US Supreme Court unanimously overturned Ali's conviction for draft evasion, citing that his beliefs as a conscientious objector were sincere and protected by the First Amendment. Following his legal victory, Muhammad Ali returned to boxing. He staged an epic comeback, culminating in the legendary "Thrilla in Manila" against Joe Frazier, a brutal three-part brawl that tested both men's limits.

Then came the "Rumble in the Jungle" in 1974. A thirty-two-year-old Ali, past his prime, faced the seemingly unstoppable George Foreman in Zaire. In a spectacle watched by millions, Ali deployed his "rope-a-dope" strategy, letting Foreman tire himself out before unleashing a devastating knockout in the eighth round. He reclaimed his title, proving that even a fallen champion could rise again.

Muhammad Ali's refusal to be drafted and his principled stand against the Vietnam War is a testament to his courage, conviction, and willingness to sacrifice his career for his beliefs. His stance made him a symbol of resistance to the war and a powerful advocate for civil rights and social justice.

**Muhammad Ali and Joe Frazier's promotional photo.**
*https://commons.wikimedia.org/wiki/File:Gatti,_Reutemann,_Cap,_Clay_y_Frazier_-_El_Gr%C3%A1fico_2831_3.jpg*

99. **On February 9th, 1964, The Beatles made their historic debut on the American television program The Ed Sullivan Show. This appearance is often regarded as a pivotal moment in the British Invasion and the band's rise to international superstardom.**

Approximately seventy-three million viewers, or over 34 percent of the American population at the time, tuned in to watch The Beatles perform live on *The Ed Sullivan Show*. It remains one of the most-watched television broadcasts in US history.

The Beatles performed a set that included "All My Loving," "Till There Was You," "She Loves You," "I Saw Her Standing There," and "I Want to Hold Your Hand." Their energetic performance and charismatic presence captivated the audience. The screams of teenage girls in the studio and the electrifying atmosphere during the performance were captured by the cameras, creating an indelible image of "Beatlemania."

Following their Ed Sullivan appearance, The Beatles embarked on a whirlwind tour of the United States, performing in major cities and receiving an overwhelmingly positive reception. Among the frenzied crowd was fourteen-year-old future Oscar-nominated actress Sigourney Weaver, who already harbored dreams of the stage. She remembers The Beatles as "explosions of mop hair and energy." Their arrival must have felt like an alien invasion, not one of spaceships, but one of catchy tunes and teenage rebellion.

Their music, style, and personalities resonated with American youth. The Beatles' success on *The Ed Sullivan Show* marked the beginning of a wave of British bands and artists, including The Rolling Stones, The Who, and The Kinks, who achieved tremendous success in the United States during the British Invasion. The cultural impact of the British Invasion extended beyond music, influencing fashion, art, and youth culture in the 1960s and beyond. It helped bridge the gap between the United States and the United Kingdom, fostering a fascination with British pop culture.

**100. Jaws, directed by Steven Spielberg and released in 1975, is widely considered the first summer blockbuster and one of the greatest films in cinematic history. However, the making of the film was fraught with challenges and setbacks.**

The film, based on Peter Benchley's novel of the same name, tells the story of a small coastal town terrorized by a great white shark. Spielberg, a relatively young and unproven director at the time, was hired to helm the project.

One of the primary challenges during production was the mechanical shark used for the film, nicknamed "Bruce" after Spielberg's lawyer. The shark, which was supposed to be the film's central antagonist, suffered numerous technical malfunctions and delays, often leaving the production team frustrated. The mechanical shark's problems forced Spielberg to adopt a more suspenseful approach by showing the shark sparingly and relying on the iconic John Williams score to build tension. This decision became a defining element of the film's success.

Shooting on the open ocean presented additional challenges. The crew faced unpredictable weather, seasickness, and difficulties in capturing underwater footage.

The film's budget and shooting schedule also ballooned, far exceeding initial estimates. The production was initially slated for a 55-day shoot but extended to 159 days.

Despite the numerous obstacles, Spielberg's determination and creativity, combined with the commitment of the cast and crew, paid off. *Jaws* was completed and released in the summer of 1975. The movie became a massive success upon its release, breaking box office records and earning critical acclaim. It was a cultural phenomenon that not only revitalized the career of its director but also profoundly impacted the film industry by ushering in the era of blockbuster films.

The film's success led to sequels, theme park attractions, and a lasting legacy in popular culture. It also demonstrated the power of suspense and storytelling over visual effects, proving that limitations can lead to creative innovation.

**101. In the early 1980s, the video game industry was booming, with home consoles like the Atari 2600 and a flood of new games hitting the market. It seemed like everyone was getting into gaming, and arcades were thriving.**

However, the industry's rapid growth led to oversaturation and quality control issues. Many video games released during this period were of poor quality and often rushed to market to capitalize on the gaming craze.

In 1983, the video game market in the United States suffered a significant crash. It began with a combination of factors. First, too many games were available, causing consumer confusion and leading to a lack of demand for new titles. Many games released during this time were subpar, leading to disappointment among players. Additionally, the cost of video games and consoles was relatively high, making them less accessible to the average consumer. Personal computers, like the Commodore 64 and the Apple II, began to offer more sophisticated gaming experiences, diverting attention from traditional consoles.

As a result of these factors, sales of video games and consoles plummeted. Major companies, including Atari, suffered huge financial losses. To combat the crisis, Atari attempted to dispose of unsold inventory of their game *E.T. the Extra-Terrestrial* by burying thousands of unsold cartridges in a landfill in Alamogordo, New Mexico, a story that later became the stuff of legend.

The crash led to the bankruptcy of several video game companies and the downsizing of others. It also profoundly impacted the industry's reputation and consumer trust. However, the crash ultimately paved the way for a fresh start and the emergence of the Nintendo Entertainment System (NES) in 1985. Nintendo's strict quality control, iconic games like *Super Mario Bros.*, and a "Seal of Quality" certification system helped revitalize the industry and rebuild consumer confidence.

# Conclusion

As we bring our journey through American history to a close, it becomes abundantly clear that this nation is a mosaic of seemingly disparate yet deeply interconnected narratives. From the humble beginnings of colonization to the untamed spirit of Manifest Destiny, from the crucible of the Civil War to the triumphs of the civil rights movement, each chapter represents a thread woven into the vibrant tapestry of American society. These stories serve as a reminder that this nation is not just a mere collection of dates, names, and events but also a living, breathing story of resilience, determination, and everlasting pursuit of freedom.

As we move forward, let us embrace past lessons and strive to amplify the voices that have long been silenced, ensuring that the arc of American history bends ever closer toward justice, equality, and unity.

If you enjoyed this book, a review on Amazon would be greatly appreciated because it would mean a lot to hear from you.

**To leave a review:**

1. Open your camera app.
2. Point your mobile device at the QR code.
3. The review page will appear in your web browser.

*Thanks for your support!*

# Check out another book in the series

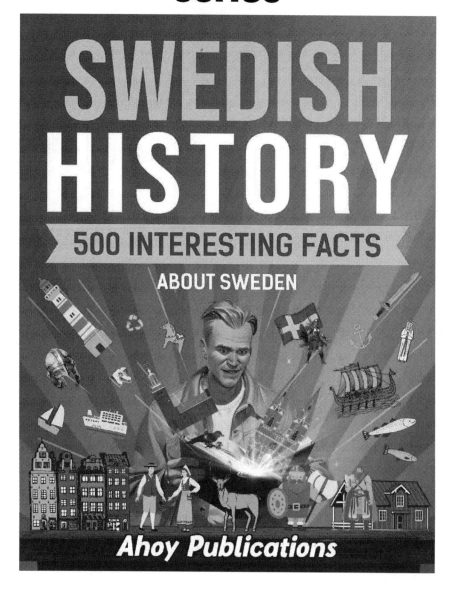

# Welcome Aboard, Check Out This Limited-Time Free Bonus!

Ahoy, reader! Welcome to the Ahoy Publications family, and thanks for snagging a copy of this book! Since you've chosen to join us on this journey, we'd like to offer you something special.

Check out the link below for a FREE e-book filled with delightful facts about American History.

But that's not all - you'll also have access to our exclusive email list with even more free e-books and insider knowledge. Well, what are ye waiting for? Click the link below to join and set sail toward exciting adventures in American History.

Access your bonus here: https://ahoypublications.com/

Or, Scan the QR code!

# Sources and Additional References

Thornton, Russell. American Indian Holocaust and Survival: A Population History Since 1492. University of Oklahoma Press, 2015.

Thornton, Russell. The Cherokees: A Population History. University of Nebraska Press, 1990.

White, Bruce M. The Stone Age of the Great Lakes. University of Michigan Press, 1965.

King, Mary Elizabeth. Ceramics for the Archaeologist. Smithsonian Institution Press, 1975.

Smith, Andrea. Native Americans: A History. St. Martin's Press, 2011.

Kickingbird, Kirke, and Herbert T. Hoover. Indian Traders of the Southeastern Spanish Borderlands: Panton, Leslie & Company and John Forbes & Company, 1783-1847. University of Oklahoma Press, 2011.

Kostiainen, Vaino. The Development of American Agriculture: A Historical Analysis. University of Minnesota Press, 2008.

Anderson, Carol. The Indian Way: Learning to Communicate with Mother Earth. Santa Fe, NM: Sunstone Press, 2014.

Dominguez, Virgil. Native American Art in the Twentieth Century. Austin, TX: University of Texas Press, 1998.

White, Richard. The Middle Ground: Indians, Empires, and Republics in the Great Lakes Region, 1650-1815. Cambridge: Cambridge University Press, 1991.

Sault, Carole A. Native American Medicine. ABC-CLIO, Inc., 2000.

Orenstein, Ruth M. Native American History. Greenwood Press, 1996.

Deloria, Vine, Jr. and David E. Wilkins. American Indian Politics and the American Political System. Rowman & Littlefield, 2000.

Mohawk, John. Native American Spirituality. Viking, 1993.

Orenstein, Ruth M. American Indian Arts and Crafts. Greenwood Press, 1994.

Nelson, S. The Role of Medicine Men and Women in Native American Culture. The Rosen Publishing Group, 2011.

Ross, David. Buffalo Hunt: Native American Hunting and the Sacred Buffalo. Capstone Press, 2007.

Stein, Rob. Native American Migration Patterns. Facts on File, 2006.

Dunn, Jill. Native American Sustainable Agriculture Practices. The Rosen Publishing Group, 2010.

Bierhorst, John. Native American Spirituality: A Critical Reader. University of Arizona Press, 2008.

Stone, Lynn M. American Indian History: An Introduction. ABC-CLIO, 2015.

"Exploring America: The Story of the U.S.A.". Raintree, 2014.

"Jamestown Settlement." Encyclopedia Virginia, http://encyclopediavirginia.org/Jamestown_Settlement#start_entry.

Taylor, Alan. The Civil War of 1812: American Citizens, British Subjects, Irish Rebels, & Indian Allies. Vintage, 2012.

Helgerson Richard L., et al., eds. "Spanish Exploration and Settlement in North America (1492–1763)." The Oxford Companion to United States History, Oxford University Press, 2001; accessed April 28 2020 from Encyclopedia Britannica online: https://www.britannica.com/topic/list-of-SpaniardsettlementsinNorthAmerica.

"Dutch Colonies in North America (1609–74)." Encyclopedia Britannica, March 15 2019; Accessed April 28 2020 from https://www.britannica.com/topic/list-of-Dutchcoloniesinnorthamericahistory.

Bradford, William. Of Plymouth Plantation. Edited by Samuel Eliot Morison, Alfred A. Knopf, 2020.

Weber, David J. The Spanish Frontier in North America. Yale University Press, 1992.

Robinson, Donald L., ed. Slavery in the Structure of American Politics, 1765-1820. Harcourt Brace Jovanovich, 1971.

Wood, Gordon S. The American Revolution: A History. Modern Library, 2002.

Foner, Eric. Give Me Liberty!: An American History. W. W. Norton & Company, 2017.

McConnell, M. A Country of Vast Designs: James K. Polk, the Mexican War and the Conquest of the American Continent. New York, NY: Simon & Schuster, 2016.

Gerson, Noel B. The Northwest Ordinance: A Bicentennial Handbook. Scarecrow Press, 1987.

Ambrosius, Lloyd E. Woodrow Wilson and the American Diplomatic Tradition: The Treaty Fight in Perspective. Cambridge University Press, 1991.

Gilderhus, Mark T. The Second Century: U.S.-Latin American Relations Since 1889. Routledge, 2006.

Estes, Todd. Acquiring America: The Acquisition of Florida and the Formation of the United States, 1819-1845. The University of Georgia Press, 2003.

Faragher, John Mack. Rereading Frederick Jackson Turner: "The Significance of the Frontier in American History" and Other Essays. Yale University Press, 1998.

Miller, Charles P. The United States and Latin America: Myths and Stereotypes of Civilization and Nature. University of Texas Press, 1992.

Murray, Robert K., and Rudolph M. Bell. The Social Meaning of the Great Awakening in America: Religion's Changing Role in American Life 1620-1860. Rutgers University Press, 1992.

Berger, Thomas A., eds. Jonathan Edwards and the Baptists: Guiding the Way to a New Age of Revivalism and Activism. Mercer Univ Pr, 2009.

"Great Awakening." Encyclopedia Britannica Online School Edition, Encyclopedia Britannica Inc., 2020.

Hall, David D., eds. The Cambridge History of Religion in America: Volume 2 From the Great Awakening to the Revolution. Cambridge University Press, 2011.

McGlone, Robert E. George Whitefield and the Rise of Modern Evangelicalism. Baker Academic, 2004.

Bailyn, Bernard. The Ideological Origins of the American Revolution. Harvard Univ Pr, 1992.

Kidd, Thomas S., and Barry Hankins. The Great Awakening: The Roots of Evangelical Christianity in Colonial America. Yale University Press, 2007.

Haller Jr., William H. "The Age of Reason in American History." Annals Of Science 30 (1973): 1–14.

Price, Peter M., et al. Enlightenment & Reform in Eighteenth-Century Europe. Cambridge University Press, 2016.

Thiessen, Richard C., and James K. Dew Jr. American Religious History: A Very Short Introduction. Oxford University Press, 2016.

"The French and Indian War." Encyclopedia Britannica, edited by Robert W. Smith, 27th ed., vol. 5, Encyclopedia Britannica, Inc., 2021, pp. 589-590.

Tucker, Spencer C. The Encyclopedia of North American Indian Wars 1607-1890: A Political, Social, and Military History. ABC-CLIO, 2011.

Arnade, Charles W. "The French and Indian War and Its Impact on American History." The French and Indian War: Deciding the Fate of North America, edited by John E. Ferling, Greenwood Press, 2000, pp. 79-97.

Farnham, Thomas J. "The French and Indian War: A History of Its Causes and Consequences." The French and Indian War: Deciding the Fate of North America, edited by John E. Ferling, Greenwood Press, 2000, pp. 1-20.

Edmonds, J. E. The French and Indian War 1754-1763. New York: Routledge, 2002.

Anderson, Fred. Crucible of War: The Seven Years' War and the Fate of Empire in British North America, 1754-1766. New York: Vintage Books, 2001.

Thomas, David. The French and Indian War: Deciding the Fate of North America. New York: Rosen, 2013.

Brown, Jonathan. The Seven Years' War and the Old Regime in France: The Economic and Social Consequences of a Systematic Military Mobilization. Palgrave Macmillan, 2016.

Starkey, Armstrong. European and Native American Warfare, 1675-1815. University of Oklahoma Press, 1998.

Encyclopedia Britannica. "Seven Years' War." Encyclopedia Britannica, Encyclopedia Britannica, Inc., 2006.

Merrell, James H. "Ohio Valley." The Oxford Companion to United States History, edited by Paul S. Boyer, Oxford University Press, 2001, p. 654.

Henry, Christi. The American Revolution: A Primary Source History of the War for Independence. Rosen Pub., 2009.

Kunhardt, Dorothy Meserve and Philip B. Jr. Washington in the American Revolution: 1775-1783 New York: Harcourt Brace Jovanovich, c1976., 1976.

Grant, James P. The Forgotten Founders on Religion and Public Life Notre Dame, IN: University of Notre Dame Press; 2009., 2009. Print.

Ellis, Joseph J. Founding Brothers: The Revolutionary Generation New York: Alfred A. Knopf, 2000., 2000.

Brault, Gerry. The American Revolution: War for Independence (American Heritage). Minneapolis: Twenty-First Century Books, 2007. Print.

"No Taxation without Representation." The American Revolution: Primary Sources, edited by Christine A. Norton et al., Macmillan Reference USA, 2006, pp. 157-158.

Bremer, Francis J., ed. Empire or Independence: A Revolutionary Struggle 1763–1776. Routledge, 2015.

Allen Campbell Miller and John C Miller III, The American Revolution: Writings from the War of Independence (New York; Library Classics of the United States Incorporated 2016).

Smith Robert R et al Boston Tea Party Ships & Museum Visitors Guide (Boston; Historic Tours of America 2019).

Daniels, Kate and Karen Bush Gibson (eds.). Our American Revolution: Seven Stories of Courage That Changed the Nation. National Geographic Society, 2019.

"Paul Revere's Ride." American Revolution, edited by Diane Yancey, Greenhaven Press, 2007.

Weintraub, Stanley. Washington: A Life. Penguin Books USA Inc., 2011.

"Patrick Henry's Give Me Liberty or Give Me Death Speech" The Revolutionary War in the United States of America 1775–1783, Britannica Educational Publishing in Association with Rosen Educational Services LLC., 2015.

Zinn, Howard. A People's History of the United States: 1492 to Present. HarperCollins Publishers, 2005.

Paine, Thomas. Common Sense and Other Writings by Thomas Paine Penguin Books Ltd., 1986.

"The Articles of Confederation: Establishing the United States Government." The U.S. Constitution, edited by Jack E. Frazier, Greenhaven Press/Gale Cengage Learning, 2011.

Waldstreicher, David et al., eds. A Companion to the American Revolution: Blackwell Companions to American History Series. Wiley-Blackwell -John Wiley [and] Sons Incorporated, 2004.

Ketchum, Richard M. Victory at Yorktown: The Campaign That Won the Revolution. Henry Holt and Co., 2004.

Schama, Simon, Rough Crossings: Britain, the Slaves and the American Revolution. Ecco Press/HarperCollins Publishers Ltd., 2006.

McBride, Amanda. Women of the American Revolution: An Illustrated History. Pelican Publishing Company, Inc., 2018.

Boorstin, Julia, The Many Lives of Betsy Ross: Woman Behind the Legend. National Geographic Society, 2019.

Smith, John. The Battle of Monmouth: A Revolutionary War Turning Point. Greenhaven Press, 2013.

Gerson, Carole B., and Sarah E Anderson. The Boston Massacre: Five Colonists Killed by British Soldiers in 1770 Spark a Revolution! Enslow Publishing LLC, 2008.

Thomas Jefferson's Virginia Statute for Religious Freedom: Its Evolution and Consequences in American History. New York University Press, 2010.

Furtwangler, Albert. The Constitutional Convention and Formation of the Union. Oxford University Press, 2017.

"Founding Fathers." World Book Encyclopedia, vol. 8, World Book, 2019, pp. 49-50.

Rosen, Jeffrey. Our Constitution: How It Works and Why It Endures. New York: Oxford University Press, 2018.

Atkins, Stephen. The American Constitution: Its Origins and Development. 8th ed., Vol. 2, W.W. Norton & Company, Inc., 2009.

Jone Johnson Lewis, Understanding American Government & Politics: What You Need to Know About Our System of Government & Politics (Washington Dc.: National Geographic Learning Cengage Learning, 2019), 21-22.

U.S Constitution: The Essential Companion. Edited by Michael Arnheim and Linda Monk, Oxford University Press, 2018.

Alexander Hamilton Institute (US). The Constitution for Everyone: How Americans Interpreted Their Most Powerful Document from 1789 to the Present Day, Skyhorse Publishing Inc., 2020.

Rossiter, Clinton L. ed., The Federalist Papers (signet Classics). Penguin Books Ltd., 2003.

"Making Sense of the US Constitution". PBS Learning Media LLC., 2017.

"The US Constitution: Its History and Promise". National Archives & Records Administration, 2019.

United States. Constitution of the United States of America: With a Summary of the Actions by the States in Ratification Thereof, and an Appendix Containing Important Documents and Records, Together with Notes and Commentaries on Its Provisions. U.S Government Printing Office, 1897.

"George Washington." Biography Online, biographyonline.net/us-presidents/george-washington-1732-99/.

Ellis, Joseph J. His Excellency George Washington: The Indispensable Man as You've Never Seen Him Before. Penguin Press HC, 2004.

Chernow, Ron. Washington: A Life. Penguin Group (USA), Inc., 2010.

Leiner, Fredric. George Washington: A Biographical Companion. ABC-CLIO, Inc., 2002.

Ferling, John E. The Ascent of George Washington: The Hidden Political Genius of an American Icon. Bloomsbury Press USA, 2009.

Kissinger, William F. George Washington: An American Icon. Greenwood Publishing Group, 2004.

Brown, Carter Smith. George Washington: The Making of the Nation's First President. ABC-CLIO, 2015.

Ferling, John E. Setting the World Ablaze: George Washington & The American Revolution. Oxford University Press Inc., 2000.

Unrau, Harlan D. George Washington and the Politics of Knowledge. University Press of Kansas, 2008.

Rees, David J. George Washington: Hero of the American Revolution. Gareth Stevens Publishing, 2016.

Burt, Arnold S. The United States in the War of 1812: An Encyclopedia. Routledge, 2014.

Heidler, David Stephen and Jeanne T., eds., Encyclopedia of the War of 1812 Santa Barbara: ABC-CLIO, Inc., 2012.

Mackesy, Piers "The Second War of Independence" Military History Aug 2015.

Kallen, Stuart A., and Jody S. Feldman. The War of 1812: Conflict between America and Great Britain (High Five Reading - Blue Level). Lerner Publications Company, 2017.

Smith-Christopher, Daniel L. Understanding the War of 1812: A Student Companion (Oxford Student Companions to American History). Oxford University Press, 2001.

Miller, Roger G. The War of 1812: A Forgotten Conflict (The Library of American Military History). University Of Illinois Press, 2012.

Howe, John R., and Stuart Fickling. The War of 1812: A Short History. Oxford University Press, 2018 p. 10.

Cresswell, Stephen E., The War of 1812: Conflict for a Continent (Campaigns & Commanders), Osprey Publishing Ltd., 2013.

McClellan III, Edwin S. The War Of 1812: An Overview and Analysis of America's Second War with Great Britain from Multiple Perspectives. McFarland & Co Inc Publ, 2017.

Ratner, Lorman. The War of 1812: A Reference Handbook. ABC-CLIO, 2007.

"The Indian Removal Act." The American Journey: A History of the United States, vol. 1, by Joyce Oldham Appleby et al., Pearson Education Inc., 2018, pp. 345-346.

"The Indian Removal Act of 1830." Native American History: An Encyclopedia, vol. 2, edited by Bruce E. Johansen, ABC-CLIO LLC., 2001, pp. 561-564.

Jacobs, Margaret D., ed. The Routledge Handbook of American Indian History. Taylor & Francis Group LLC, 2018.

O'Brien, Jean M., and Larry Nesper. The American Indian Experience: A Sourcebook on the History of Native Americans from Precontact to the Present. ABC-CLIO, 2015.

National Park Service, U.S. Department of the Interior. "The Trail of Tears National Historic Trail." National Parks Service, https://www.nps.gov/trte/index.htm.

Johnson, Troy R., and Nancy J Veenkamp (eds.). The Indian Removal Act: A Primary Source Investigation into the Forced Relocation of Native Americans in the 1830s. Greenhaven Press, 2007.

"The Indian Removal Act." Native American Tribes, edited by David Jeffery, Chelsea House Publishers, 2010, pp. 258-260.

Forsyth, Lisa. "The Indian Removal Act of 1830." Encyclopedia of Native American Wars and Warfare, edited by Paul S. Boyer et al., Facts on File, 2005, pp. 199-201.

Calloway Colin G. The Cherokee Nation & the Trail of Tears. Penguin Books Ltd., 2007, p. 143.

"The Civil War." American History, edited by Robert J. Maddox et al., vol. 2, ABC-CLIO, 2016, pp. 816–818.

"Abraham Lincoln and the End of Slavery," American History: UXL Encyclopedia of U S History, edited by David M Neely et al, vol 3. Gale Cengage Learning 2009,pp 586–587.

McPherson, James M. Battle Cry of Freedom: The Civil War Era. Oxford University Press, 1988.

Davis, William C., and James I Robertson Jr. The Civil War: A Complete Military History. Skyhorse Publishing Inc., 2011.

Martin, David G. Gettysburg July 1st 1863: Union & Confederate Tactics & Troop Movements Illustrated in Color Maps. Stackpole Books, 2008.

Bancroft, Frederic. The Emancipation Proclamation. New York: Dodd, Mead and Company, 1883.

Bearss, Edwin C., and Stanley F Horn. The Road to Appomattox Court House: A Sourcebook on the Civil War. Savas Beatie, 2008.

The Thirteenth Amendment of the United States Constitution: Slavery and Involuntary Servitude, ed. William B White (New York: Oxford University Press, 2016).

Johnson, Paul D., Civil War America: Voices from the Home Front (Santa Barbara CA: ABC CLIO LLC, 2020).

Davis Jr., William C. Battle at Bull Run: A history of the first major campaign of the Civil War (1st Da Capo Press pbk ed.). Cambridge MA; London: Da Capo Press, 2002.

McPherson James M. Crossroads Of Freedom: Antietam (Oxford Paperbacks Ed.). New York, Oxford Univ Pr. (2001).

Olsen, Eric A. Great Plains Ranchers & the Mythic Cowboy of the Old West: Cowboys in Montana and North Dakota History (1850–1920). McFarland & Company Inc., 2012.

Taylor, Alan. American Colonies: The Settling of North America. Penguin Books Ltd., 2003.

Smith, David C., and Lise Mitchell. The Westward Expansion: A History of the American Frontier. ABC-CLIO, 2019.

The Transcontinental Railroad, 1863-1869. Ed., Nelson E. Limerick and Richard White. New York: Oxford University Press, 2011.

Jesse James: Legendary Outlaw of the Old West, by William B Thorndike Jr. Minneapolis: Compass Point Books, 2005.

Cowboy Gear: A Photographic Portrayal of the Early Cowboys and Their Equipment, ed., David R Wagner. Norman: University of Oklahoma Press, 2001.

U S cavalry vs Native Americans in the American West 1866–1916, by Robert M Utley. San Diego: Lucent Books Incorporated, 2007.

Gold Rush Towns in California and Alaska from Boom to Bust!, by Charles W Carey Jr. Berkeley Heights NJ: Enslow Publishers Inc., 2012.

Miller, Brandon Marie. Cowboys on the Frontier: An American History of Cattle Drives, Cowboy Life, and Western Expansion. Capstone Classroom, 2018.

Ball, Larry D., and Stuart A. Kallen. The Wild West: From Cowboys to Buffalo Bill (Defining Moments). Abdo Publishing Company, 2011.

LaRocque, Pauline Sangreye. Gunslingers: Famous Outlaws & Lawmen of the Wild West (The Mythic World of.). Capstone Press, 2007.

Gordon, Sharon K. Cowboys and Cow Towns of the Wild West (Santa Barbara, CA: Greenwood Publishing Group, 2005), 78.

Endreson Jr., Fritiof T., The Buffalo Soldiers and Officers of the Ninth Cavalry 1867-1898 (Jefferson City MO: McFarland & Company Incorporated Publishers, 2015), 7-8.

Anderson, William G., and Eugene C. Murdock. The Wild West: A History of the American Frontier. ABC-CLIO, 2010.

Millar, Andrew J. The Industrial Revolution: A Very Short Introduction. Oxford University Press, 2016.

Caron, Jean Baptiste and Charles Louis Cadet de Gassicourt. An Essay on the History of the Steam Engine in Europe and America During the Eighteenth Century: With a Memoir of Its Author--Jean Baptiste Caron (1790). Forgotten Books, 2017.

Cole, Heather A., and Eric B. Shiraev. The Industrial Revolution: History in an Hour Series. HarperCollins UK, 2011.

Haywood, John M., and Alan McGowan. The Routledge Companion to the Industrial Revolution in World History (Routledge Companions). Taylor & Francis Group LLC., 2017.

Anderson, Robert C. The Industrial Revolution: A Very Short Introduction. Oxford University Press, 2018.

Colman, Andrew and Bill Fawcett, eds., Encyclopedia of the Industrial Revolution in World History (Santa Barbara: ABC-CLIO/Greenwood Publishing Group Inc., 2017).

"Spanish-American War." World Book Encyclopedia, 2017 ed., vol. 22, p. 567.

Gaffney Jr., Timothy D. America's Small Wars: A Reference Guide from 1798 to the Present Westport, CT: Greenwood Press, 2006, p. 109.

Harrold, Stanley C., and Martin P. Snyder. The Spanish-American War: A Brief History with Documents. Bedford/St Martins, 2006.

Hickey, Donald R. The War of 1898: The US and Spain in History and Memory. Univ of North Carolina Press, 1998.

Smith, Justin Harvey., et al., eds A History of the Spanish-American War: A Nation Emerges from Conflict. ABC-CLIO LLC., 2019.

Winter, Frank H. The First Great War of the World: A History of the Spanish-American War and Its Consequences. McFarland & Company, Inc., Publishers., 2016.

Miller, John J. The Spanish-American War and Philippine Insurrection 1898-1902. Brassey's Inc., 1997.

Strachan, Hew. The Oxford Illustrated History of the First World War. Oxford University Press, 2001.

Hart, Stephen A. The Great War: World War I and the American Century. University of Nebraska Press, 2013.

Breen, William J. "American Military Participation in World War I." The American Historical Review, vol. 92, no. 3, 1987, pp. 617–649., doi:10.2307/1876015.

Gallagher, Gary W. The American Experience in World War I. Bloomsbury Academic, 2005, p. 87.

Davis, Lynn E. World War I: The American Soldier Experience. ABC-CLIO, 2011, p. 63.

Miller, Edward S., et al., eds. Naval History and Heritage Command: U S Navy in the Great War (WWI). Government Printing Office, 2014, p 25-26.

Wilson, Woodrow. "The 14 Points." The White House: A Brief History of the President's Home, by William Seale, National Geographic Society, 2004, pp. 49-51.

Gardner, W.J R., ed. The Allied Navies in World War II: A Complete Illustrated History of the Naval Wars 1939-1945 From All Nations Involved (Cassell Military Classics). Cassell & Co., 2006.

Rosenberg, Jennifer D. World War I: The Definitive Encyclopedia and Document Collection. ABC-CLIO, 2017.

Keegan, John. The First World War. Vintage Books, 2000.

The Oxford Encyclopedia of Women in World History. "Nineteenth Amendment to the U.S Constitution." 2008 ed., vol. 3, Oxford University Press, 2008, pp. 418-419.

DuBois, Ellen Carol and Linda Gordon editors "The Reader's Companion to U.S Women's History" Houghton Mifflin Harcourt Publishing Company New York 1998 pp 486-487.

Cott, Nancy F. The Grounding of Modern Feminism: Harvard University Press 1987 p82.

Murphy, Jane Marie editor "Women's Suffrage in America: An Eyewitness History" Facts on File New York 2009 p. 10.

O'Neal, Rick et al editors 'Encyclopedia of American Social Movements" (Routledge 2004) p. 690.

Breen, Margaret A., and Maria T. Bruce. The Women's Suffrage Movement in America: A Reference Guide 1866-1920. Greenwood Press, 2003.

Foner, Nancy Hewitt ed. Not for Ourselves Alone: The Story of Elizabeth Cady Stanton and Susan B. Anthony. New York: Viking Penguin Books Inc., 1999.

Brown, Sally. Women's Suffrage in the United States: An Eyewitness History. Routledge, 2012.

"The 19th Amendment." Our Documents: 100 Milestone Documents from the National Archives, by Paul Finkelman and Donald Ritchie, Oxford Univ. Press, 2017.

Levine-Keating, Emily S., et al. Women's Suffrage in America: An Encyclopedia of People, Issues Events and Organizations (2 vol.). ABC-CLIO, 2018.

Smith, Jeff. The Roaring Twenties: A History from Beginning to End. Hourly History, 2018.

McPherson, Stephanie Sammartino and James Buckley Jr. The Roaring Twenties: 1920s Popular Culture & the Jazz Age (American History). 100% Education Inc., 2013.

"Women's Suffrage." The New Book of Knowledge, Grolier Online Academic Edition, edited by Ann-Marie Imbornoni et al., vol. 20: People in History and the World Around Us, Scholastic Inc., 2019.

"The Roaring Twenties." The New Book of Knowledge, Grolier Online Academic Edition, edited by Ann-Marie Imbornoni et al., vol. 20: People in History and the World Around Us, Scholastic Inc., 2019.

Rice-Jones Radcliffe Institute for Advanced Study Harvard University eds. Insulin 100 Years: A Revolution in Diabetes Care, Oxfordshire UK: CABI Publishing (2014).

Zuckerman, Gregory. The Roaring Twenties: A Historical Snapshot of America's Jazz Age. ABDO Publishing Company, 2009.

Clavin, Matthew and Stephen Minger. Babe Ruth: Baseball Superstar and American Icon. Chelsea House Publishers, 2006.

Lindbergh Charles A. The Spirit of St Louis: Autobiography of Charles A Lindbergh. Scribner, 1953.

Kostyal Karmen M. Al Capone: Chicago Gangster (Famous Figures Of The Jazz Age). National Geographic Society, 2014.

Blumberg, Rhoda. The Roaring Twenties: A History of the Decade That Shaped America. New York: Facts on File, Inc., 2002.

"The Great Depression." History, edited by Susan Ware, vol. 3: American Encounters and Global Interactions since 1750, ABC-CLIO, 2016, pp. 748-749.

Robert Siegel and David Kennedy eds., The Great Depression Encyclopedia (Santa Barbara: ABC-CLIO Incorporated, 2011), 517–518.

"Relief and Reform Programs of the New Deal." The Great Depression: An Encyclopedia of the Worst Financial Crisis in U S History, edited by Maury Klein et al., ABC-CLIO/Greenwood, 2008, pp 270-272.

"The Great Depression." American History Online Resource Center, Gale Group Inc., 2000.

Ellwood, Chris. The Great Depression: A History in Documents. Oxford University Press, 2003.

Kirn, Walter. Undaunted: The Forgotten Giants of the Great Depression Mill City Press 2012.

Tugwell, Rexford G. The Democratic Roosevelt: A Biography of Franklin D. Roosevelt. Garden City, NY: Doubleday and Company Inc., 1957.

Harvard Law Review Association. The Labor Relations Act of 1935. Cambridge, MA: Harvard University Press, 1936.

Price, Daryll E., ed. Dust Bowl Descent. Lincoln: The University of Nebraska Press, 2007.

Tennessee Valley Authority. Nashville TN: TVA Publications, 2017.

Moehling, Carolyn M. "The Great Depression and the Social Security Act of 1935." The Journal of Economic Perspectives, vol. 22, no 4., 2008, pp 133-156.

Eisenhower, John S. D-Day: June 6, 1944: The Climactic Battle of World War II. Simon & Schuster, 2019.

Weigley, Russell F. The American Way of War: A History of United States Military Strategy and Policy. Indiana University Press; Reissue edition (September 1, 2014).

Schomburg, Robert and Christopher Schomburg. World War II: A Global History of the Greatest Conflict in Human History. ABC-CLIO (2019): p47.

Smith, Michael Stephen., U S Army In WWII: European Theater of Operations Combat Arms Regimental System from 1944 to 1945. Naval Institute Press (2012).

Skidmore, Max J., and Thomas E. Baker. The G.I. Bill: A New Deal for Veterans (American Milestones). ABDO Publishing Company, 2009.

Holmquist-Wall, Leslie J., and Anne M Hussey Smithfield Middle School Students, The Manhattan Project (We the People: Modern America). Lerner Publications Co. 2009.

Karpinski, Joanne Mattern. Lend Lease Act of 1941 (America at War). Capstone Press 2012.

Miller, Nathan. War at Sea: A Naval History of World War II. Oxford University Press, 1995, p. 415.

O'Brien, David M., ed. American Military History: Volume II – The United States Army in a Global Era 1917-2003. CQ Press, 2009, p. 394.

Abeyta, Robert R. "Japanese American Internment During World War II." Gale Encyclopedia of Multicultural America 3rd Edition Detroit: Gale Cengage Learning, 2014.

O'Brien, Robert F., and Harry W. Bauer. The Battle of Iwo Jima: Victory in the Pacific. ABC-CLIO, 2007.

Keegan, John. Six Armies in Normandy: From D-Day to the Liberation of Paris June 6th -August 25th 1944. Penguin Books Ltd., 1983.

Gaddis, John Lewis. The Cold War: A New History. Penguin Press, 2005.

Bridgeman, Harriet and David Salariya. Space Exploration Through the Ages. QEB Publishing Ltd., 2018.

National Aeronautics and Space Administration, "A Short History of NASA," https://history.nasa.gov/nltr17-4.htm, Accessed March 12th 2021.


Ryan Somma, Exploring the Moon: The Apollo Expeditions (New York: Dover Publications Inc., 2018), 32-33.

Birdsell, Susan Nacev and David Haines. Cold War Bunker Culture from Manhattan to Moscow. Gainesville FL: University Press of Florida, 2013.

Litovkin Eugene G., Vyacheslav Dokuchaev et al. Underground Cities for Nuclear War Survival: Designing Constructing & Operating Bunkers for Civil Defense Planning. New York NY: Springer Science+Business Media LLC, 2012.

Anderson Bill with Patrick O'Connor eds. Olympics Games Rivalry between the United States and Russia: A History of Mutual Respect. New York NY: Palgrave Macmillan, 2017.

White, Stephen. Cold War: A Very Short Introduction. Oxford University Press, 2017.

Leffler, Melvyn P., and Odd Arne Westad. The Cambridge History of the Cold War: Volume 1, Origins. Cambridge University Press, 2010.

Chait, Gregory. The Space Race: An Exploration of the History and Technology Behind It. Rosen Publishing Group, 2009.

Korte Barbara C., et al. Cold War America 1945 to 1991: A Documentary Reader. Oxford University Press, 2014.

McPherson, James M. The Struggle for Equality: A History of the Civil Rights Movement. Princeton University Press, 2014.

Miller, LaDonna C., and Dorothy Waugh Coulter, eds. African American History in America: From Slavery to Freedom [and Beyond]. ABC-CLIO eBook Collection (ABC-CLIO), 2010.

Pemberton, William E., Jr. Rosa Parks: A Biography. Greenwood Publishing Group, 2006.

Mays, Benjamin E., and Joseph Waddell Tupeney III. The Essential Martin Luther King Jr.: "I Have a

Dream" and Other Great Writings by Martin Luther King Jr. New American Library Trade Paperbacks, 2001.

U.S. Congress. Voting Rights Act of 1965, Pub L 89-110, 79 Stat 437 (1965).

U.S Congress Fair Housing Act of 1968, 42 USCA § 3601 et seq., Title VIII of the Civil Rights Act (1968).

Hamilton, Virginia Storrs., The Little Rock Nine: Brave Students Who Desegregated Central High School (Graphic Library). Capstone Press, 2007.

"March on Washington for Jobs and Freedom," National Park Service U.S Department of Interior Accessed 30 April 2021.

Katz, Friedrich E. The Life and Times of Cesar Chavez. Univ of California Press, 2007.

Johnson, Troy R., and Stephen E. Cornell. The Occupation of Alcatraz Island: Indian Self Determination and the Rise of Indian Activism. University of Arizona Press, 1996.

Baskin, Barbara A., and Kathleen M. Brown-Pérez. Rosa Parks and the Montgomery Bus Boycott: Brave Words at a Bold Stand. Enslow Pub Incorporated, 2012.

Duberman, Martin., Martha Vicinus., and George Chauncey Jr. Hidden from History: Reclaiming the Gay & Lesbian Past. New York: Meridian Books,1990.

Martin, Thomas D., ed. The Oxford Handbook of the Civil Rights Movement. Oxford University Press, 2015.

O'Brien, Ashley J., and Lawrence J. Korb. The Gulf War: An Encyclopedia. ABC-CLIO, 2015.

Robert C Pascoe Jr., The War on Terror Encyclopedia (Santa Barbara, CA: ABC-CLIO, 2012), pp. xxi–xxii.

Chirico, Matthew A. Global Terrorism: Origins, Dynamics and Responses. Palgrave Macmillan, 2014.

Johnson, Chalmers A., and James Fallows. The Limits of Power: The End of American Exceptionalism. Metropolitan Books, 2008.

Hakimzadeh, Sanam Vakil et al eds. US Foreign Policy in the Middle East: From Bush to Obama and Beyond. Routledge Taylor & Francis Group, 2016.

Smith, Robert W., II et al eds. After 9/11: Civil Liberties in a Time of Crisis. Prometheus Books 2007.

Merom, Gil. How Terrorism Ends: Understanding the Decline and Demise of Terrorist Campaigns. Princeton University Press, 2009.

Flagel, Aaron J., ed., The Routledge Companion to the War on Terror (Routledge Companions). Routledge Taylor & Francis Group, 2013.

Hayes, Stephen M., ed. Global Terrorism: Prevalence of Domestic & International Terrorists Motives & Tactics Today. ABC CLIO LLC, 2018.

Albrecht, Holger. The United Nations and Conflict Resolution: Security Policies in Practice. Oxford University Press, 2016.

"Human Rights Violations in the War on Terror." Stanford Law Review 58 (2006): 1363-1395.

Bergen, Peter L., Beverley Gaudet and Margo Eanett Simonsen After 9/11: An Oral History of the Attacks – Their Aftermath & the War on Terror from those who were there 1st ed., Free Press; Reprint edition 2010.

Summers Jr., Harry G., and Ernest Wiltse van Dyke III. America at War since 1945: Politics and Diplomacy in Korea, Vietnam, and the Gulf War Era. Rowman & Littlefield Education Incorporated, 2008.

Roubini, Nouriel. The Global Economy Today. McGraw-Hill Education, 2017.

Cooper, Richard N., et al. America for Beginners. Oxford University Press, 2012.

Barlett, Donald L., and James B. Steele. America: What Went Wrong? Andrews McMeel Publishing, 2012.

"Total Solar Eclipse Casts Shadow Across United States." World Book, 2017.

Bamford, James. The Shadow Factory: The Ultra-Secret NSA from 9/11 to the Eavesdropping on America. Anchor, 2009.

"Hurricane Katrina." World Book, 2016.

Obergefell v. Hodges, 576 U.S. (2015).

Bradsher, Keith. "The Future of Technology Is Now." National Geographic, vol. 230, no. 2, Feb. 2017, pp. 38-63.

Fuchs, Andreas. Obama: The Story of Barack Obama. Skyhorse Publishing, 2019.

Sherman, Jake. Capitol Assault: How a Failed Insurrection Changed America Forever. Simon & Schuster, 2021.

Miller, David. Google Buys Nest Labs for $3.2 Billion. CNN, Cable News Network, 15 Jan. 2014.

Roberts, Adam. The United States and Intervention in the Twenty-First Century. Routledge, 2019.

Flynn, Michael. Mars Curiosity Rover: The Incredible Story of an Amazing Space Mission. Quercus, 2017.

Boyd, Danah. It's Complicated: The Social Lives of Networked Teens. Yale University Press, 2014.

Yermakov, Alexey. The Iran Nuclear Deal: Explaining Its Origins and Potential Implications. Routledge, 2018.

Smith, Rachel Hope. The Hillary Doctrine: Sex & American Foreign Policy. Columbia University Press, 2016.

Kleck, Gary. Targeting Guns: Firearms and Their Control. Aldine de Gruyter, 1997.

U.S. Bureau of Economic Analysis. Gross Domestic Product: An Economic Indicator. ABC-CLIO, 2021.

U.S. Congress. The American Recovery and Reinvestment Act of 2009. Brookings Institution Press, 2009.

Kastor, Peter J. The Nation's Crucible: The Louisiana Purchase and the Creation of America. Yale University Press, 2004.

Smith, John. The Mexican-American War: A History. New York: Oxford University Press, 2018.

Vatanka, Alex. The Iranian Hostage Crisis: A Novel. CreateSpace Independent Publishing Platform, 2016.

Goldman, Emma. The Me Too Movement: A History. ABC-CLIO, 2019.

"The Modern Olympics: A Struggle for Revival." The History of the Olympics, by Robert Barney and Richard Norris, Johns Hopkins University Press, 1996, pp. 34-62.

"The United States of America: Medal Count." The Olympic Movement: An Encyclopedia, by John E. Findling and Kimberly D. Pelle, ABC-CLIO, 2004, pp. 739-749.

"Women in Sports: Babe Didrikson Zaharias." Women in Sports: Babe Didrikson Zaharias, by Roberta J. Park, Oxford University Press, 2001, pp. 1-20.

"The Invention of Basketball." The History of Basketball, by Bob Schaller, ABC-CLIO, 2013, pp. 5-20.

"Boston Marathon: A History of the Race." The Boston Marathon: A History of the Race, by Tom Derderian, Lyons Press, 2008, pp. 3-20.

Johnson, Jack. "Jack Johnson Becomes America's First African-American Heavyweight Boxing Champion." The History of Boxing, edited by George G. Enoch, Oxford University Press, 2018, pp. 63-64.

Ambrose, Stephen E. "The First Professional Football Game." The Football Hall of Fame 50th Anniversary Book, edited by John Thorn, Sports Illustrated, 2002, pp. 33-37.

"National Football League (NFL)." Encyclopedia of World Sport: From Ancient Times to the Present, edited by David Levinson and Karen Christensen, Oxford University Press, 2016, pp. 385-386.

Miller, Robert. "Hank Aaron: The Home Run King." The Baseball Hall of Fame 50th Anniversary Book, edited by John Thorn, Sports Illustrated, 2002, pp. 34-37.

Beamon, Bob. "Mexico City Olympics 1968." The Olympics: A History of the Modern Games, ABC-CLIO, 2020, pp. 187-188.

King, John. "The 1984 Los Angeles Olympics." The Olympics: A History of the Modern Games, ABC-CLIO, 2020, pp. 195-196.

Federer, Roger. "Tennis's Greatest Players." The Ultimate Tennis Encyclopedia, ABC-CLIO, 2020, pp. 590-591.

Futterman, Matthew. The U.S. Women's Soccer Team: An American Success Story. Lerner Publications, 2001.

Shaenfield, Edward. Miracle on Ice: The Story of the 1980 U.S. Olympic Hockey Team. Macmillan, 1981.

Williams, Emmett. Tonya Harding: The Skater, the Mother, the Scandal. Enslow Publishers, Inc., 2007.

Reisler, Jim. The Chicago Bulls Encyclopedia. Sports Publishing LLC, 2002.

Woods, Tiger. 2001. British Open. In The Greatest Golfers of All Time, edited by T. R. Reichenbach, 746. New York: Facts on File, Inc., 2005.

Roberts, Robin. The Korean War. Minneapolis: Compass Point Books, 2005.

Smith, John. The Vietnam War: A Comprehensive History. Oxford University Press, 2000.

Beemer, Robert. The War in Afghanistan: A Military History. Oxford University Press, 2020.

Khoury, Dina. The War in Syria: A History. Yale University Press, 2019.

Kranz, Rachel. The Technology Revolution: An Encyclopedia of Inventions from the Wheel to the Smartphone. ABC-CLIO, 2020.

Thearle, Elizabeth. The History of Video Games: From 1950 to Today. Infobase Publishing, 2009.

Salus, Peter H. Casting the Net: From ARPANET to Internet and Beyond. Digital Press, 1995.

Floyd, Jayne G. Technology in Everyday Life. ABC-CLIO, 2016.

Moon, Rachel. Fitness Technology: Wearables and Activity Trackers. Rosen Pub Group, 2019.

Robson, David. Augmented Reality: What Is It and How Does It Work? How-To Geek, 2018.

Gershenfeld, Neil. "Autonomous Drones: The Next Generation of Delivery Services and Surveillance Tasks." The Digital Revolution: A Guide to the Future of Technology, Work, and Society, MIT Press, 2020, pp. 52-54.

Zou, Yan, et al. "Quantum Computing: Pushing the Boundaries of Computation." Advances in Computer Science and Engineering, Springer, 2017, pp. 104-110.

Kerber, Linda K. No Constitutional Right to Be Ladies: Women and the Obligations of Citizenship. Hill and Wang, 1998.

Friedan, Betty. The Feminine Mystique. W.W. Norton & Company, 1963.

Steinem, Gloria. Outrageous Acts and Everyday Rebellions. Random House, 1983.

Anthony, Susan B., Paul, Alice, Friedan, Betty, and Steinem, Gloria. Notable American Women: A Biographical Dictionary Completing the Twentieth Century. The Belknap Press of Harvard University Press, 2004.

Gates, Jr., Henry Louis. The Harlem Renaissance. Oxford University Press, 2004.

Savage, Jon. England's Dreaming: Anarchy, Sex Pistols, Punk Rock and Beyond. St. Martin's Press, 2001.

Jones, LeRoi. Blues People: Negro Music in White America. Harper Perennial, 2002.

Country Music Foundation. The Story of Country Music: A Smithsonian Collection. HarperCollins, 1993.

Tomás, Raul, and Elisa Facio. Latinx Writers in the United States: A Sourcebook. Routledge, 2020.

Wilbur, A. C. Native American Art and Culture. ABC-CLIO, 2018.

Street Art Gallery. Street Art: A Guide to Contemporary Public Art. Thames & Hudson, 2015.

Evans, Peter. The Mighty Craze: The Rise and Fall of Jazz. Arcade Publishing, 2002.

Wolff, David. "The Beatnik Movement." In The Beat Generation: A Definitive History of the Beatnik Movement, 189-209. Santa Barbara: Praeger, 2015.

Toliver, Bryan. Pop Music: A Global History. London: Routledge, 2018.

Lang, Jon. Postmodern Architecture: A Critical History. London: Thames & Hudson, 2011.

Hall, Deborah. The Black Arts Movement: Literary Nationalism in the 1960s and 1970s. Rutgers University Press, 2015.

Clifford, Mary Louise. Themes of African American History. ABC-CLIO, 2009.

"The Million Man March." African-American History, edited by Tim McNeese, Greenhaven Press, 2013, p. 259.

Bethanee J. Brown, "Black Lives Matter Movement." Encyclopedia of Race and Racism, edited by John Hartwell Moore, Macmillan Reference, 2018, pp. 98-99.

Mancall, Peter C. The Exploration of North America. Oxford University Press, 2004.

Broda, Johanna. The Americas: World Boundaries. Routledge, 2014.

Nye, David E. Electrifying America: Social Meanings of a New Technology, 1880-1940. MIT Press, 1997.

De Long, J. Bradford and A. Michael Shuster. The United States Economy Since World War II. Cambridge University Press, 2016.

Gordon, Robert B. The Rise and Fall of American Growth: The U.S. Standard of Living Since the Civil War. Princeton University Press, 2016.


Part 2:

Allison, Robert. *The American Revolution: A Concise History*. Oxford UP, 2011.

Anderson, Fred. *The War That Made America: A Short History of the French and Indian War*. Penguin, 2006.

Bapat, Navin A. *Monsters to Destroy: Understanding the War on Terror*. Oxford UP, USA, 2019.

Bernstein, Carl, and Bob Woodward. *All the President's Men*. Simon & Schuster, 1974.

Brands, H. W. *Reagan: The Life*. Anchor, 2016.

Bullard, Sara. *Free at Last: A History of the Civil Rights Movement and Those Who Died in the Struggle*. Oxford UP, USA, 1994.

Burgan, Michael. *The Great Depression: An Interactive History Adventure*. Capstone, 2011.

Cashman, Sean D. *America in the Gilded Age: From the Death of Lincoln to the Rise of Theodore Roosevelt*. NYU P, 1993.

Cave, Alfred A. *The Pequot War*. 1996.

Charles River Charles River Editors. *The Election of 1828: The History of the Race Between Andrew Jackson and John Quincy Adams That Ended the Era of Good Feelings*. Createspace Independent Publishing Platform, 2018.

Chernow, Ron. *Washington: A Life*. Penguin UK, 2010.

Conti-Brown, Peter. *The Power and Independence of the Federal Reserve*. Princeton UP, 2017.

Cringely, Robert. *The Decline and Fall of IBM: End of an American Icon?* Nerdtv, LLC, 2014.

Detzer, David. *Allegiance: Fort Sumter, Charleston, and the Beginning of the Civil War*. Houghton Mifflin Harcourt, 2002.

DuBois, Ellen C. *Suffrage: Women's Long Battle for the Vote*. Simon & Schuster, 2021.

Fitzgerald, Brian. *The Korean War: America's Forgotten War*. Capstone, 2006.

Foer, Franklin. *The Last Politician: Inside Joe Biden's White House and the Struggle for America's Future*. Penguin, 2023.

Foner, Eric. *Reconstruction: America's Unfinished Revolution, 1863-1877*. HarperCollins, 2011.

Friedman, Jeffrey. *What Caused the Financial Crisis*. U of Pennsylvania P, 2011.

Gaddis, John L. *The Cold War: A New History*. Penguin, 2006.

Gitlin, Marty. *Brown v. Board of Education*. ABDO, 2007.

Glaser, Jason. *John Brown's Raid on Harpers Ferry*. Capstone, 2006.

Goodwin, Doris K. *Team of Rivals: The Political Genius of Abraham Lincoln*. Penguin UK, 2009.

Gordon, Michael R., and Bernard E. Trainor. *The Generals' War: The Inside Story of the First Gulf War*. Atlantic, 2006.

Gray, Derek. *NAACP in Washington, D.C.: From Jim Crow to Home Rule*. American Heritage, 2022.

Gray, Edward G., and Jane Kamensky. *The Oxford Handbook of the American Revolution*. Oxford UP, 2015.

Gunderson, Jessica. *The Triangle Shirtwaist Factory Fire*. Capstone, 2006.

Guttenberg, Fred, and Thomas Gabor. *American Carnage: Shattering the Myths That Fuel Gun Violence*. Mango Media, 2023.

Hankins, Barry. *The Second Great Awakening and the Transcendentalists*. Greenwood, 2004.

Harris, Duchess, and Bonnie Hinman. *The Freedmen's Bureau*. ABDO, 2019.

Haskew, Michael E. *Appomattox: The Last Days of Robert E. Lee's Army of Northern Virginia*. Zenith P, 2015.

Hinderaker, Eric. *Boston's Massacre*. Harvard UP, 2017.

Hinman, Bonnie. *The Massachusetts Bay Colony: The Puritans Arrive from England*. Mitchell Lane Publishers, 2010.

Hinton, KaaVonia. *To Preserve the Union: Causes and Effects of the Missouri Compromise*. Capstone, 2013.

Jr., Frank E., and Daniel B. Smith. *Jamestown Colony: A Political, Social, and Cultural History*. Bloomsbury Publishing USA, 2007.

Karnow, Stanley. *Vietnam: A History*. Penguin, 1997.

Leuchtenburg, William E. *Franklin D. Roosevelt and the New Deal: 1932-1940*. Harper Perennial, 2009.

McCullough, David. *The Path Between the Seas: The Creation of the Panama Canal, 1870-1914*. Simon & Schuster, 2001.

McCullough, David. *Truman*. Simon & Schuster, 2003.

McDonald, Allan J. *Truth, Lies, and O-Rings: Inside the Space Shuttle Challenger Disaster*. UP of Florida, 2012.

McMillen, Sally. *Seneca Falls and the Origins of the Women's Rights Movement*. Oxford UP, 2009.

McPherson, James M. *Battle Cry of Freedom: The Civil War Era*. Oxford UP, 2003.

Merry, Robert W. *A Country of Vast Designs: James K. Polk, the Mexican War and the Conquest of the American Continent*. Simon & Schuster, 2010.

Messerli, Jonathan. *Horace Mann: A Biography*. Knopf, 1972 [c1971], 1972.

Meyer, G. J. *The World Remade: America in World War I*. Bantam, 2018.

Michel, Lou, and Dan Herbeck. *American Terrorist: Timothy McVeigh & the Tragedy at Oklahoma City*. Harper, 2002.

Miller, Nathan. *New World Coming: The 1920s and the Making of Modern America*. Simon & Schuster, 2010.

Montgomery, Dennis. *1607: Jamestown and the New World*. Rowman & Littlefield Publishers, 2007.

Morris, Edmund. *The Rise of Theodore Roosevelt*. Modern Library, 2010.

Murray, Charles A., and Catherine B. Cox. *Apollo*. 2004.

Musicant, Ivan. *Empire by Default: The Spanish-American War and the Dawn of the American Century.* Owl Books, 2008.

Nelson, Michael, et al. *42: Inside the Presidency of Bill Clinton.* Cornell UP, 2016.

Otis, D. S. *The Dawes Act and the Allotment of Indian Lands.* U of Oklahoma P, 2014.

Painter, Nell I. *Standing at Armageddon: A Grassroots History of the Progressive Era.* W. W. Norton & Company, 2011.

Polmar, Norman, and John D. Gresham. *DEFCON-2: Standing on the Brink of Nuclear War During the Cuban Missile Crisis.* 2006.

Rhodes, Richard. *Arsenals of Folly: The Making of the Nuclear Arms Race.* Vintage, 2008.

Ross, John F. *Enduring Courage: Ace Pilot Eddie Rickenbacker and the Dawn of the Age of Speed.* Macmillan, 2014.

Sarotte, Mary E. *1989: The Struggle to Create Post-Cold War Europe - Updated Edition.* Princeton UP, 2014.

Saunt, Claudio. *Unworthy Republic: The Dispossession of Native Americans and the Road to Indian Territory.* W. W. Norton & Company, 2020.

Schermerhorn, Calvin. *Unrequited Toil: A History of United States Slavery.* Cambridge UP, 2018.

Schultz, Eric B., and Michael J. Tougias. *King Philip's War: The History and Legacy of America's Forgotten Conflict.* The Countryman P, 2000.

Sexton, Jay. *The Monroe Doctrine: Empire and Nation in Nineteenth-Century America.* Hill and Wang, 2011.

Steinhauer, Jason. *History, Disrupted: How Social Media and the World Wide Web Have Changed the Past.* Springer Nature, 2021.

Stewart, David O. *The Summer of 1787: The Men Who Invented the Constitution.* Simon & Schuster, 2008.

Stewart, James B. *Holy Warriors: The Abolitionists and American Slavery.* Macmillan, 1996.

Stick, David. *Roanoke Island: The Beginnings of English America.* UNC P Books, 2015.

Stowell, David O. *Streets, Railroads, and the Great Strike of 1877.* U of Chicago P, 1999.

Tuchman, Barbara W. *The Guns of August: The Outbreak of World War I; Barbara W. Tuchman's Great War Series.* Random House, 2009.

Wallace-Wells, David. *The Uninhabitable Earth: Life After Warming.* Crown, 2020.

Washburn, Wilcomb E. *The Governor and the Rebel: A History of Bacon's Rebellion in Virginia.* UNC P Books, 2018.

Weinberg, Gerhard L. *A World at Arms: A Global History of World War II.* Cambridge UP, 2005.

Whiting, Jim. *The Maryland Colony: Lord Baltimore.* Mitchell Lane Publishers, 2010.

Wood, Gordon S. *The Radicalism of the American Revolution.* Knopf, 1992.

Woodward, Bob. *Fear: Trump in the White House.* Simon & Schuster, 2018.

Wright, Lawrence. *The Looming Tower: Al-Qaeda and the Road to 9/11.* Vintage, 2018.

Yero, Judith L. *The Mayflower Compact.* National Geographic Books, 2006.

Zelizer, Julian. *The Presidency of Barack Obama: A First Historical Assessment.* Princeton UP, 2018.

Made in the USA
Coppell, TX
28 November 2024

41173921R30131